Learning to Teach Design and Technology in the Secondary School

Design and technology embraces work with food, resistant materials, systems and control and textiles. It requires pupils to work both practically and theoretically, to investigate and research, design, plan, make and evaluate. It is a subject which is based on the needs of people, and so has a 'real world' context and relevance for the pupils. It should also be interesting, exciting and fun.

Learning to Teach Design and Technology in the Secondary School aims to help student teachers in their task of learning and developing their professional practice. It provides the theory underpinning important issues, and links this to practical classroom situations. Topics covered include:

- areas of subject knowledge content and how these can be audited and developed
- the importance of health and safety in design and technology work
- the integration of ICT into teaching and learning
- planning lessons and classroom management
- assessment in design and technology
- design and technology and its links with the community.

The book is designed to help student teachers to develop their subject knowledge, teaching skills, understanding of the wider issues and the ability to reflect on classroom practice.

Related titles

Learning to Teach Subjects in the Secondary School Series

Series Editors
Susan Capel, Canterbury Christ Church College; Marilyn Leask, De Montfort University, Bedford; and Tony Turner, Institute of Education, University of London.

Designed for all students learning to teach in secondary schools, and particularly those on school-based initial teacher training courses, the books in this series complement *Learning to Teach in the Secondary School* and its companion, *Starting to Teach in the Secondary School*. Each book in the series applies underpinning theory and addresses practical issues to support students in school and in the training institution in learning how to teach a particular subject.

Learning to Teach English in the Secondary School
Jon Davison and Jane Dowson

Learning to Teach Modern Foreign Languages in the Secondary School
Norbert Pachler and Kit Field

Learning to Teach History in the Secondary School
Terry Haydn, James Arthur and Martin Hunt

Learning to Teach Physical Education in the Secondary School
Susan Capel

Learning to Teach Science in the Secondary School
Tony Turner and Wendy DiMarco

Learning to Teach Mathematics in the Secondary School
Sue Johnston-Wilder, Peter Johnston-Wilder, David Pimm and John Westwell

Learning to Teach Using ICT in the Secondary School
Edited by Marilyn Leask and Norbert Pachler

Learning to Teach Design and Technology in the Secondary School

A companion to school experience

Edited by

Gwyneth Owen-Jackson

RoutledgeFalmer
Taylor & Francis Group

LONDON AND NEW YORK

First published 2000
by RoutledgeFalmer
11 New Fetter Lane, London EC4P 4EE

Simultaneously published in the USA and Canada
by RoutledgeFalmer.
29 West 35th Street, New York, NY 10001

Reprinted 2003 (twice)

RoutledgeFalmer is an imprint of the Taylor & Francis Group

Typeset in Bembo by
J&L Composition Ltd, Filey, North Yorkshire
Printed and bound in Great Britain by
TJ International Ltd, Padstow, Cornwall

British Library Cataloguing in Publication Data
A catalogue record for this book is available from the British Library

Library of Congress Cataloging in Publication Data
Owen-Jackson, Gyneth, 1956–
Learning to teach design and technology in the secondary school: a companion to school experience / Gwyneth Owen-Jackson.
p. cm. – (Learning to teach subjects in the secondary school series)
Includes bibliographical references and index.
ISBN 0–415–21693–1 (pbk.: alk. paper)
1. Technology – Study and teaching (Secondary) 2. Design – Study and teaching (Secondary) I. Title. II. Series.
T65 .O94 2000
607.1′2–dc21 99–087308

ISBN 0-415-21693-1

Contents

Illustrations

Figures

Tables

Tasks

Contributors

Louise Davies (MA, BEd Hons) was a teacher of Home Economics in secondary and special schools in London, a Senior Lecturer at South Bank University and Deputy Project Director/Research Fellow at the Royal College of Art Schools Technology Project (1993–1997). She is now a part-time Principal Subject Officer for Design and Technology at QCA, advising on national curriculum and examinations for primary, secondary and post-16. She is also a freelance education consultant working with the Open University Learning Schools Programme, Denford Ltd, QCA KS1/2 and KS3 Schemes of Work and OFSTED inspections of initial teacher education. She is on the editorial board of the *Journal for Design and Technology Education* and is the chair for the DATA Special Needs Advisory Group.

Jim Newcomb (MA, BA Hons) taught in secondary comprehensive schools and was an Advisory Teacher for Design and Technology with Gwent LEA. Since 1993 he has been a Senior Lecturer in the Department of Education at the University of Wales College at Newport, supporting undergraduate and postgraduate primary and secondary design and technology provision. He has worked as an Associate Lecturer on the Open University's PGCE course since 1995 and operates as that institution's Subject Specialist Tutor for secondary design and technology within Wales. He is a member of DATA's Primary Design and Technology Advisory Group and has just completed the first year of an EdD, with the intention of developing research on the extent to which Key Stage 2 children are encouraged to operate as 'reflective practitioners' during practical problem-solving activities.

Frank Banks has taught science, engineering science and technology in a number of secondary schools in the north of England and in mid-Wales. He worked as a primary advisory teacher for science and technology before joining the staff of the University of Wales, Swansea. Since 1992 he has worked at the Open University, where he has written on a number of courses for technology teachers and is currently a Sub-Dean in the School of Education. His research interests are teacher professional knowledge and the links between school science and technology. He is the editor of *Teaching Technology*, also published by Routledge.

Howard Denton (BEd, MPhil, PhD) is Programme Leader for Industrial Design and Technology with Education at Loughborough University. His main teaching interests are the training of teachers of design and technology and the teaching of design practice. His main research interests lie in the areas of group- and team-working in design practice and design and technology education. In addition he has worked and published in the areas of simulation and design, ergonomics education and design and technology teaching and learning at school and undergraduate levels.

Chris Hopkins has been a secondary teacher of design and technology for twenty years. He currently is Head of Department at an outer-London school. He has previously worked with the Institute of Education on the Maths and Technology project, and he has written a number of books and run several courses. In addition to teaching, he is now working with the Open University as a Subject Specialist Tutor for Design and Technology.

John Young has fifteen years' experience of working in industry, from light engineering to retail management, and he has taught design and technology for over ten years at a City Technology College. He has worked on developing relevant programmes of study for engineering courses, been involved in teacher training at the CTC and has worked with the Open University as a Subject Specialist Tutor.

Acknowledgements

Thank you to all the authors in this book for the contributions that they have made, and thank you to those schools, teachers and students who allowed their work to be used.

Acknowledgement is given to ACCAC (previously the Curriculum Council for Wales) of Castle Buildings, Cardiff for their permission to use the diagram in Chapter 8. Publications from ACCAC are available from their order line 070 71223 647 (English language) 070 71223 646 (Welsh language).

I want to thank Jennifer for her practical support, encouragement and patience throughout the production of this book.

Introduction

How true is the phrase that 'good teachers are born not made'? There may be a grain of truth in it, but all professionals need training and practice to improve their knowledge, skills and performance. It is true that it is useful to have a good grasp of your subject knowledge in order to teach well, but you need to know how to convey that knowledge to others in a way that they will understand. It's also true that if you get on well with young people you could be a good teacher, but you need to know what it is you are teaching them and why.

There are basic skills involved in teaching which you can be told about, which can be demonstrated to you and which you can practise. Good, effective teaching, though requires you to be able to decide from moment to moment in the classroom which of those skills you need to call on, and then to be able to use them well. Teachers are individuals with different personalities and characteristics and so will make different professional judgements; no one can say that there is one right way to teach. In addition, good teachers continue to be learners themselves and will continue to develop their skills, knowledge and teaching style, so that teaching becomes a continual process of personal and professional development. This can be rewarding and exciting, and has benefits in the classroom.

Nowhere is this process of development more obvious than in design and technology, since the subject itself depends on the continual development of new materials, new machinery, new processes, new knowledge. Design and technology is also relatively new to the school curriculum, as Chapter 1 explains, and so the challenge is there for you to be involved in the development of a curriculum which is interesting, motivating, exciting, fun, relevant and, at the same time, demanding, pushing pupils' learning forward. This is not an easy task but certainly an interesting one. Modern society needs technologists, people who can solve problems, be creative, be aware of social, moral and ethical considerations, and who can practically apply theoretical knowledge. We need to engage pupils' interest and encourage them to continue their studies – this applies to all pupils, girls and boys. Traditionally, the areas of design and technology have been divided, with girls working in food and textiles and boys working in resistant materials and electronics. This is now no longer appropriate. So much of our everyday lives requires a technical and technological understanding that *all* pupils should have an entitlement to a relevant and appropriate course of study. It is important that we help pupils to understand the knowledge and processes, as well as to develop the skills, many of which will help them in whatever career path they follow.

Design and technology is also able to embrace the experiences of pupils from different ethnic backgrounds. In design work there is the opportunity to talk about and appreciate Eastern and Asian patterns and symbols as well as European ones. When talking about the materials used, it is possible to include examples from a range of cultures; open-ended design briefs allow pupils to design and make products which meet their own specified needs. In looking at the development of products, it is possible to bring in cultural and social developments as well as historical ones. Design and technology should also allow pupils to investigate the context of their work and the social, moral, ethical, environmental issues involved, and this may lead to considerations of the needs and values of different cultures and populations. These are not additions to the work of design and technology but should be an integral part of it.

ABOUT THIS BOOK

This book aims to help you develop:

- competence in basic teaching skills in design and technology
- awareness of how to develop your subject knowledge
- ability to reflect critically on what you are doing.

It is one of a series and you are recommended to read it alongside the core text *Learning to Teach in the Secondary School* (Capel *et al.*, 1997). The core book will give you a broader overview of the issues whilst this one aims to put them into a design and technology context. The wider view, however, will aid your professional development.

As in the core text, each chapter in this book is organised as follows:

- *introduction* to the content of the chapter
- *objectives* outlining what you should know, understand or be able to do after having read the chapter and carried out the tasks
- *content*, including *tasks*, to help develop your knowledge, skills and understanding
- *summary* of the main points of the chapter
- *further reading* selected to help you find out more about the content of the chapter.

Chapter 1 looks at the development of the subject, whilst Chapters 2–5 consider the subject knowledge required in the different areas: resistant materials, food, control and systems and textiles. Chapters 6 and 7 look at issues that affect all areas of design and technology, namely those of health and safety and information and communications technology. Chapters 8–11 cover various aspects of teaching, such as pupils' learning, planning lessons, teaching and assessment. Chapter 12 considers how design and technology can involve the local community. Chapter 13 looks at getting your first job and continuing your own professional development.

Theory and practice are interwoven in the text, and examples of relevant classroom practice are used to explain or illustrate the points being made. The tasks, too, combine theory with practice, sometimes asking you to read and reflect, sometimes to carry out a classroom-based activity. Where activities involve other members of staff, for example where you are asked to observe other teachers in the classroom, *you must ask permission from the person concerned before you carry out the task*. It is also good practice to discuss your observation with the person afterwards, and be aware of any sensitive or confidential issues.

ABOUT YOU

We recognise that you will have a wide range of needs as a student teacher, depending on your background and previous experience. We cannot recommend, therefore, one best way to use this book: you may wish to read it all the way through or you may read sections of it alongside any other studying you are doing, or you may choose to dip in and out of it.

We recognise also that you are studying in different places and on different types of initial teacher education (ITE) courses. We have tried to address as many of your potential needs as possible, but there will be times when you will need to refer to the specific requirements of your own situation, whether it be in the school or in the wider national context. You will also need to consider the outcomes, or competences, that you are working towards on your course; again, these may be specific to your own situation.

TERMINOLOGY USED IN THE BOOK

Schoolchildren have been referred to throughout this book as 'pupils' to avoid confusion with students on ITE courses. The person who has responsibility for your professional training has been called your 'mentor': this may be a tutor in the college or university where you study or it may be a teacher in the school where you are based.

The terms 'he/him' and 'she/her' have been used equally and each is taken to include both genders.

The subject has been referred to throughout as 'design and technology', although Chapter 1 acknowledges that it may take a different name in different places. We thought that it would be confusing to refer to the subject by different names so chose to use the same one throughout; please substitute a different title if that is appropriate for where you are.

1 Design and technology in the school curriculum

Gwyneth Owen-Jackson

INTRODUCTION

Design and technology is one of the newest subjects in the school curriculum, in fact it's likely that you didn't study it when you were at school. It's also known by different names – technology in Scotland, South Africa and other parts of the world; design and technology in England and Wales; technology and design in Northern Ireland. One of the important aspects, therefore, of studying design and technology, and especially being a teacher of it, is being clear about what it means, what is taught under this heading and why it is on the curriculum at all.

This chapter explores some definitions of design and technology and looks, briefly, at its history. It also considers the rationale for the inclusion of the subject on the school curriculum.

OBJECTIVES

After reading this chapter you should be able to:

- give a definition of design and technology;
- understand its historical development;
- explain why it is included on the school curriculum.

WHAT IS DESIGN AND TECHNOLOGY?

Task 1.1 Defining design and technology

Write down, in your own words, what your definition, or understanding, of design and technology is.

You have certainly chosen an interesting subject to teach. Design and technology is interesting because it is a relatively new subject on the school curriculum and, as such, is still developing its identity.

Task 1.2 Comparing design and technology content

If possible, talk to a design and technology student or newly qualified teacher from another school. Compare what is taught in design and technology in your school with the other school:

- Are there similarities in the content of the topics?
- Are the same materials, equipment and processes used?
- How is the content structured and delivered?
- What are the differences, and what are the reasons for them?

The dictionary defines design both as a noun, meaning 'a plan or project, a purpose . . . a draft', and as a verb, meaning 'to plan, contrive or intend, to invent a pattern for'. Technology is defined as the 'science of industrial and mechanical arts'. These everyday meanings are fine for the individual words, but do they help you to understand 'design and technology' as a composite term, or as it is taught in schools? The following definitions have all been applied to the school subject of design and technology:

> D&T is an essentially practical activity, concerned with developing pupils' confidence to tackle a variety of issues, drawing on a broad base of knowledge and skills. It is developed in response to perceived needs and opportunities, takes place within a context of specific constraints, depends upon value judgements at almost every stage and enables the individual to intervene to modify and improve his or her environment.
>
> (Somerset County Council, 1990, p. 113)

> It is an active study, involving the purposeful pursuit of a task to some form of resolution that results in improvement (for someone) in the made

world. It . . . uses knowledge and skills as a resource for action rather than regarding them as ends in themselves.

(Assessment of Performance Unit [APU], 1991, p. 17)

Design and Technology involves applying knowledge and skills when designing and making good quality products fit for their intended purpose.

(Department for Education [DfE], 1992, p. 13)

Technology is the creative application of knowledge, skills and understanding, to design and make good quality products.

(National Curriculum Council [NCC], 1993, p. 5)

design and technology capability [requires pupils to combine] their *designing* and *making skills* . . . with *knowledge and understanding* . . . in order to design and make products.

(DfE, 1995, p. 6)

[it is] . . . a distinctive creative process that combines intellectual and practical skills through purposeful practical activities . . . it involves a series of identifiable activities including:

- investigating a need or design opportunity
- developing design proposals, and modifying them in light of evaluation
- planning for implementation of design solution
- making of the proposed solution
- evaluating the effectiveness of the process they are engaged in and the product they have made.

(Design and Technology Association [DATA], 1995a)

[D&T] helps to prepare young people for living and working in a technological world . . . by teaching the technical understanding, design methods and making skills needed to produce practical solutions to real problems.

(DfE, 1996)

Process-centred capability, the ability effectively to pursue an activity from inception to completion, is the central requirement of Design and Technology capability. It requires the development of knowledge and skill, but that is not the point of it all. The point is to be able creatively to make use of that knowledge and skill in tackling tasks in the made world.

(Kimbell *et al.*, 1996, p. 113)

> . . . [T]echnology is a distinct form of creative activity where human beings interact with their environment to bring about change in response to needs, wants and opportunities.
>
> (Scottish CCC, 1996, p. 3)

> Technology is the use of knowledge, skills and resources to meet human needs and wants, and to recognise and solve problems by investigating, designing, developing and evaluating products, processes and systems.
>
> (South African National Curriculum, 1996)

> Design and technology contributes to the school curriculum by preparing all young people to participate in a rapidly changing technological world. It enables them to understand how to think and intervene creatively to improve the world, combining their knowledge with understanding of aesthetics and function. It helps pupils to become discriminating and informed users of products [and] broadens their understanding of industrial production and commercial practices.
>
> (Qualifications and Curriculum Authority [QCA], 1999, p. 122)

Task 1.3 Looking for common elements in design and technology

Read through the above definitions again, and from them list what you think are the common elements running through them.

These definitions range over time and are from different countries, but from reading through them you should have been able to identify some common elements. Compare the list you drew up in Task 1.3 with the list below:

- combining knowledge and skills
- intellectual activity and practical activity
- meeting human needs and wants
- consideration of values
- involvement with the 'real' world and real tasks.

This may help to lead you to an understanding of what design and technology is, and what it might be. Look back at Task 1.1 and see how many of the common elements from the above definitions were in your own definition.

THE DEVELOPMENT OF DESIGN AND TECHNOLOGY

The reason for the lack of just one definition, this lack of certainty about design and technology, is partly due to its historical development. Most countries, from the point at which they introduced state educational systems, have included some form of craft work on the curriculum, although this was not always offered to all pupils. The 'crafts' being taught were usually those of metalwork, woodwork and domestic work, in order to train pupils for manual or domestic labour or, in the case of girls, their future roles as housewives and mothers. In this form the subjects were concerned only with passing on to pupils traditional knowledge and skills. Pupils were required only to learn the knowledge, not to understand it, and to copy and practise the making skills.

Over time there were changes in society, such as the rise of feminism and calls for equal opportunities. There were changes in the world of work, with increasing industrialisation and computerisation, which led to employers requiring different kinds of knowledge and skills from their employees. There were also changes in educational philosophies, with a move to more child-centred learning. These changes all had some impact on the craft curriculum and led to developments which broadened the scope of the various subjects. In Britain, metalwork and woodwork became craft, design and technology (CDT), while cooking and needlework became domestic science, and later home economics.

These changes in society and employment continued, and in some cases at a more rapid pace than ever before, so that even CDT and home economics were not meeting the needs of pupils. There was a need for pupils to be taught how to find and use new information, how to be flexible and adaptable, how to continue to learn new knowledge and skills, and how to be creative. This area of the curriculum responded to these needs by adapting both its content and pedagogy.

In England and Wales, the introduction of the national curriculum was an opportunity for debate and discussion and led to 'design and technology' being introduced as a new subject, compulsory for all pupils aged 5–16. The original form in which this new subject appeared was a 'federation' of art, business studies, CDT, home economics and information technology, to reflect the creative, practical, technical and industrial aspects of the new subject. However, this proved to be unmanageable in practice and had a detrimental effect on teachers and on the quality of pupils' work. This led to a revision and, after a prolonged debate, a new design and technology national curriculum was published in 1995. In this version, the subject joined together work in resistant materials, systems and control, food and textiles and drew on other curriculum areas in the teaching of these. The 1995 Orders were reviewed again in 1999, there was some simplification in the programmes of study and assessment, but no major changes were made. This latest national curriculum, for England only, is implemented from September 2000.

In Northern Ireland, where the subject is technology and design, a similar development took place, although with variations on the content encompassed, it being mainly resistant materials and systems and control. Home economics remains as a separate subject and textiles is not included.

In Scotland, where there is 'national policy' and national guidelines for 5–14 year olds, technology was introduced in 1996. This followed a review, seeking to build on the 1985 recommendations that there should be 'technological activities' in both primary and secondary education and to develop 'a coherent, national framework for this important area of the curriculum' (Scottish CCC, 1996). Again, this is not exactly the same in its content or assessment as the technology education found in other countries but there are many similarities.

Other, similar, national guidelines for design and technology, or technology, can be found in Botswana, South Africa, parts of Germany, Australia and other countries.

Task 1.4 Developments in design and technology

Talk to colleagues in the department where you work about changes they have experienced in their teaching of design and technology. When you have done this, and have built up a picture of how the subject has developed, try to imagine what changes you might experience over the next ten years as a teacher of design and technology.

WHY TEACH DESIGN AND TECHNOLOGY?

There are various rationales which can be put forward for including design and technology in a recommended school curriculum. Many of these are linked to the various definitions and historical developments just discussed.

Task 1.5 Why teach design and technology?

Before reading the rest of this section, think about your own view of the rationale for teaching design and technology. You have chosen to teach this subject, but why? What do you think it offers pupils that is different to other curriculum experiences? Why do you think it is included on the school curriculum?

Kimbell *et al.* believe that studying design and technology presents pupils with opportunities 'for exercising unique ways of thinking about the world and *for intervening constructively to change it*' and that 'the *process* of trying to create change requires pupils to engage in a challenging, enriching, empowering activity' (Kimbell *et al.*, 1996, p. 29). In their work they also describe various interpretations of technology that they found in schools, each of which is underpinned by a different rationale. Each rationale, although applied here to design and technology, can also be related to education generally; some have a liberal view of education, some a more economic view and others a social view.

One view is of technology as a 'competence', requiring a knowledge of things and how they work. This view justifies the teaching of design and technology because of the employment and vocational benefits it brings, both to pupils and to employers. Another view is of technology as a social phenomenon worthy of study for its impact on the development of society: here the study is more sociological than technological and its rationale is that it will provide pupils with a more general, liberal education.

Harrison also acknowledges the role that technology education plays in preparing young people for the workforce and as citizens in a technological society. He further identifies the rationale that technology is part of 'the culture' of a place and time and that the curriculum should be introducing and passing on to pupils information about the culture in which they live. Finally, like Kimbell, he identifies the learning-related rationale, that technology facilitates learning 'in the context of the solving of technological problems' (Harrison, 1996, p. 6).

If you look back to the definitions of design and technology given in the previous section, I'm sure you will be able to match each of these to an underlying rationale.

Task 1.6 Your view of design and technology

Think about the various rationales which have been discussed and decide which most closely matches your own.

How did you arrive at this view: was it shaped by your own educational experience, by people you have met or things you have read?

Think about how your rationale for learning design and technology will influence the way you teach the subject.

It will also be interesting for you to look at the curriculum or guidelines which you have to follow in your school. Read carefully the aims identified in each scheme of work. In reading through them, can you see what rationale drives it, what prompted the selection of knowledge and skills that it contains? If you can, then it will help you to interpret the curriculum or guidelines in your own teaching.

I wish now to raise a note of caution. As design and technology continues to develop in various countries, questions are still being asked about its role and its place in the curriculum. In 1996 a conference was held in London to discuss 'The Contribution of Design and Technology to the Curriculum'. In the report which was published it stated that 'There was widespread agreement that design and technology is an important element in the education of all pupils.' It then summarised some key points which had been made during the conference, namely that design and technology

- is a valuable vehicle for the development of values and cultural education
- is a significant aspect of pupils' preparation for citizenship

- provides realistic and personally involving contexts for pupils to develop transferable skills
- fosters skills such as decision-making and resource management, and qualities such as adaptability
- provides opportunities for partnership with business and industry
- develops pupils' understanding of the world of work
- gives pupils scope to draw together and use knowledge and skills gained in other parts of the curriculum.

(School Curriculum and Assessment Authority [SCAA], 1997, p. 3)

I'm sure you will agree that all of these points are important outcomes from learning design and technology. However, my concern is that design and technology may come to be seen as a 'servicer' to the needs of others, as nowhere in the key points is reference made to the importance of essential elements of design and technology, such as learning the following:

- to evaluate products critically
- to recognise opportunities to improve systems or products
- to be creative
- to be organised
- to gain a better understanding of materials
- to use tools and equipment confidently
- to make quality products.

As teachers of design and technology, we need to think carefully about why we are teaching the subject, as this will influence what we choose to teach and how we teach it, and we need to be sure that we are maintaining the integrity of the subject and serving the learning needs of the pupils as best we can.

SUMMARY

I presume you have chosen to become a teacher of design and technology because you enjoy your specialist study. I hope that this chapter has helped you to see where your specialism fits into the wider picture, to understand the constituent elements of design and technology and why they are there. But teaching is much more than passing on subject knowledge, so I hope that you have now also developed your own understanding of what design and technology is, why it is so, and what it contributes to pupils' learning. These are important things for you to learn because design and technology, more than almost any other subject, seems to have to keep on explaining what it is and why it is important. Also, it is not a static subject, it will continue to evolve. It is therefore important that, in keeping up with these changes, you do not lose sight of the principles of what you are teaching and why.

FURTHER READING

Banks, F. (1994) *Teaching Technology*, London: Routledge

Kimbell, R., Stables, K. and Green, R. (1996) *Understanding Practice in Design and Technology*, Buckingham: Open University Press

2 Teaching resistant materials

Howard Denton

INTRODUCTION

The area known as resistant materials covers work primarily in metals, timbers and plastics. It may also, in some schools, include electro-mechanical systems and compliant materials such as textiles. If teaching in all these areas sounds daunting, don't panic!

If you are a post-graduate student, your first degree is unlikely to have covered the breadth of knowledge and skills required for resistant materials. However, teaching in a design and technology department is a team operation; you and your colleagues support one another and senior management will have recruited a team with complementary skills who can work together. Throw yourself into your new professional role and continue to learn as you teach.

This chapter aims to help you identify the knowledge and skills you will need to teach resistant materials through analysing the curriculum guidelines or syllabus that you will be following. This is particularly important because as you move on in the teaching profession you will adopt new syllabuses, and inevitably any national curriculum or guidelines in place now will change. It is vital, therefore, to develop your ability to analyse curricula and syllabuses and identify from them:

- the knowledge and skills you need to teach
- the level to which you need to teach them
- what you already know (and what you don't know)
- where you need support or development.

This process is often referred to as a knowledge and skills audit.

Whilst the range of syllabuses and any national guidelines may look complex, they can all be simplified to a basic framework. It is easier to look at this framework in three phases as this is the way the subject is usually approached and planned in schools: foundation (11–14 years), examination (14–16 years) and post-16.

Working through this chapter will help you to identify a suitable framework for yourself and your situation, and you can then flesh this out to see what knowledge and skills you need to teach at each level. You will also be guided to audit your own knowledge and skills and to build an action plan to develop any areas identified and to gain support from colleagues with complementary skills.

OBJECTIVES

By the end of this chapter you should:

- have an improved understanding of the knowledge and skills you will need to teach resistant materials
- be able to identify specific subject knowledge and skills required to be taught in a range of foundation and examination courses
- be able to use the above to identify areas for personal development and the means by which that could be achieved
- be able to use the above to identify any areas where you need to collaborate with colleagues in order to ensure pupils have a full experience.

ESTABLISHING A FRAMEWORK OF KNOWLEDGE AND SKILLS AT FOUNDATION LEVEL

In the lower school (pupils aged 11–14 years) you will not have the immediate prospect of preparing pupils for examinations, but you must give them the foundations for that work. You will, also, almost certainly be working to some form of national guidelines but, as indicated above, these will change over the years. It is important, therefore, for you to build a conceptual framework to help you understand the requirements placed on you. A good framework is easily adjusted over time as it is based on the central tenets of the subject.

Task 2.1 Familiarising yourself with curriculum guidelines

Obtain a copy of the current guidelines or curriculum that you are required to work to. Read through the document asking yourself the following questions:

- How do I know which specific tools and processes I need to teach?
- At what level of detail do I teach them?

It is important to have some understanding in these areas before you can start to establish the framework, so some guidance is given below.

How do I know which specific tools and processes I need to teach?

Unless the documents you are working to give specific information, which is unusual, the answer is that it is your professional decision. This can be alarming to the new teacher. You have a great deal of autonomy to teach in the manner you wish, as long as you meet any criteria laid down in the document, but there are ways of finding out what needs to be taught.

First, it is important to find out what pupils already know and what they have done in their previous schools. The best way of doing this is by visiting their primary schools; you could ask to do this as part of your teaching practice or induction. Talk to primary school staff and collect any schemes of work that identify what has been taught. Remember that much design and technology work at primary level may be taught along with other subjects in general projects, so you may need to look hard to find it. You will soon realise that different primary schools will cover different areas; this means you need to identify any common ground that all your pupils have covered. You will, of course, have to recap some of these aspects, don't assume that they remember perfectly, as it's unlikely that they will. At the same time do acknowledge their prior learning, as pupils find it insulting to have their existing knowledge ignored.

Second, look carefully at the way the subject is taught in your school. Analyse it, work with these schemes and, as you gain confidence, develop your own schemes which borrow best practice as you see it. Introduce fresh ideas a bit at a time. One of the best ways of doing this is to work through a project yourself, not just the design work but also the making. This is very useful for several reasons:

- You can carefully list all the knowledge and skills you use which you would have to teach.
- It boosts your sensitivity to the pupils' experience.
- It helps you get around the workshop facilities.
- It clearly identifies any gaps in your knowledge or skills, and you can then do something about them.

Try this first with a project from the first year in secondary school. Be careful to look closely at what you are doing and relate it to working with young pupils: for example, you will use a steel rule without thinking twice, but on arriving in a secondary school pupils will not have used one before. Unless you point out that the measurement starts from the end of the ruler they sometimes assume that the one centimetre mark is the start of the scale because this is what they are used to with wooden rules. You have to spot these things and get them over to pupils.

Third, talk to experienced staff, perhaps using school projects as the basis for discussion. List the skills and knowledge they state and don't be alarmed if they appear to demand skills and knowledge you don't have. Be prepared to learn from them. Experienced staff usually enjoy teaching skills to students and new teachers and it boosts their opinion of you if you are seen as 'willing to learn and take advice'. This can be helpful when they are writing your reference or induction report.

It is also worth considering that there may be an overlap in teaching across other subjects. You should try to identify these, as knowing what is taught elsewhere may save you teaching from scratch. You will still need to put the material into a design and technology context, but this will help pupils' learning as it is reinforcement. Examples of overlap include the use of mathematics to calculate angles and dimensions when designing, or the scientific principles of fair testing when pupils investigate and evaluate existing products, or you might use art, historical or sporting contexts as a basis for design.

At what level of detail do I teach them?

To answer this you have two main sources: the syllabus or guidelines you are working to, including past papers if available, and the experience of colleagues. The syllabus will contain content and areas for assessment. In the new national curriculum for England there is one main area for assessment, the attainment target 'design and technology', and pupils can be assessed as operating at one of eight levels. Level descriptions are provided, which give some indication of what to look for in a pupil's work. For example, Level 5 states that pupils will:

> draw on and use various sources of information, using their understanding of the characteristics of familiar products when developing and communicating ideas. They work from their own detailed plans, modifying these where appropriate. They work with a range of tools, equipment, components and processes with some precision. They use checking procedures as their work develops and modify their approach in the light of results. They evaluate their products after testing, showing understanding of the situations in which their designs will have to function and an awareness of resources as a constraint. They evaluate their predictions and use of information sources.
>
> (QCA, 1999, p. 131)

Compare this with Level 6, which states:

> Pupils draw on and use a range of sources of information, and demonstrate an understanding of the form and function of familiar products. During planning they develop detailed criteria for their designs and use them to formulate or explore design proposals. They work with a range of tools, equipment, components and processes showing understanding of their characteristics. They use checking procedures as

> their work develops and modify their approach in the light of results. They evaluate the effectiveness of their own use of information sources, using the results to inform their judgements. They evaluate their products in use and identify ways of improving them.
>
> (QCA, 1999, p. 131)

Task 2.2 Looking for progression in curriculum guidelines

Re-read the above statements carefully. Note down the key points they cover then look for points that indicate some degree of progression between the two levels.

You should have seen that the statements look at planning, the use of tools and techniques, and evaluation. In terms of progression, we can see that pupils should progress by analysing existing products for specific criteria and then be able to draw up their own criteria for design work. In making they develop an understanding of practical skills, 'knowing that' as well as 'knowing how'. Note that no specific techniques or tools are mentioned. Providing that the tools used are appropriate to the task, the level requirement is fulfilled. Finally we see that evaluations should become more precise.

You should now be able to work your way through any syllabus or guidelines and start to get a feel for the progression pupils should experience and at what level you need to teach different year groups. This may seem daunting at first, and when you are assessing work you will need to refer to the level descriptions, or other guidance, frequently. However, it is like learning a foreign language, at first you think in your own language and translate back and forward slowly, but eventually you find you can actually think in the new language and work very quickly.

It is important to remember that you are working with and assessing individual pupils, who may achieve different levels of attainment in different areas of the work. A clear understanding of the above will help you plan work for individual pupils within your class and to produce differentiated learning materials (see Chapter 8 for information on differentiation in pupils' learning).

When do I teach specific knowledge and skills?

You should plan to introduce skills and knowledge to pupils logically and try to make them relevant to the pupils. Teach a skill, such as using a coping saw, when they need it and not before. Learning also needs reinforcement: teach the skill, recap at the end of the lesson, and then check learning with quick questions a week or so later. Skills which involve potential dangers will need recapping yet again.

Task 2.3 Looking for progression in schemes of work

Look at a project taught to pupils in the first year in the school and another from their second year. List the skills and knowledge required for each, in some detail. For example, to list 'marking out' would be inadequate: marking out using which techniques and tools?

Identify what is new in the second year project. Does this provide a logical progression for the pupils?

There is more on progression in Chapter 8.

DRAWING UP A FRAMEWORK

After working through the questions and points above, you should now be in a position to establish a basic framework from the curriculum guidelines or syllabus you are currently using. Remember, at this point you need to keep it fairly general so that you can use it as a basis for interpreting other curricula guidelines and syllabuses in parallel and in the future.

Looking more closely at your curriculum guidelines or syllabus, you will probably identify requirements for teaching aspects of: materials and components; systems and control; structures; quality; health and safety; and designing and making. So the basic framework you draw up will cover these aspects. You now need to learn how to use the framework to identify specific knowledge and skills you need to teach. There are several sources of information:

- the curriculum guidelines or syllabus you are currently working with
- talking to experienced teachers
- schemes of work and examples of project work around you in the school
- material from professional organisations and other support agencies
- textbooks.

Your aim is to develop a list of knowledge and skills and some indication of the depth you will need to teach them. Do this first at a foundation level. The process is then repeated for examination courses. Once you have the lists, you can use them in two basic ways: (a) as an audit of your own knowledge and skills and (b) as a planning structure to assist you in covering syllabuses fully.

Designing skills

Turn to the curriculum guidelines or syllabus you are working to at foundation level and read it carefully. Make short notes on the key points relating to design skills to be taught as this will help you to analyse the critical content; simply reading is not adequate. Notice that the list will probably outline a form of design line, a sequence of operations. This does not imply that design is a linear process and always starts at the same point and follows the same sequence. You do not even need to teach all the points listed each time. It may be appropriate to select a few specific ones and focus on them, as long as over the whole foundation level you have covered what is required.

Task 2.4 Listing the design skills you will be required to teach

Take a sheet of A3 paper and draw two lines down it to give you three equal columns. Don't worry about being neat as this is a working sheet. At the top left write 'Designing Skills' as a title and below this start by writing the list of design skills that you noted down from your reading of the foundation syllabus or guidelines. Space them over the whole column.

Now, on a new piece of paper do a brainstorm on each point (see the example in Figure 2.1). Discuss the brainstorm diagram with your mentor or other colleagues: this may help you to expand the diagram or get a feel for the depth you will need to work to. The brainstorm can then be used to generate a list which you write in the middle column of the A3 sheet as a working summary.

Repeat this process for all the design skills you identified. The right-hand column is for you to note the areas where you need to develop your own knowledge.

Making skills

Again, look at the curriculum guidelines or syllabus and make notes on those parts relating to making skills. Again, typically these are generic and not very specific. An example from the new national curriculum for England states that:

> pupils should be taught to:
> a) select and use tools, equipment and processes, including computer-aided design and manufacture (CAD/CAM), to shape and form materials accurately, and finish them appropriately . . .
>
> (QCA, 1999, p. 126)

This does not say which tools, equipment and processes need to be taught – you and your colleagues are the ones who must decide these details.

When you have done Task 2.5 your centre column list will be looking substantial, but it is still only a slightly fleshed-out skeleton. As you look closely you will see that some of the points in the centre column need further expansion. For example, from

Figure 2.1 Brainstorm diagram, based on the design skill of identifying appropriate sources of information

Note: This brainstorm is not complete, you should be able to add to it. The important point is that you have identified a range of sources of information which pupils could use in design work. Notice the way the branches sub-branch appropriately.

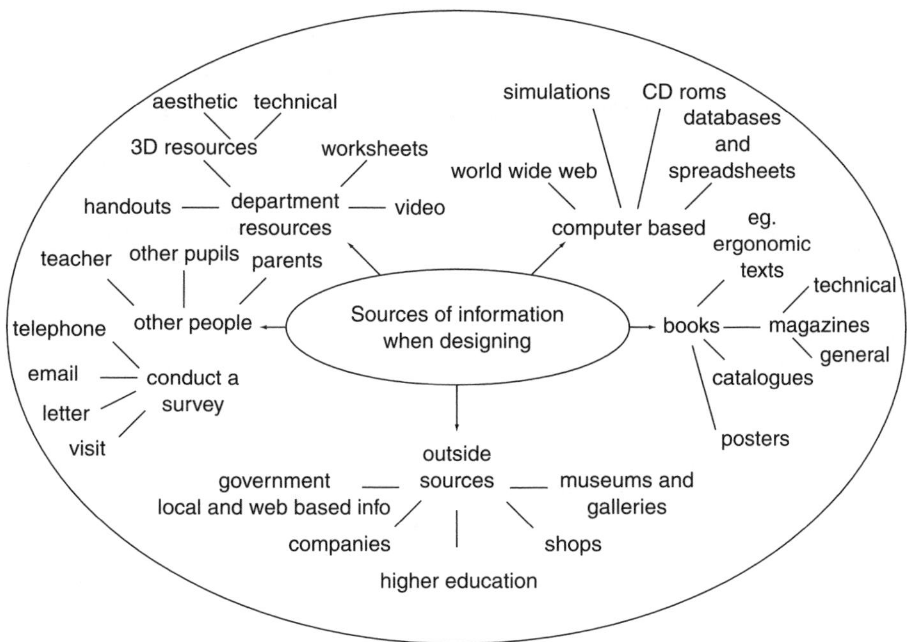

Task 2.5 Listing the making skills you will be required to teach

Repeat the activity that you carried out in Task 2.4, using 'Making Skills' as a title and brainstorming the making skills that you noted down from your reading of the foundation level curriculum guidelines or syllabus.

As an example, Figure 2.2 brainstorms the processes involved when making involves shaping and forming materials.

the brainstorm diagram in Figure 2.2, consider the process of 'joining-adhesives'. You can develop this further, either on your own or with colleagues. Remember, it may also refer to combining materials, so you should consider adhesives to join metals to plastics or rubber to metal, and other combinations. An example of how you might expand it is given in Figure 2.3.

You should now go back to your 'Making Skills' list and start to look at each part using the brainstorm technique. This will take time but it is important that you make

Figure 2.2 Brainstorm diagram showing processes involved when shaping and forming resistant materials

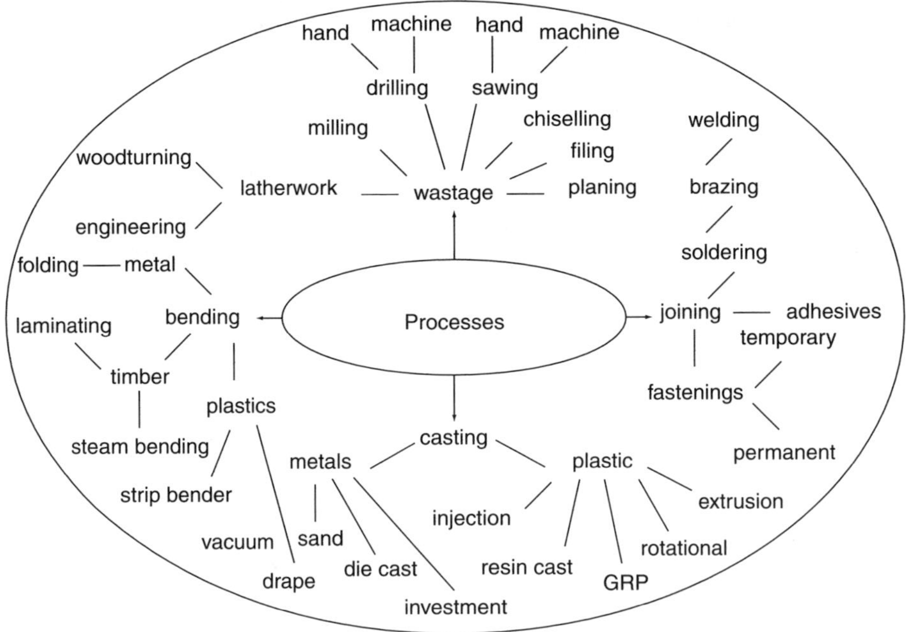

the effort if you are to develop a deep, rather than superficial, understanding. Notice that you need two phases for each exercise; first try it yourself, or working with other trainees, then see if the staff at your school can expand on the diagram. You should also look at textbooks. Look, particularly, for advice on when various processes might be introduced.

Once you have each brainstorm expanded to the limit, you should then simplify the range of points into a list. If all this is done on a word processor it can build into a highly useful planning document which you can easily adapt.

The above processes could then be used against each of the sections in the curriculum or guidelines. If done thoroughly this will give you several A3 sheets which describe the knowledge and skills you will need to teach and, therefore, will need to be familiar with. Remember these lists are goals not specific requirements at this stage of your career. Very few entrants to design and technology teaching have a comprehensive range of skills and knowledge, usually they have great expertise in specific areas. You should, therefore, put a lot of energy into trying to develop and expand on your skills and knowledge. Use your time in school to learn from teaching staff. They are usually more than happy to help you gain those basic 'craft' skills, for example, that so much of the subject is based on. In turn, you can help them develop skills that you have but which they may lack.

Figure 2.3 Brainstorm diagram showing the many uses of adhesives

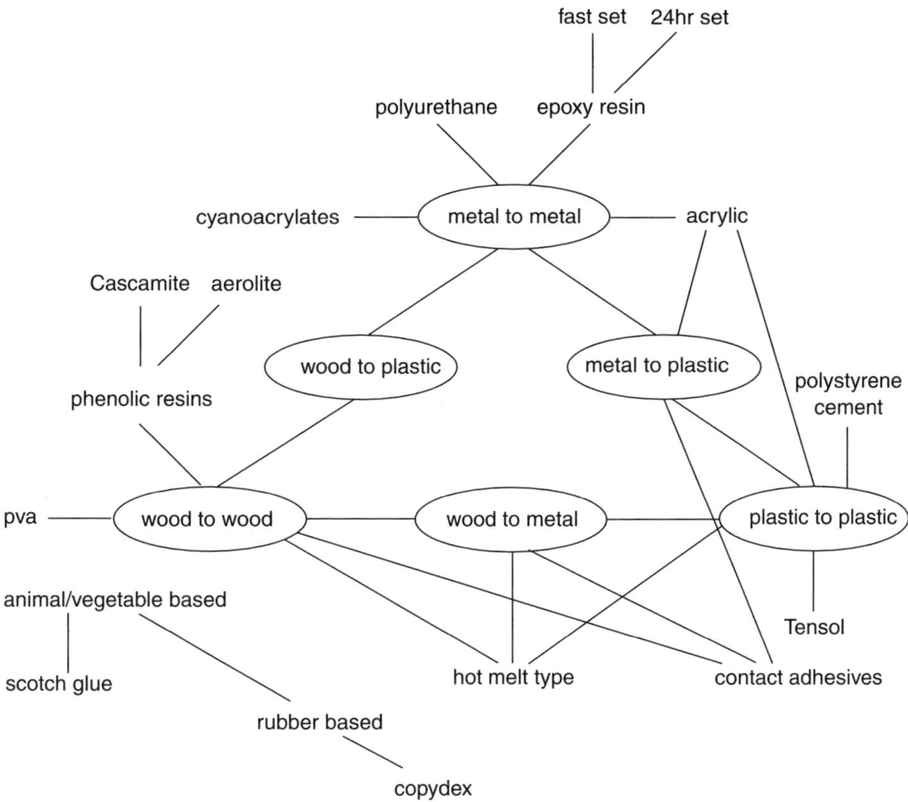

AUDIT AND DEVELOP YOUR OWN KNOWLEDGE AND SKILLS

You can use the lists you have developed to audit your own knowledge and skills in order to:

- identify where you need to develop
- prioritise this development
- look at ways in which the knowledge and skills can be gained.

The process is simple and you will probably have already subconsciously done it while compiling the lists. Look carefully at the centre column and identify areas in which you feel comfortable and those in which you feel you need to develop. You might use a code against each section: a tick for where you feel confident, 1 for some knowledge which needs brushing up, 2 for only a little knowledge, needing a reasonable amount of developing and 3 for no knowledge at all.

The next step is to prioritise your areas for development. Remember some important principles:

- Nobody will have a sound grasp of all these areas; you must collaborate with other teachers in ensuring pupils get full coverage.
- Your subject learning will never stop; you will continue to develop in the profession, and new technologies will come into being which you will need to grasp in the future.
- Use experienced colleagues to help you identify the areas of priority for you, but beware of the teacher who simply wants to clone him/herself and the training they did 30 years ago – they must be able to look forward!

Having started the third column on your A3 sheet, you could entitle it 'For Action'. You need to identify how you are going to gain or develop those areas you have identified. Some ways in which this can be done are reading text books and practising the skills. Maybe you could work with colleagues with complementary skills or attend specific training courses. The essential message, however, is that you cannot allow your subject knowledge and skills to remain static. Design and technology is about innovations; you must, therefore, constantly be at the fore of knowledge and skills in the area.

Read widely. Remember the role of fantasy in design, even of a technological nature, just think how interesting the authors Terry Pratchett or Douglas Adams would be as designers. Read a good quality newspaper and look for news of both design and technological developments, but also note the social and environmental contexts and impact of these developments. Watch and record television documentaries and programmes such as 'Tomorrow's World'. Be prepared to share some of these observations with your classes at key points such as the last five minutes of a lesson.

Remember, too, that a teacher of design and technology should practise her/his subject. I meet many teachers who have not designed or made anything for years. Always try to have a personal 'design and make' project on the go and try to extend yourself. Allow pupils to see the project in its development and be prepared to discuss it with them if they show interest, as they probably will. Such activity, besides developing your own skills, will develop your credibility with pupils and boost your teaching.

BUILDING ON THE FRAMEWORK: EXAMINATION LEVEL

In order to identify the knowledge and skills to teach resistant materials to examination level, you need to repeat the process you went through above. This may appear a big job, but remember that examination work is built on earlier work, so you have been through most of it already.

Start by getting the appropriate syllabus in front of you, ideally one with which you are going to work. Check on the front that it is current, i.e. that it shows the date for the year pupils will be examined, not the current year. The layout of syllabuses differs between examination boards but you should have little difficulty identifying the section that deals with the content. Here you should find a very similar basic structure to the one used in analysing the foundation level curriculum or guidelines. If the syllabus title is 'Design and Technology: Resistant Materials', or something similar, it will be straightforward to identify the knowledge and skills. Some syllabuses are entitled 'Design and Technology' and then have a 'common core' of content with additional specialist sections such as graphics, food, textiles and resistant materials. In this case you would look at both the common core and resistant materials specialism. If a common core is used, it will take areas from the basic framework such as 'quality' and 'health and safety', but all the elements are likely to be present, even if in a different order.

Your task now becomes one of finding areas of knowledge and skills that you have not previously covered at the lower level, and identifying the depth to which you will have to teach. Remember, teaching one aspect in too much depth can lead to you not covering the whole syllabus and so disadvantaging pupils. Long-term planning is all important: you must have plans to show when and how the whole syllabus will be covered (Chapter 9 gives more details on planning).

Task 2.6 Listing what you will be required to teach at examination level

Look at the specific syllabus you will work with and identify the basic framework, in the order the syllabus presents it, making brief notes on the content. Note the similarity to your foundation level framework.

Now use the same technique as in Task 2.4. On separate A3 sheets you can list the designing skills, the making skills and knowledge and understanding that you will be required to teach.

Brainstorm each point to fill in the detail. You will find a lot more detail in these syllabuses, so give yourself space on your A3 sheets. As you expand the framework, move on to a word processor to make it easier to adapt it as you gain experience or move to teaching different syllabuses, although you will be surprised how similar the underlying frameworks will be.

In the third column on each sheet you can identify where you feel confident and where you need to develop your own skills and knowledge.

POST-16 WORK

Post-16 work in design and technology includes A levels and vocational qualifications in areas such as manufacturing and engineering. If you are going to be teaching these, you need to analyse the subject content and audit your knowledge and skills as you did before. Remember, it is only by direct personal analysis that you will gain a deep understanding of the subject requirements.

A levels are relatively straightforward to analyse as they build more directly on the previous phases of foundation and examination work. The procedure you should follow is the same as in previous sections. You should, however, find the process much faster as it incorporates work at previous levels. Providing you have listed these carefully, you will find the detailed framework can be fleshed out relatively quickly.

Teaching at A level is frequently a team task; few staff will have the breadth and depth of expertise to cover an A level syllabus on their own. If you are required to teach an A level group, you are likely to be working with staff with complementary knowledge and skills, which you can use to help develop your own.

Analysing a vocational qualification programme is more difficult as the units are set out in a different way, but the knowledge and skills required are made explicit (although these are still not specific on which materials, tools and processes you need to teach) and once you have listed these, you will easily be able to proceed as before.

As a student or newly qualified teacher, your 'leading edge' knowledge and skills in specific areas can have particular value to post-16 groups. You could, for example, set up a display of some of your own final project work. This is likely to promote discussion which you can steer to relevant areas of the syllabus.

SUMMARY

Years of experience in training teachers of design and technology have shown me that many are shocked and disturbed by the fact the national curriculum or guidelines and syllabuses are remarkably vague as to what and how to teach the subject. This should, however, be seen as valuable professional freedom to be used and enjoyed. There are many skills that will be important to you as a teacher, but the first should be the skill of analysing curriculum guidelines and syllabuses to see what you are required to teach and what pupils are expected to learn and experience. Once you have a good grasp of that, you can enjoy the professional autonomy of putting together learning experiences that will motivate and stretch all pupils. You will have to learn a lot of very basic material very quickly, and be sensitive to the details of skills which you take for granted and which you are now responsible for teaching. This chapter should have shown you how to go about this process. Note that you cannot do it simply by reading lists from a book – it must be done by active analysis on your part. This leads to better learning and skills which you will use time and time again in your teaching career.

Although resistant materials may be your specialist area, it is recommended that you also read the subject knowledge chapters on the other areas, as these contain other ideas for ways of auditing and updating subject knowledge which you can adapt for your own use. Reading these other chapters will also give you an overview of the whole subject of design and technology.

FURTHER READING

Denton, H.G. (1990) 'The role of group work in the delivery of Design and Technology in the National Curriculum', *Design and Technology Teaching*, vol. 22, no. 2, pp. 90–91

Denton, H.G. and Atkinson, S.E. (1988) 'Strategies for teaching coursework for A level design' in Eggleston, J. (ed.) *The Best of Craft Design and Technology*, Stoke on Trent: Trentham Books

Design and Technology Association (1995) *Minimum Competences for Students to Teach Design and Technology in Secondary Schools*, Wellesbourne: DATA

Norman, E. (ed.) (1995) *Advanced Design and Technology*, London: Longman

3 Teaching food technology

Gwyneth Owen-Jackson

INTRODUCTION

This chapter considers the knowledge required by a design and technology teacher specialising in food technology. It is not, however, a course in food studies, rather it indicates what may be included in a food technology curriculum, and how the principles of design and technology may be taught through the medium of food. The requirements of food technology at foundation and examination level are discussed, as is the contribution that food technology specialists can make to some vocational courses.

Food technology has its roots in home economics and, prior to that, domestic science. These earlier subjects involved pupils preparing food for family meals, managing resources and concern for the quality of family life. The change to food technology means a greater emphasis on commercial food production with pupils being taught to design food products suitable for different consumer needs and circumstances.

If food technology is your specialist area, it is likely that you will have a degree in home economics, food science or catering; you may also have relevant industrial experience through working for a food manufacturer or in catering. A background such as this will have given you some of the knowledge and skills required to teach food studies. However, the scope of food technology within design and technology is broad, so it is unlikely that any qualification or industrial experience you have will cover all the elements you may be required to teach. It may be necessary for you to develop specific aspects of your knowledge and skills in order to feel confident with all the aspects within the teaching programme.

If you find that you need to develop knowledge and skills in particular areas, you will find references in the Further Reading section, at the end of this chapter, which will help you.

OBJECTIVES

By the end of this chapter you should:

- have audited your own subject knowledge and be aware of any development of subject knowledge which may be required
- be familiar with the subject content of examination syllabuses in food technology
- be aware of vocational courses where food specialists may contribute.

FOOD TECHNOLOGY CURRICULA

The general principles of a design and technology course require you to teach pupils to design and make food products.

Designing

The question has been asked 'How can pupils design with food?', but if you consider the activities that make up what is generally understood as 'designing', you will see that they can be applied to food. The design process is complex but it can be broken down into a number of stages:

- identification of a need for design
- research for further information
- application of theoretical knowledge to the problem
- generation of possible solutions
- testing of the ideas
- selection of best-fit solutions
- modelling, or making, the solution.

In reality, design is not a linear process as presented here. Designers will be engaged in research and evaluation throughout the process, and modelling may occur at several points. However, rather than despair at the complexity, consider how these activities may be applied to the design of a food product:

- The identification of the needs of a specific group of consumers, or a manufacturer, may be presented to the pupils or may arise out of other activities, e.g. they could be asked to design a new food product for teenage healthy eaters or for a manufacturer who wishes to boost seasonal sales.
- Research can be carried out to help pupils further understand the needs of consumers or they may research existing products, e.g. the nutritional needs of teenagers or seasonal products already available.

- Theoretical knowledge may have to be specifically taught, e.g. nutrition, properties of foods, methods of making, sensory analysis.
- Pupils could then suggest possible recipes, foods or dishes, which may be entirely novel or may be adaptations of existing products.
- Testing of a range of ideas could involve nutritional analysis, costing and making up dishes to test for taste, colour and texture.
- From the test results one or two recipes could be developed further to produce solutions which meet the identified need.

If you analyse these processes, using the brainstorm method described in Chapter 2, you will be able of think of many more activities involved at different levels.

In industry, food designers are usually required to work to a specification. This will list the criteria which the product must meet, for example in relation to:

- cost
- size
- shape
- ingredients
- flavour
- colour
- nutritional value.

In school you may set a specification for pupils to work to, which may be simple or more complex. At foundation level, it is likely that pupils will only be able to deal with one or two criteria, for example, to produce a product with specific ingredients to a limited cost. As they become more experienced, the criteria can be made more complex and could include ingredients, cost, nutritional value, cooking methods and shelf-life. Working to a specification requires pupils to think much more carefully about the dish they are designing, to make sure that it meets the criteria. Their design, though, may be an adaptation of an existing recipe. It would be unrealistic to expect pupils to invent something new each time, as this takes time and resources way beyond those available. However, you only have to look at the wide range of varieties of products available (for example Cheddar cheese with ginger, spring onions or ham, or the wide and ever-increasing variety of soup flavours) to see that adaptations can easily be made to existing products.

Task 3.1 Designing with food

If your subject background has not involved design work, then try working through the design process described above, to design a new savoury snack food suitable as a lunch-time food for office workers.

As you do this, note what you do, how you do it, and your reactions to each stage.

In order to teach designing with food, you need to be familiar with it yourself. When you have done Task 3.1 think about how you would teach this to pupils:

- What subject knowledge would you need?
- What would the pupils need to know or learn?
- How would you take them through the process?
- What might they feel about the work?

If there are any areas that you are not sure about, then undertake further practice by working to other design briefs, perhaps those used in your school, and talk through your work with your mentor or tutor until you feel confident that you understand the process.

Making

There will be a range of practical skills that you will want pupils to acquire, but these should be relevant to their design tasks. However, to allow pupils to acquire specific skills which you have identified, you may choose to present them with a particular task requiring them to use specific making skills, so giving you an opportunity to teach these. As an example, if you want them to learn pastry-making skills, you could set a design brief asking them to develop a new snack product with a pastry case.

It is important also that each skill taught has a meaningful purpose within the overall scheme of work. This means that it should be carefully planned to relate both to the designing and the knowledge and understanding parts of the pupils' programme of learning. Making skills range from the simple (e.g. making a sandwich) to the complex (e.g. boning and rolling a chicken). In planning which skills will be taught and when, you should consider the level of difficulty involved and should structure the learning so that pupils move from easy to more difficult tasks. Beware, too, of assuming that simple foods involve simple making tasks; one of the most difficult dishes for young pupils to get right is scones, a simple product but getting the right consistency in the mixture can be problematic!

When selecting suitable practical work for pupils it is also important to remember:

- pupils often provide their own ingredients, so you have a responsibility to ensure that a good end-product is possible and that the cost is not prohibitive
- the time available – practical lessons include preparation and clearing away as well as cooking time
- the suitability of the practical work for the learning purpose
- experimental work – pupils may investigate through experiments rather than practical work. This would require you to provide ingredients and may require specialist equipment.

Task 3.2 Identifying making skills

From the curriculum guidelines that you have to follow, or the examination syllabus, identify the making skills that are involved.

Try to list them in sequential order, from the simplest to the most difficult.

Discuss with your mentor which making skills pupils find the simplest and which the most difficult.

As with designing, your own subject knowledge should include the ability to carry out, with confidence and skill, a wide range of making skills. You will also need to know what to do if pupils go wrong in their making, for example how to put right a pastry mix that is too wet or too dry or will not roll out, and how to rescue a lumpy sauce. This means that your knowledge has to be more than superficial, not just a knowledge of 'knowing how', but also 'knowing that'. In other words, you need to understand what is happening when ingredients are being manipulated. If there are areas that you are not sure about, the best way to develop these is through continual practice. Also try to watch your mentor or other colleagues teaching making skills and note what they say as well as what they do. Books listed in the Further Reading section below will also help to develop your knowledge of food science.

Consider not only whether you can carry out these making skills, but also whether you can explain what you are doing at each stage, and why. The teaching of making skills usually involves you carrying out some form of demonstration, in which you will need to explain to pupils what is happening and why it is done. Whilst practising your making skills, try talking about the ingredients, the weights and proportions of ingredients, the processes, health and safety and quality control factors. You can do this at home, either when you are alone, or with your family or friends as an audience!

Knowledge and understanding

To assist with their designing and making, pupils need to have acquired, or be taught through the task, a range of theoretical knowledge about food commodities. This is the subject knowledge which you will need to be confident about. Most food studies curricula cover similar aspects, these include:

- nutrition
- food science, viz. the chemical and physical properties of foods
- sensory analysis and evaluation
- energy, and how it is used in food preparation
- methods of cooking food
- food preservation

- health and safety
- quality.

For all of these aspects, you will be expected to have a high level of knowledge and understanding. Let us examine each of these in turn.

Nutrition will require you to know about all the major nutrients, their functions and dietary sources. You should also know the recommended dietary requirements for these nutrients, and the nutritional requirements of different groups of people. You should be able to provide advice on healthy eating and how this can be achieved, and should keep up to date with new and developing knowledge.

In *food science*, you will need to have knowledge of the chemical composition of nutrients, and how these are changed by heat, cold and processing. You will also need to know about the physical properties of food commodities and how these are utilised in the making of food products.

Sensory analysis involves knowing about the range of techniques available, how to carry these out and record the results.

In terms of *energy* used in cooking, you will need to know how this is transferred into food and the effect it has on it. Also, you will need some knowledge of energy costs, conservation and efficiency. There is also human energy to consider, a knowledge of the basal metabolic rate and the need to maintain an energy balance.

You will also need to know about methods of *food preservation*: what causes food spoilage and how this can be prevented; the effects on food of various preservation techniques and how each method works; also, the causes and effects of food poisoning.

Health and safety issues are detailed in Chapter 6, but you should be familiar with the relevant legislation and be able to apply health and safety procedures in all practical work. It is highly recommended that if you do not already have a Basic Food Hygiene Certificate, you contact your local authority Environmental Health Office to ask about classes and obtain this certificate. It is a simple course, requiring six hours of teaching and assessed by a short test. Once you have this you may apply to the Institute of Environmental Health Officers for registration to allow you to teach the course in your school.

The making of *quality products* is an important issue and you should, therefore, know about quality assurance and quality control systems and be able to apply the Hazard Analysis and Critical Control Processes (HACCP) system. If you are not sure what this means, then you need to take the Basic Food Hygiene Course (referred to above), or read up in textbooks or talk to colleagues. As described below, the focus of food technology is now on commercial production, and the issues of health and safety, and quality, are vital to all food manufacturers and consumers.

As food technology now focuses on industrial practice, you will also be required to know about the above areas from an industrial perspective, for example:

- the role of ingredients in products
- sensory evaluation techniques used in the food industry
- consumer behaviour and food choice
- large-scale preparation and production methods

- food preservation, storage and shelf-life
- costing
- health and safety legislative requirements.

Task 3.3 Teaching design and technology through food

Obtain a copy of the curriculum for design and technology which is relevant to where you teach and look at what is required to be taught. This chapter has given some examples of how some aspects could be taught through food. Now try to think of other food-related activities which would teach aspects of designing and making.

The Design and Technology Association has produced a paper entitled *Minimum Competences for Students to Teach Design and Technology in Secondary Schools* (1995b). This paper outlines the competences which they believe are required by newly qualified teachers. The paper outlines the subject-specific knowledge in each of the four areas and so provides a useful guide to the type and depth of knowledge required.

For each of the material areas (food, textiles, resistant materials and control and systems) there is a list of the subject knowledge required to teach the 11–14 age group (tier 1) and to the 14–18 age group (tier 2). As a food specialist, it is tier 2 which should be your guide. This is shown in Table 3.1.

Table 3.1 Minimum competences for food technology

DESIGNING AND MAKING

1.1 Understand the use of Dietary Reference Values to design products to meet specific nutritional specifications, e.g. to meet the needs of groups with particular conditions such as coeliacs, diabetics.

1.2 Include the range of sensory assessment techniques used in the food industry in the development and trialling of new products and in modifying existing products to meet new criteria and expectations.

1.3 Match the techniques to the product; understand the role of sampling and use of statistical analysis in the presentation of results.

1.4 Understand and use the planning and manufacturing procedures for large-scale production.

1.5 Use knowledge of the complexity of consumer behaviour in food choice.

1.6 Use a greater range of advanced food preparation skills.

1.7 Understand the use of commercial food preparation techniques and processing.

COMMUNICATION SKILLS

2.1 Use more accurate representations, and show understanding of the importance of concept development in the food process.

2.2 Apply more rigorous standards of scientific investigation to evaluate changes to product specification.

Table 3.1 Continued

2.3 Apply more depth of understanding of use of nutritional modelling and costing databases.
2.4 Display more precision in the presentation, showing understanding of production schedules and quality control, a greater skill in the use of photography and a range of communication strategies.

PRODUCTS AND APPLICATIONS

3.1 Apply scientific knowledge of the role of ingredients in product formation; use greater depth of knowledge and understanding of nutrition and sensory analysis; understand the pricing mechanism used in industry in a free market economy.
3.2 Show a greater depth of knowledge and understanding (of the legislative framework related to the development, production and sale of food products).
3.3 Understand marketing techniques in the food manufacturing and retail industries.
3.4 Show a greater depth and breadth of understanding (of the political and ethical influences on the design, production and sale of food products).

TECHNOLOGICAL CONCEPTS

4.1 *Materials and components*
4.1.1 Apply more detailed scientific knowledge of the functional components of food.
4.1.2 Use knowledge of the physical, chemical, biological and nutritional composition of foods to select ingredients to meet detailed specifications for food products.
4.1.3 Apply Hazard Analysis and Critical Control Processes (HACCP) to food production processes and quality control measures.
4.1.4 Use knowledge of commercial preservation techniques.
4.2 *Control and systems*
4.2.1 Understand systems of quality control and quality assurance used in the food industry.
4.3 *Energy*
4.3.1 Understand a greater depth of knowledge (of energy transfer, conservation and efficiency in the preparation and manufacture of food products), including industrial applications.
4.3.2 Understand basal metabolic rate (BMR) and the factors affecting BMR, the concept of homeostasis and applications to individuals.

INFORMATION TECHNOLOGY RELATED SKILLS

5.1 Use statistical analysis of sensory evaluation data.
5.2 Show use of industrial applications of IT in food manufacturing.

Source: Design and Technology Association, 1995b, pp. 25–28

Task 3.4 Audit your own subject knowledge and skills

Conduct an audit of your own existing subject knowledge against that listed in the *Minimum Competences* paper, shown in Table 3.1, and against the designing and making skills you previously identified.

Do this by drawing two lines down a sheet of A3 paper, to give three columns. In the first column you can list the areas involved in the various aspects, such as designing, making, subject knowledge. For example, the *Minimum Competences* paper lists under 'Making', 1.6 'Use a greater range of advanced food preparation skills'. In the second column you can put the detail into this. For this your earlier analysis in Task 3.2 will have helped you think about what food preparation skills you will need to know and teach, or you could use the brainstorm technique referred to in Chapter 2. Discuss your list with your mentor or other teachers to make sure that you have covered the full range of skills.

In the third column you should indicate whether you feel confident that you have each skill. You must decide whether you have it but it needs a little practice; or you have it but it needs a lot of practice; or you may know nothing about it at all and need some training.

Where you have identified the need for practice or training, plan how and when you will cover these.

An area which is increasing in importance is the development of pupils' skills of graphical presentation. This can be developed through all the areas of design and technology, in food it can be done *inter alia* through:

- information-giving tables and charts
- sensory analysis star diagrams
- posters of information, with photographs, drawings, tables, charts
- food labels with sketches, drawings, tables, charts
- photographic presentation of finished dishes.

Computer programs can also be of value here – they are discussed in Chapter 7.

EXAMINATION SYLLABUSES

In secondary schools the examination syllabuses are also a major determinant of what is taught and so you should ensure that your subject knowledge meets these requirements.

There have been a range of examinations available over the past few years but these seem to have been rationalised. Most examination boards now offer full and short courses in all the materials areas of design and technology, including food technology, and in graphics products. Syllabuses from the different boards vary slightly but cover much common ground. The commonly required knowledge for most food technology examinations includes:

- designing and making
- basic food commodities and components, their composition, structure and characteristics
- properties of foods, including nutritional values
- human nutritional needs and preferences
- hygiene, health and safety issues in relation to food
- food preservation and storage
- food preparation and cooking equipment
- food preparation and cooking methods
- convenience foods
- food manufacturing processes and systems
- product development
- product packaging and retailing
- food quality, including organoleptic qualities, food tests and presentation.

In designing, and planning to make, pupils will have to call on the knowledge and skills they have developed in learning about food commodities and food production. Table 3.2, from the London Examinations GCSE Design & Technology Food Technology Syllabus, shows how areas of food knowledge relate to the process of design. Again, this uses a linear approach to design in order to set out clearly the processes involved. In reality, pupils could undertake these processes in a number of different ways, perhaps employing one step several times and another not at all.

Making skills require pupils to be able to select and use food preparation equipment appropriate to the task. There is no prescribed list of equipment which pupils need to learn about; this is where you need to use your professional judgement as to what is appropriate.

There is also a requirement for pupils to be aware of industrial processes of food production, through simulation exercises, visits, videos or speakers. It will therefore be important that you are familiar with industrial processes and systems, such as commercial production methods, industrial equipment and the use of flow-charts and workflow charts.

You will see from this that the list of requirements is much the same at examination level as foundation level, and that what distinguishes them is the depth and complexity of knowledge taught. For example, it is more likely that at foundation level pupils will be taught the names of the different nutrients and their sources, whilst at examination level they will be taught the chemical structure of the nutrients. At foundation level they may be taught that flour thickens a sauce, and at examination level they will learn how this happens.

Table 3.2 Food technology subject knowledge and its links with design

DESIGNING WITH FOOD

When designing with food, pupils will develop design tasks, both open and within set parameters, which provide alternative strategies to possible problems. They should:

- *Illustrate logical development of design procedures* and plans of action that will achieve the stated objectives.
- *Provide alternative strategies* to possible problems, e.g. design a vegetarian dish using Quorn or other meat substitute; alter the ratio of ingredients in a dish; try different processing techniques as in recipe adaptation/modification.
- *Plan the development of new products*, including considerations of shape, size, volume, texture, flavour, costs, marketing, etc.
- *Apply understanding* of storage of food products; the specific conditions required to ensure a safe shelf-life, e.g. temperature, environments, sell by/use by dates. Carry out research through experimental work.
- *Understand the manufacture potential/implications* of batch production, e.g. market forces, costs, sensory qualities of product, consumer preferences, profit, labour, etc.
- *Recognise and take account of user preference*, e.g. by survey, observation, availability of resources, etc. Also particular issues, e.g. for Vegetable Chilli, what can be used as an alternative to meat? Produce dietary calculations to meet needs. Be aware of conflicting demands and how to resolve them, e.g. certain ingredients may be too expensive, therefore a cheaper alternative must be found.
- *Carry out consumer research strategies*. Discuss ideas. Set up and manage taste panels, e.g. Hedonic scale, etc. Consider users with particular needs, e.g. nutritional/physical, etc.
- *Apply understanding* of portion control and other considerations in relation to cost, etc., the effect of outside forces, e.g. mechanical, energy as in temperature.
- *Apply understanding of the functional properties* of ingredients, e.g. when thickening a liquid using starch, understanding that proportions are critical; make realistic suggestions on how to achieve intentions, e.g. pupils suggest a range of healthy puddings for the school dining room. Carry out recipe adaptation, etc.
- *Understand how to produce a dietary analysis* of chosen recipe, e.g. interpret data concerned with nutritional needs, food composition, dietary and eating trends, regional patterns of food consumption, etc. Apply and communicate information appropriately. Data bases, etc. Bar coding systems.
- *Understand the sequence of steps* in food production and processing – resources, times, efficiency of throughput, hygiene and safety, appropriateness for purpose.
- *Make modifications*, e.g. re-organise time, alter seasonings, adding liquid to sauces to achieve consistency desired, noting all modifications. Review actions, use and compile data.
- *Analyse and test* ingredients, e.g. assess proportions of ingredients to

Table 3.2 Continued

identify the way forward. Check against specification, e.g. sensory qualities, consistency, uniformity, etc. Understand the importance of having control in a test; produce and develop flexible strategies and plans.
• *Carry out sensory analysis*, e.g. use triangle, rating and other appropriate tests to judge final products and to assess and rank opinions, etc. Test consumer reaction to pricing, comparability etc. with similar products using prototypes.

Source: Based on University of London Examinations and Assessment Council, 1998, p.10

Task 3.5 Reviewing the examination syllabus

Obtain a copy of the examination syllabus used in your school. Read through this and carry out an audit as you did in Task 3.4.

On an A3 sheet write in the first column the areas for study listed by the examination board. In the second column put the detail in to expand each of these areas, perhaps talk to colleagues to help with this. In the third column indicate what level of knowledge and skills you already have and what you need to develop.

You may teach pupils beyond the age of 16 A level for Advanced, Higher or to vocational qualifications. In England, Wales and Northern Ireland the AS/A level qualifications have been reviewed and new syllabuses will be in place from September 2000 with the first new AS examinations in 2001 and the first new A levels in 2002. There is currently only one suitable course for food specialists, viz. Design and Technology: Food. This is designed to further develop pupils' capability in design and technology as well as their values and attitudes and their knowledge and skills in relation to food. In addition to designing and making, pupils will be required to study in detail:

- food commodities
- nutrition
- properties and functions of foods
- processing of foods, with the emphasis on industrial and commercial practice
- product development
- packaging and labelling
- quality issues
- health and safety
- food marketing and consumer issues.

It is also a requirement for these new courses to provide opportunities for pupils to develop key skills, namely:

- communication
- application of number
- information technology
- working with others
- improving their own learning
- problem-solving.

However, it is a statutory requirement for the design and technology courses to include in their assessment the key skill of communication, so this will need to be built in to the teaching programme.

Task 3.6 Auditing your knowledge and skills against post-16 requirements

Obtain a copy of the latest post-16 syllabus in your area, this should be one that will be examined in one/two years' time, not one showing the current year. If your school does not teach post-16, then contact one of the examination boards to obtain a copy of the syllabus.

Carry out an audit of your knowledge and skills against those listed in the syllabus, following the procedure described in Task 3.4.

Food technology specialists can also contribute to the teaching of vocational courses in areas of study including manufacturing, health and social care, and hospitality and catering. When studying manufacturing, pupils develop knowledge and skills and an understanding of manufacturing principles and practice which apply across a range of industries, including the food and drink sector. They study manufacturing organisations and production systems, product design and development, production planning, manufacturing processes and quality. Food production may be the major focus of their work, or it may be a contributor, but you will need to be familiar with industrial and manufacturing processes in order to teach this.

The hospitality and catering course relates to those industries. Pupils study aspects of hotel and catering provision, customer care, hotel tasks and management in addition to food purchasing and preparation skills, nutrition, hygiene and safety. There are additional, optional units available in environmental health, nutrition awareness and food science which the school may choose to offer to pupils.

Health and social care is a course that prepares young people for work in these fields. It contains units of work in 'Understanding health and well-being' and 'Planning diets'.

If you are asked to deliver units of work in vocational courses, it is likely that it would be those in which you had a specialism and you would be working with a team of teachers who, together, would cover the whole course. If you need to develop subject knowledge in these areas, then an industrial or work placement would be ideal. Talk to your mentor, tutor or person responsible for staff development in the school, about the possibility of organising this. If this is not possible then try to arrange one or two visits for yourself, in your own time, to local manufacturers. Many companies now produce promotional or educational literature which may be helpful; reading trade and professional journals will also give you some background knowledge.

SUMMARY

The subject knowledge that a teacher possesses is important in many ways, particularly for the student teacher and newly qualified teacher. Good subject knowledge means that you have a depth of knowledge to draw on and this will help you in both your preparation and classroom performance.

When planning lessons, you may still need to search out information but you will know how information links together. In the classroom it will enable you to be more confident when teaching and answering questions, for example knowing which foods contain complementary nutrients, or in practical lessons dealing with the problems children often face such as pastry that just will not bind together. In assessing pupils you will have a better understanding of their responses. During your initial training course, having good subject knowledge means that you will be able to focus on learning about teaching.

It is likely that there will be gaps in your subject knowledge and this chapter should have helped you to identify what these are. This will allow you to plan to develop your knowledge and skills throughout your course, through the support of tutors, mentors, other courses or self-study.

Food technology may be your specialist area but it is recommended that you also read the subject knowledge chapters on the other areas as these contain other ideas for ways of auditing and updating subject knowledge which you can adapt for your own use. Reading these other chapters will also give you an overview of the whole subject of design and technology.

Design and technology, though, is an area where subject knowledge is never static – new materials, new equipment, processes and products mean that you will be constantly updating your knowledge throughout your career. This is discussed further in Chapter 13.

FURTHER READING

Campbell, A. M., Penfield, M. P. and Griswold, R. M. (1980) *The Experimental Study of Food*, London: Constable

Davidson, S., Passmore, R., Brock, J. F. and Truswell, A. S. (1981) *Human Nutrition and Dietetics*, Edinburgh: Churchill Livingstone

Fox, B. A. and Cameron, A. G. (1995) *Food Science, Nutrition and Health*, London: Edward Arnold

Rutland, Marion (ed.) (1997) *Teaching Food Technology in Secondary Schools*, London: David Fulton

4 Teaching control and systems

Jim Sage

INTRODUCTION

Control and systems is a complex area of design and technology as it covers systems, control systems and the use of electronics, microprocessors and computers, pneumatics, mechanisms and electro-mechanical devices in control systems. The basic structure of the knowledge and understanding of control and systems, and some connections between them, are shown in Figure 4.1.

This chapter outlines a core of experience and indicates how it can be taught discretely or related to work in other areas of design and technology. The place of electronics and computer control within the area of control and systems is discussed, as well as how developing pupils' understanding of systems can lead to enhanced skills in product analysis and product design.

OBJECTIVES

By the end of this chapter you should:

- have audited your own knowledge and understanding of control and systems
- be familiar with the key ideas in this area
- be aware of a range of teaching approaches and strategies for delivering this content.

Figure 4.1 Aspects of control and systems

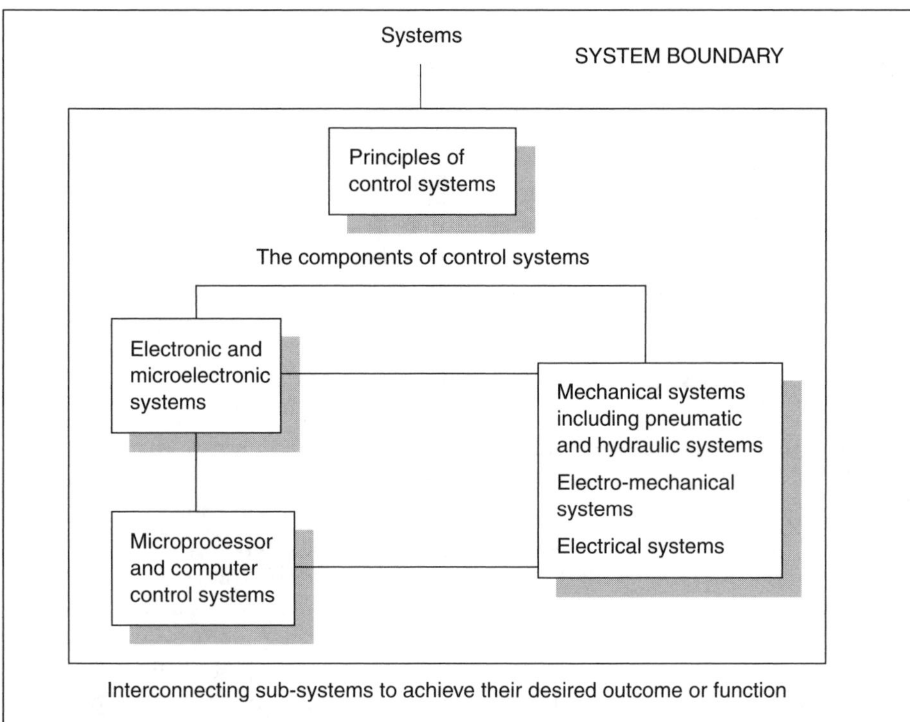

KEY STRANDS WITHIN CONTROL AND SYSTEMS

In order to help pupils develop their knowledge and understanding in a way that enables them to transfer it to their designing and making, it is useful to identify the key strands that need to be developed. These strands are:

- an understanding of the principles of systems
- the use of an 'input–process–output' model to describe systems
- the use of systems diagrams (block diagrams, flow diagrams, control system diagrams) to represent this process
- an understanding of the principles of control systems
- open and closed-loop (feedback) control, sequential control systems
- knowledge of a range of sub-systems
- electrical and electronic
- mechanical, including pneumatics and hydraulics
- electro-mechanical
- microprocessor and computer control

- an understanding of how to interconnect sub-systems to achieve their desired outcome or function
- knowing how to analyse the performance of systems
- use this knowledge and understanding to design and make products and systems containing control systems.

However, each strand should not be considered in isolation, dividing the area of systems and control in this way is an aid to planning rather than a suggested model for teaching. Although discrete teaching units may be required for some aspects, activities for pupils should make links between the strands to present a more coherent and cohesive view of control and systems. This is developed later in the chapter.

Progression through these strands

Table 4.1 presents each of these strands and key experiences within them. These are laid out to show the progression through them. The earlier experiences are suitable for pupils aged 11–14 years, the middle experiences are suitable for all pupils in the 14–16 age range, irrespective of the course they are following or their material specialism, and the later experiences are appropriate for 14–16 year olds specialising in control and systems and for post-16 courses. They are also relevant to some vocational courses, such as engineering and manufacturing.

As pupils move through the middle and later experiences described in Table 4.1, design and make activities should encourage them to make use of current designing and manufacturing practices and technologies. The coverage of concepts, ideas and

Task 4.1 Checking your understanding of control and systems

Table 4.1 can be treated as a list of content which you can use to check your own understanding of control and systems. Take a sheet of A3 paper and draw two lines down it, to give you three columns.

In the first column you can write out the points listed as pupil experiences in Table 4.1. In the second column you can identify those aspects where your knowledge is secure, where it requires some checking to clarify certain points, or where you have little or no understanding.

You can then use this to produce an 'action plan' showing, in the third column, what strategies you will use to strengthen and develop your understanding.

You will find the list of suggested further reading at the end of this chapter useful.

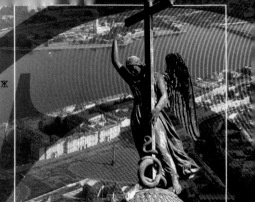

ЭРМИТАЖ
The State Hermitage Museum

Входной билет в
Государственный Эрмитаж

Дата:07.08.2004
Цена:350.00р.

ЭП 759947

Основная категория ИГ

ИНН 7830002416 ОКПО 02175184

001 103 100318688001

07-08-2004 12:58:43 001-1072538

ГОСУДАРСТВЕННЫЙ ЭРМИТАЖ
приглашает Вас посетить:

ДВОРЕЦ МЕНШИКОВА
Университетская наб., 15

ЗИМНИЙ ДВОРЕЦ ПЕТРА I
Дворцовая наб., 32

ЭКСПОЗИЦИЮ В ГЛАВНОМ ШТАБЕ
Дворцовая пл., 8

ДНИ И ЧАСЫ РАБОТЫ:
ВТОРНИК, СРЕДА, ЧЕТВЕРГ, ПЯТНИЦА, СУББОТА
10.30-18.00
ВОСКРЕСЕНЬЕ
10.30-17.00

ГОСУДАРСТВЕННЫЙ ЭРМИТАЖ

THE STATE HERMITAGE MUSEUM
cordially invites you to visit its branches:

MENSHIKOV PALACE
15 Universitetskaya Emb.

WINTER PALACE OF PETER I
32 Dvortsovaya Emb.

EXHIBITION IN THE GENERAL STAFF BUILDING
8 Dvortsovaya Square

OPENING TIMES
TUESDAY, WEDNESDAY, THURSDAY, FRIDAY, SATURDAY
10.30 am to 6.00 pm
SUNDAY
10.30 am to 5.00 pm

www.hermitagemuseum.org

Don't forget to visit HERMITAGE MUSEUM E-STORE: www.shop.hermitagemuseum.org

Просьба сохранять билет до конца посещения

Table 4.1 Key strands and experiences in control and systems

Key strand	*Key experiences*
SYSTEMS	*Early experiences*: Systems have inputs, processes and outputs; pupils should recognise these in existing products and products they have analysed and made. Complex systems can be broken down into sub-systems to help analyse them; each sub-system has input, process and output stages. Types of control systems including mechanical, electrical, electronic and pneumatic, including the use of switches in electrical systems, sensors in electronic switching circuits and the interconnection of mechanical systems to achieve different kinds of movement. How different types of system and sub-system can be interconnected to achieve the required function. The importance of feedback in control systems. Examples of ON/OFF feedback control. *Middle experiences*: Defining systems and sub-systems using systems boundaries. The language and principles of systems and control: • open loop control • closed loop (feedback) control ON/OFF only • sequential control. Ways of representing systems, such as block-flow diagrams, flow-charts. *Later experiences*: Analysis of more complex, multi-stage control systems. Industrial applications of control systems, in a wide range of contexts such as automated production systems, process control, material handling systems. The language and principles of systems and control: • open loop control • closed loop (feedback) control ON/OFF • proportional control • sequential control. Use of control systems diagrams using appropriate conventions.

Table 4.1 Continued

Key strand	*Key experiences*
SUB-SYSTEMS 1: Electrical and electronic systems. The specific content should be driven by function rather than covering every type of component and sub-system; the functions to be covered are: • sensing • switching • timing and sequencing • power supplies • matching different electronic sub-systems and the need for signal conditioning and interfacing.	*Early experiences*: Investigate a range of products and applications containing electrical and electronic sub-systems. Use of switches and other simple components to control electrical circuits. Use sensors in transistor switching circuits. Use of single/two transistor switching circuits as process • using switches and sensors as inputs • motors, solenoids, electrical heaters, lamps and LEDs as outputs • use of devices such as relays and transducer drivers as simple interfaces. Use sensors in ON/OFF feedback control systems. *Middle experiences*: Electronic systems involving feedback to achieve ON/OFF control. Use comparator to compare actual with set level. Use logic to process signals from more than one sensor. 555 timer – as an example of the use of an IC configured in a variety of ways using external components to achieve a desired outcome such as a pulsed or timed input. Use of an electromagnet /solenoid /linear actuator as an output device. *Later experiences*: Introducing a range of ICs that can be used to achieve particular functions. Example: Use of op-amp configured as non-inverting, inverting and differential amplifier; timers, controllers. Combinational and sequential logic. Monitoring and analysing the performance of the above electronic systems and sub-systems including quantitative analysis. Interfacing the above electronic sub-systems with other systems and sub-systems. Extending the range of electronic components used through these experiences: for example switches, resistors – fixed and variable, potentiometers, capacitors, transistors, thyristors, relays, timer IC, basic logic, operational amplifiers, range of output devices.

SUB-SYSTEMS 2: Mechanical systems including pneumatics and hydraulics. Electro-mechanical systems. The specific content covered should be driven by function rather than covering every type of component and sub-system; the functions to be covered are: • the use of mechanical systems to provide a range of different types of motion • the use of mechanical systems to control the speed and direction of motion • the use of mechanical systems to transmit or change the magnitude of force/torque • latching and locking systems • the interconnection of mechanical systems to achieve the desired output • the control of mechanical systems.	*Early experiences*: Investigate a range of products and applications containing mechanical sub-systems. Identify what the mechanical system is doing: • changing the type of movement • changing the force/torque applied or distance moved • interconnecting different mechanical systems to achieve a particular output. Building mechanical systems to achieve a particular function. Changing the type of motion: • cams, gears, cranks etc. • levers and linkages • force and distance multipliers. • 3-port valve and single acting cylinder. *Middle experiences*: Use electrical switches to control electro-mechanical systems – e.g. motors, solenoids, linear actuators. Use microswitches as limit switches in electronic circuits to control electro-mechanical systems. More complex pneumatic systems including the use of air muscles. Qualitative and quantitative analysis of the performance of mechanical systems. *Later experiences*: Open and closed-loop control of electric motors: on/off; reversing; speed control; servo and stepper motors. Electronic control of solenoids, solenoid operated valves, linear actuators, smart wire (shape memory alloy), linked to mechanical systems. The performance of mechanical systems: • quantitative analysis of mechanical systems, including energy transfers in mechanical systems. • efficiency of mechanical system and methods for maximising the efficiency. Interfacing electro-mechanical systems with other systems and sub-systems. Electronic and microprocessor control of electro mechanical sub-systems.

Table 4.1 Continued

Key strand	*Key experiences*
THE USE OF COMPUTERS & MICROPROCESSORS IN CONTROL SYSTEMS	*Early experiences*: Experience of using a computer and interface to control external devices. *Middle experiences*: Use of computer to control a wider range of external devices – interconnecting with range of other sub-systems. Selection of the most appropriate control system to perform a particular function. *Later experiences*: Microprocessor control. PLC control. Use of PICs in control systems. Use of language- and graphic-based control programs. Selection of the most appropriate control system to perform a particular function. Interfacing microprocessor and computer control systems with other systems and sub-systems. Applications of microprocessor and computer control in a range of contexts.
INTERCONNECTING SUB-SYSTEMS	*Early experiences*: Interconnecting sub-systems to achieve a desired outcome or function (some simple examples: electronic circuit controlling motor, solenoid, linear actuator, water pump such as a 12 volt car windscreen washer, through a relay; pneumatic piston operating a lever; electronic control of a pneumatic piston using a solenoid operated valve). *Middle experiences*: In many systems the processing is electronic – understanding of basic electronic processing systems. The processing can be done using a microprocessor or a computer. Electronic, microprocessor and computer control can be used with: electrical systems; electro-mechanical systems – solenoids, motors, electromagnets, etc.; mechanical systems; pneumatic /hydraulic systems. Structures to support control systems. Matching sub-systems and the use of interfaces between different systems and sub-systems. Selection of power supplies.

Later experiences:
The use of quantitative analysis in the design of structures to support control systems.
The use of a quantitative approach to the selection/design of the interfaces used and to the selection of power supplies.

ANALYSING THE PERFORMANCE OF SYSTEMS

Early experiences:
Investigating the use of control systems in products and other applications.
Simple qualitative observations of input and output, such as making measurements of distance, force, number of rotations.

Middle experiences:
Investigating the use of control systems in products and other applications:

- simple qualitative observations of input and output such as making measurements of distance, force, angle turned through, number of rotations, electric current and potential difference
- establishing the relationship between input and output in simple systems, e.g. simple gear systems, levers, and using these relationships to analyse the performance of the system/sub-system.

Representing systems using block diagrams, flow diagrams, systems diagrams to aid the analysis.

Later experiences:
Investigation of systems and sub-systems including a systematic and quantitative analysis of the performance of systems including efficiency. This should cover mechanical, electronic, electrical, electro-mechanical and pneumatic systems and the evaluation and analysis of a range of control and other products.
Representing systems using block diagrams, flow diagrams, systems diagrams to aid the analysis.
The application of this understanding to control systems and products used in a range of different contexts covering a range of different materials.
Using a systems approach for:

- product evaluations
- analysing a range of systems including production systems and factory layouts using work-flow diagrams and other similar methods, quality assurance systems and procedures, organisational systems used in commercial and industrial organisations
- hazard analysis, e.g. HACCP
- project management
- organising their own work.

Table 4.1 Continued

Key strand	*Key experiences*
DESIGNING AND MAKING CONTROL SYSTEMS	*Early experiences*: Designing single sub-systems, e.g. electrical circuit with appropriate choice of switch or electronic circuit with a sensor. Designing combination of sub-systems, e.g. using an electrical or electronic circuit to switch a motor or electromagnet on/off at appropriate times or in response to certain inputs. Designing more complex systems but making use of kits such as systems electronics, mechanisms and pneumatics kits. The use of computer programs in the design of sub-systems and systems. *Middle experiences*: At this stage activities should relate to industrial practices and the application of systems and control. Use of kits for investigating and evaluating design decisions and for rapid prototyping. Designing control functions within the context of the overall product or system design. The use of computer programs in the design of sub-systems and systems. Construction techniques appropriate to making products containing different types of control system. Analysing the performance of the sub-systems and the complete systems and fault finding and rectification techniques. *Later experiences*: Syllabuses should enable pupils to design and make systems and products incorporating control systems within a variety of contexts, including industrial and commercial, and making use of a range of different materials and components. Pupils' work on control systems should also develop their understanding of structures. Using a systems (systematic) approach to designing alongside more intuitive approaches. Computer modelling of systems and sub-systems. Computer-aided design of control systems and sub-systems. Use of kits for investigating and evaluating design decisions and for rapid prototyping. Designing control functions within the context of the overall product or system design. Construction techniques appropriate to making products containing different types of control system. Analysing the performance of the sub-systems and the complete systems and fault finding and rectification techniques.

SYSTEMS AND CONTROL IN MANUFACTURING	*Middle experiences*: Analysing the sequence of processes used in the manufacture of familiar products. The place of control systems within the manufacturing process. *Later experiences*: Analysing the sequence of processes used in the manufacture of familiar products. The place of control systems within the manufacturing process. The role of control systems as the scale of production increases and the impact of this on design, the materials used, production techniques, the workforce, quality control and assurance, costs (social, economic, environmental issues). The role of control systems in product design such as CAD/CAM, Total Product Modelling (TPM) and Electronic Product Definition (EPD). The use of control systems in quality control and quality assurance.

knowledge should have a clear emphasis on function rather than specific technologies, for example, pupils should be encouraged to identify an appropriate integrated circuit rather than designing complex combinations of smaller sub-systems in order to gain experience of these sub-systems. This more detailed knowledge should be acquired through focused tasks and investigations as necessary and appropriate.

Task 4.2 Planning the use of a range of teaching and learning strategies

Select an idea for a project with a significant control component. This could be one you will be teaching or use an idea from Table 4.3.

Plan in outline a variety of focused tasks that could be used to help pupils develop their knowledge and understanding, design ideas and the skills needed to realise their ideas.

TEACHING PUPILS ABOUT SYSTEMS AND SUB-SYSTEMS

It is important that pupils have a good understanding of the nature of systems and sub-systems and ways of representing systems. The system boundary is very important in establishing and defining the limits of the system being investigated. When teaching this aspect, it is useful to take pupils through examples to establish the key features of systems and sub-systems (see Sage and Thomson, 1996). Pupils should then reinforce their understanding by applying the process described to other familiar situations.

Using kits to teach pupils about control and systems

The use of kits in investigating and using control and systems is recommended because they allow pupils to:

- investigate types of control system and sub-systems and achieve reliable results
- interconnect different types of control system; for example, the use of electronic control with mechanical, electro-mechanical and pneumatic systems
- develop, model and evaluate design ideas
- make models and simulations of complex systems and investigate these
- produce prototypes to evaluate design ideas and possible design solutions quickly.

This does not detract from the need for pupils to design and make control products. There is a range of equipment available that allows pupils to produce quite complex products once they have modelled their ideas using kits – for example, the use of cheap and readily available integrated circuits including microcontrollers and pneumatics components that can be built into products.

USING A SYSTEMS APPROACH TO ANALYSE AND EVALUATE PRODUCTS

As explained earlier, a systems approach can be used to evaluate products. This activity is easier and more rewarding if pupils can investigate actual products. A bank of suitable products should be assembled and added to over time. It is also possible to build up a bank of ideas for products using cuttings from newspaper articles and magazines. Suitable products include:

- toys
- domestic appliances and kitchen equipment
- tools and other workshop equipment
- devices designed for use by people with particular disabilities
- security devices.

Provide pupils with a range of products and take them through an example to establish the key features of the processes used to analyse and evaluate products:

- identify whether electrical, electronic, mechanical or pneumatic (or hydraulic) systems have been used
- work out what the function of the system is
- identify the inputs and outputs for the complete system
- identify any sub-systems and their inputs and outputs
- work out how the sub-systems link together
- use an input–process–output systems diagram to explain how it works.

This activity can be more effective if pupils work in small groups, taking one or two products or applications each, and then report their findings to the rest of the class. For examples of using this approach, refer to *Control Products* (RCA, 1997).

> **WARNING**: Pupils should not be allowed to dismantle mains electrical appliances.

Task 4.3 Using a systematic approach to product analysis

> Choose a suitable product and go through the process described above and note any particular difficulties you experience.
>
> Consider how you might present this activity to pupils. What products could you use? How would you guide them through the analysis? How would they record their analysis?

USING A SYSTEMS APPROACH TO DESIGNING

The input–process–output model can also be used as an approach to designing. Obviously this process is more suitable for some products than others, but pupils should be taught the process to add to their design repertoire. They should first of all be encouraged to define what they want to achieve, then to describe the task that the system needs to perform. You can help pupils to describe as fully as possible what they want to achieve by guiding them through the questions shown in Table 4.2.

Once the pupils have answered all the questions, they could use a systems diagram to show how the sub-systems relate to each other, showing the inputs and outputs for each. This means:

- identifying the inputs and outputs for the overall system
- identifying any sub-systems
- identifying the inputs and outputs for each sub-system
- drawing the systems diagram for the complete system.

However, it is not suggested that this is the only approach that pupils should be taught; there are times when a more intuitive and less systematic approach to evaluating and

Table 4.2 Using the input–process–output model in designing

Output	*Input*	*Process*
What do you want to happen? What output do you want? What could you use to achieve this? What are the advantages and disadvantages of each method? What appears to be the best output sub-system at this stage?	When and how do you want the output to happen? What do you want to cause it to happen? Do you want the system to respond to a change or an event? How can you detect this change or event? What do you want to trigger the output? What detection/sensing devices could you use? What are the advantages and disadvantages of each method? What appears to be the best input sub-system at this stage?	The information from the input will need to be processed to drive the output. Do the input and output sub-systems match? If not, what needs to be done to make them match? Do you need to re-think either the input or the output, or both?

designing products is more useful. Pupils could be asked to consider when, where, why, how and for what type of products this approach would be suitable.

LINKING CONTROL AND SYSTEMS TO OTHER MATERIALS

It is difficult to think of a control and systems product that does *not* make use of other materials! Many projects based on other materials will include the application of control systems. Activities related to control and systems should be included in work using resistant materials, graphics products, textiles and food. Table 4.3 shows some contexts for projects linking control systems to other areas of design and technology.

Links could be made to other subjects, in particular science and mathematics, as pupils could explore the scientific and mathematical principles behind the operation of the products (see Sage, 1996). Some possible links are shown in Table 4.4.

Table 4.3 Possible contexts for linking control and systems to other material areas

	Material areas	*Examples*
Environmental control	Food Electronics/systems and control Ceramics	Temperature control in food storage area Environmental control in a greenhouse Monitoring the temperature in a kiln
Process control	Food Textiles	Temperature control, flow of fluids Temperature control during dyeing
Presentations and performances	Systems and control Resistant materials/ structures	Lighting, special effects Animatronics, revolving stage, raising/lowering flaps, trap doors
Point-of-sale displays Dynamic displays	Graphic products Resistant materials could be combined with textiles	Using flashing LEDs 'Animatronics' using control systems graphics to produce informative and eye-catching displays
Safety and security systems	Electronics Graphic products	Buildings Items on display in shops, museums
Toys and educational aids	Resistant materials, textiles, graphic products	Electrically powered, electronically controlled mechanical systems
Aids for people with disability or elderly people	Resistant materials, electronics	Picking things up, applying force, warning devices and alarms
Novelty items given away for advertising and publicity Promotional pop-ups	Graphic products, food, textiles, resistant materials with electronics	Corporate image Theme park Using pop-ups in displays, providing information, attracting attention, etc. Pop-up books for children or adults

Table 4.3 Continued

	Material areas	*Examples*
Providing information for people	Graphic products, resistant materials with electronics	Signs and signing, warning signs, direction indicators
Fun with control	Resistant materials, graphic products, textiles	Items designed to make use of control to provide entertainment or stimulate interest
Personal radios	Resistant materials, graphic products	An example of a product designed around an electronic circuit
Modelling production lines	Food, textiles, resistant materials graphic products	Quality control, moving items/materials handling, packaging operations, cutting, folding operations, filling containers

CONTROL AND SYSTEMS AND MANUFACTURING

This covers all aspects of manufacturing including research and development, product design, production, quality assurance and quality control, and marketing. As pupils move up the school, there is an increasing emphasis on industrial approaches to manufacturing and designing for manufacturing, as opposed to designing one-off products. As the scale of production increases, control systems are used more extensively in manufacturing for a wide variety of reasons:

- repeatability
- working to tighter tolerances
- using automated systems for tedious, repetitive tasks
- increasing the speed of the process and productivity
- quality control
- safety – working in hostile environments
- reduction of waste
- controlling continuous processes
- control of complex processes
- reducing the possibilities or effects of human error
- reducing maintenance and repair times through the use of warning and safety systems.

Table 4.4 Links between control and systems and aspects of science and mathematics

Aspects of science and mathematics	*Links to control and systems*
Science:	
systematic enquiry (experimental and investigative science)	• research, investigative focused practical tasks
Electricity:	
• ways of controlling the current in electrical circuits	• electronics
	• sensors used in a potential (voltage) divider
• measuring current and voltage	• evaluating control products
• V-I-R characteristics	• analysing the performance of systems
• electromagnetism	• relays, solenoids, motors
Forces:	
• types of force	• mechanical and pneumatic systems
• effects of forces	• structures used in control products
• pressure	• evaluating control products
• measuring and calculating forces and pressure	• analysing the performance of systems
Energy transfers:	
• quantifying energy transfers	• evaluating control products
• work, energy and power	• analysing the performance of systems
• efficiency	• designing systems
Mathematics:	
• solving numerical problems	• evaluating control products
• understanding and using equations and formulae	• analysing the performance of systems
	• designing systems
• understanding and using measures	
• processing and interpreting data	

With older pupils you could cover different scales of production, and provide opportunities for them to design products or systems for one-off, batch and large-scale production. In the case of products designed for large-scale production, it is not expected that they should manufacture the products on this scale, but they should make a working prototype and consider in detail all of the issues associated with scaling up the production, including design decisions, the materials used, quality issues and the manufacturing processes to be used. Case studies from industry can be used to develop pupils' understanding of control systems and their applications within manufacturing, and to inform their own designing and making, as well as develop their understanding of manufacturing. It is even better if pupils can be taken on industrial visits, but this can be difficult. If visits are used, they need to be well planned and pupils given a clear focus for the visit. (For more details on planning visits see Chapter 12.)

At the higher level pupils should also develop an understanding of:

- the place of control systems within each stage of the manufacturing process
- the role of control systems as the scale of production increases and the impact of this on design decisions, the materials used, production techniques, the workforce, quality control and assurance, costs (social, economic, environmental issues)
- the role of control systems in product design such as CAD/CAM, total product modelling (TPM) and electronic product definition (EPD)
- the use of control systems in quality control and quality assurance.

Additionally, pupils should understand the need for increased sustainability and how this relates to manufacturing and technological activity. They should be provided with opportunities to develop an understanding of the role of control systems in: monitoring environmental impact; environmental control; and in the manufacture of products and systems with reduced environmental impact.

CONTROL USING MICROPROCESSORS AND COMPUTERS

You are probably familiar with the terms 'hardware' and 'software' when you are talking about computers. If you make an electronic product such as an electronic game, you have made a piece of electronic hardware. Computers are also electronic hardware but they need programs or software to make them run. If you want to use a computer as a controller you need another piece of hardware known as an 'interface'; this takes inputs and passes information to the computer. The computer can act on this information and pass further information back to the interface. The interface also has outputs which pass information to the process or device being controlled. You will also need a piece of software, the control program, to control this process. There is another type of software which is embedded into a product, known as 'firmware'. Normally firmware is programmed into read-only memory in a microprocessor-based system. The engine management systems used on modern cars is an example of firmware. It is also very widely used for microprocessor control operations in industry.

Computers can be very useful in control systems but they can also cause some problems: the computer may not be available when you need it; they are bulky and not easy to carry around; it can be an expensive way of doing something that can be done more cheaply and easily; and you will need to use a suitable interface with your computer. Microprocessors can overcome some of these problems.

Although computers are used for control in schools, they are rarely used for this purpose in industry; industrial control is usually done using a programmable logic controller (PLC). PLCs can be programmed to carry out a particular function; they can be thought of as a 'computer-in-a-box' without the keyboard and visual display unit (VDU). If a PLC can be thought of as a computer-in-a-box, then a peripheral interface controller (PIC) can be considered as a 'computer-on-a-chip' (integrated circuit). PICs are very cheap and offer tremendous potential for use in schools.

Computer control systems do have some design advantages:

- many inputs and outputs can be controlled – usually at least eight inputs and outputs
- the system can be altered or adjusted very easily
- the system can be programmed quite easily to record what it does, to provide management information; for example, it could record the total number of parcels of different sizes and run a small program to predict when a truck will be needed for a pick-up. It could provide the data for a chart to show how busy the system was during a month to help plan working hours.

There is a choice of software applications for designing a computer control system. You could use language style such as CoCo, Control IT, Smart Move, and other similar programs, or graphical style – these are programs that allow you to design a control system as a two-dimensional flowchart – Logicator and Flowol are two examples.

The design of a computer control system can be split into these main tasks:

1 designing the control program
2 designing the electrical connections and mechanisms
3 testing the complete system
4 refining the complete system.

USING COMPUTERS TO TEACH ABOUT CONTROL

Control and systems as an area is often seen as part of information technology (IT), and computer control can appear to be an attractive way of teaching this as it appears 'high tech' and interesting, provides motivation, appeals to many pupils, and appears to have relevance to the use of control in a wide range of contexts. However, computer control:

- does not necessarily teach pupils the principles of control
- does not reflect control in industrial and other contexts where microprocessor control – using PLCs or PICs – is more common (in other words, you will not see a keyboard and screen)
- may provide pupils with knowledge of one type of control only, e.g. sequential control.

In many cases where computers are used to teach pupils about control, the control process is often sophisticated but what is controlled is trivial, e.g. traffic lights.

Experience shows that pupils can work through complex problems and use good software to design programs to control devices and systems without fully understanding the principles of control. The approach suggested here is to ensure that pupils have a full understanding of the basic principles and then to present them with a range of ways of achieving the control they need. Using a computer is obviously one way of achieving control but it is not the only way, and should not be used as the main means of teaching pupils about control systems.

A decision-tree, as shown in Figure 4.2, can be used to enable pupils to make an informed and well-considered decision about whether to use a computer in their control system. You may need to talk them through it to make sure that it is fully understood before they apply it themselves. They should go through the following steps:

Figure 4.2 A decision-tree to help you decide whether to use a computer in your control system

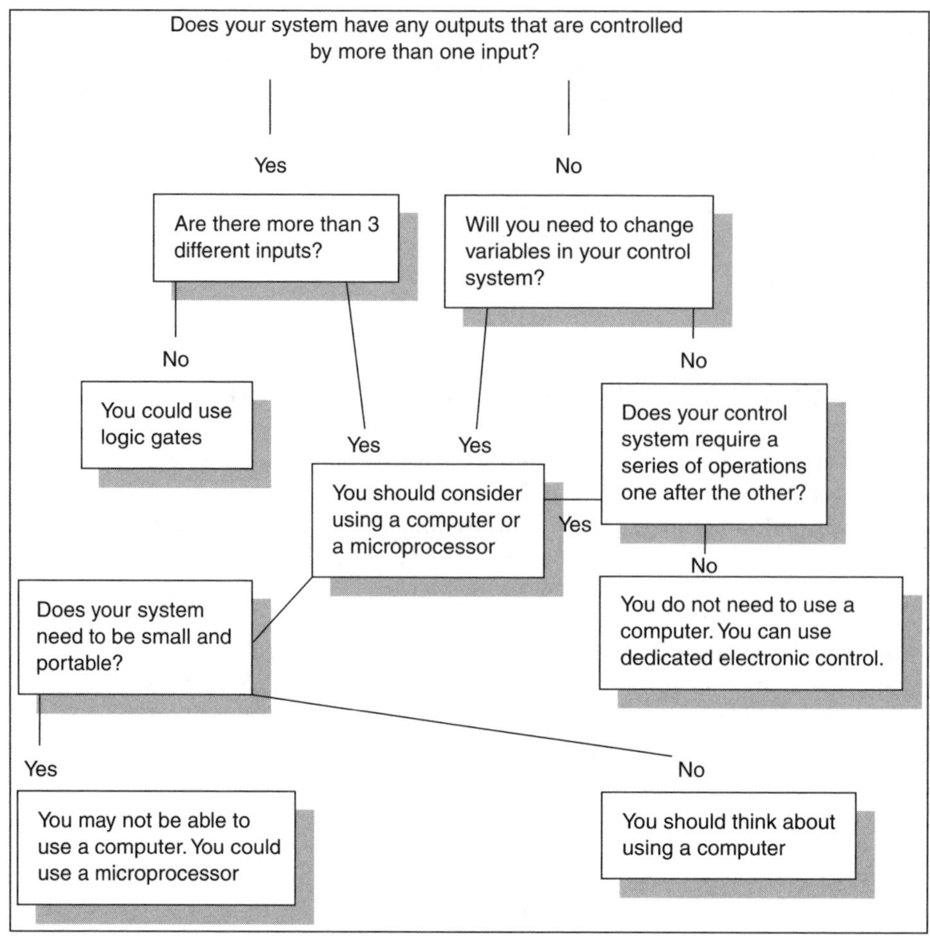

- Make a list of all the inputs to their control system.
- Next to each input write down if it is digital or analogue.
- Make a list of all the outputs from their system.
- Next to each output write down which input or inputs control it.

Having done this, they can use the decision-tree to help them decide if it would be useful to use a computer or microprocessor in their control system.

THE PLACE OF ELECTRONICS IN CONTROL AND SYSTEMS

Pupils should be encouraged to design and make products that include parts that are electronic, reflecting the wide range of electronic products available. This enables them to develop a broad approach to product development rather than being restricted by working in one or two materials. The emphasis must be on product design where pupils consider the possibilities made available using electronics alongside those available using other materials and technologies; often this will involve combining electronics with these other materials (see Table 4.3). This means that pupils need to be taught an approach to designing and making electronic circuits that produces a range of desired outcomes. This approach must make electronics accessible to the majority of pupils and not just the more able.

This means that the majority of pupils need to be introduced to electronics through a systems approach, where they learn how to assemble a set of sub-systems to achieve the outcome they require. The idea of sub-systems needs to be extended beyond meaning 'a board available in the systems kit'; a 555 timer IC is a useful sub-system in its own right. A small number of pupils will extend their understanding beyond this to a point where they can design sub-systems for themselves but this is not the primary focus of design and technology; the requirements of this group can be catered for through specialist electronics courses.

The assembly of sub-systems is best done using suitable computer software where the sub-systems can be assembled, investigated and tested on screen. Pupils can then use this to produce circuit diagrams, printed circuit board layouts and components lists. This approach to designing replicates the 'real world', moving pupils some way towards the use of computer-aided design (CAD) and electronic product definition (EPD). It also means that breadboarding and other techniques are used effectively as a means of testing final ideas further down the design process, rather than as a designing tool.

This approach requires:

- some understanding of the function of electronic sub-systems
- an understanding of the need for matching sub-systems
- the skills to assemble the final electronic circuit and integrate it effectively into the product to meet the requirements of the specification.

The first two of these points can be achieved using electronics systems kits providing hands-on, practical experience. This also allows pupils to model and investigate complete systems to extend their understanding of the possibilities that electronic products can provide. The third point requires pupils to acquire skills in soldering, mounting components, testing, fault-finding and assembly. They should also consider these issues within the wider context of designing for manufacture by asking questions like 'How would I design or make this differently if I were making several thousand rather than one?' This allows the introduction of information about techniques used in the manufacture of electronic products to avoid electronics in schools being seen as the development of a hobby skill.

In designing electronic systems, pupils should always be encouraged to look for the integrated circuit (IC) that does the job they need to be done. Increasingly, pupils will need to made aware of the use of 'firmware' and have suitable programmable devices available for their own use in designing and making products. The role of 'discrete' components in this process is an understanding and practical experience of using external components to configure an IC to do a particular job. One justification for the continued existence of the 555 timer IC is that it is useful for doing just that. The characteristics of components are best covered in science where there is a clear place for investigating current–voltage relationships for a range of components. The key problem here is the transfer and re-working of this knowledge to make it useful in design and technology, and activities need to be built into any electronics programme to support this transfer and to make it as effective as possible.

Task 4.4 Planning for progression

- Consider a project that you are likely to be teaching.
- Establish a clear set of learning objectives for this project.
- Now place the project into a sequence, remembering that tasks earlier in the sequence should establish basic learning outcomes that lead into the project. Tasks later in the sequence should build on the learning outcomes and develop the pupils further.

SUMMARY

You should now have carried out your subject knowledge audit, feel confident that you know the key principles, and have planned a programme to develop the areas where you have identified uncertainties. You should also now be able to put together a sequence of lessons which would allow pupils to develop their knowledge and understanding in a coherent progression.

A wide range of teaching and learning strategies can be used to teach pupils about control and systems. However, it is important to emphasise that you can use discrete activities to develop knowledge, skills and understanding in particular areas of control and systems, but should also include more integrated tasks, where pupils can apply their knowledge, skills and understanding to the wider context of designing and making. Remember, too, that work in control and systems relates to work in other areas of design and technology.

Control and systems may be your specialist area but it is recommended that you also read the subject knowledge chapters on the other areas, as these contain other ideas for ways of auditing and updating subject knowledge which you can adapt for your own use. Reading these other chapters will also give you an overview of the whole subject of design and technology.

Like all aspects of design and technology, control and systems is a constantly developing field and you will need to make sure that you keep your own knowledge and skills up to date.

FURTHER READING

Association for Science (1995) *Education Science with Technology Project*, particularly *Understanding Control*; *Investigating and Designing Control Systems*; *Understanding Sensors*; *Energy Transfer*, Hatfield: ASE (tel. 01707 267411)

Institution of Electrical Engineers publications, *Electronics Education* – a magazine for schools published three times per year which is an excellent source of project ideas and information. Also *Systems File*, which is an extremely useful source of electronic sub-systems. Both publications available from: Publications Sales Department, IEE, PO Box 96, Stevenage, Herts SG1 2SD (tel. 01438 313311, fax 01438 313465)

NAAIDT/DATA/NCET *IT* in *D&T: The Modelling Pack* and *The DITT pack*. Both are available from: BECTa (formerly NCET), Milburn Hill Road, Science Park, Coventry CV4 7JJ

Nuffield Foundation (1996) *Design and Technology Project*, London: Addison Wesley Longman

Royal College of Art Schools Technology Project (1997) *Design & Technology*, London: Hodder & Stoughton

Science and Technology with Electronics, *Module 3: Learning Electronics through Systems*; Pub: NEMEC, SSTF, University of Southampton, Southampton, SO9 5NH

Technology Enhancement Programme (1994) *Technology 14–16*, London: The Engineering Council

Video

How to Make Automata, Cabaret Mechanical Theatre, Covent Garden, London WC2E 8RE

5 Teaching textiles technology

Patsi Barnes

INTRODUCTION

Textiles technology has evolved from needlework, with several face-lifts along the way. Gone are the days when making a garment could become an entire year's work! The subject now encompasses the far broader use of textiles within the home and industry in its widest sense, for example the use of polyester in the making of car seat-belts.

There are some obvious similarities in content between textiles technology in design and technology and creative textiles, which may be offered in the art and design department. Both will use primary and secondary sources for inspiration in producing ideas and use many similar, if not identical, techniques to produce an article. However, the emphases are decidedly different with artistic interpretation being paramount in creative textiles, whilst a knowledge of fibres, manufacturing and producing a quality finish are required for textiles technology.

If textiles is your specialist area you will most likely have a degree relating to textiles technology, creative textiles, embroidery, fashion and clothing studies or industrial management and manufacturing. Whilst this will have given you an excellent grounding in the knowledge of textiles, it is unlikely you will have covered all the elements you are required to teach. It may be necessary for you to develop specific aspects of your knowledge and skills in order to feel confident with all the aspects within the teaching programme.

It is a valuable experience to have the help and support of your colleagues, not just as a student or new teacher, but throughout your teaching career. The sharing of skills and expertise among staff can only enhance the learning of the pupils. A common approach across all areas within the design and technology department, for example having the same format for presentation of work, is also seen as giving 'gravitas' to the subject. There is certainly much to recommend sharing the teaching during the planning stage to make full use of the strengths of each member of the department.

Teaching textiles bears several similarities to resistant materials: both use materials that are longer-lasting than food; measurements must be accurate for an item to be successful; and the length of time needed to produce an outcome is similar. The general requirements for design and technology capability are shown in Figure 5.1 and this chapter will show how these apply within textiles technology.

OBJECTIVES

By the end of this chapter you should:

- have audited your own knowledge and understanding of the subject and the skills you will be required to teach
- have examined the 'design and make' process
- be familiar with the subject content of examinations for textiles technology
- be aware of areas where help from other colleagues in your department, and others, can extend your knowledge and will benefit the learning of your pupils
- recognise that cross-curricular links with other subjects assist learning, understanding and development.

Figure 5.1 Aspects of design and technology capability

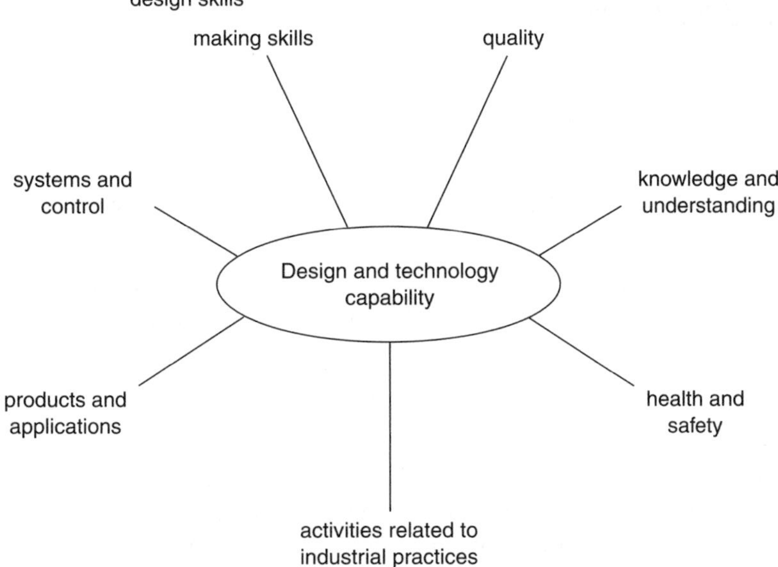

KNOWLEDGE AND UNDERSTANDING

The areas of construction and industrial manufacturing, along with the creative element within textiles, combine to produce a well-rounded curriculum which enables skills, processes and knowledge to be developed. Elements of study within these three areas are outlined in Table 5.1. You may need to undertake further study in some of these elements to ensure a solid foundation from which to teach and provide a varied diet for your pupils.

The constant development of new fibres and fabrics is worthy of mention here. Unless the school can afford to replace a class set of books on a regular basis, it is likely you will need to keep an eye open for magazine and newspaper articles to update your knowledge. Tencel is one example of a new fibre which is very widely used but features only in the latest publications. Use of the world wide web will also help you to keep up to date with information on developments in fibres, fabrics and processes.

The Design and Technology Association (DATA) has produced a paper entitled *Minimum Competences for Students to Teach Design and Technology in Secondary Schools* (1995b). The paper outlines the subject-specific competences required by newly qualified teachers in each of the four areas, and so provides a useful guide to the type and depth of knowledge necessary.

For each of the material areas (food, textiles, resistant materials, systems and control) there is a list of subject knowledge required to teach the 11–14 age group (tier 1) and the 14–18 age group (tier 2). As a textiles specialist, it is tier 2 which should be your guide, as shown in Table 5.2.

Task 5.1 Auditing your subject knowledge

Take a sheet of A3 paper and draw two lines down it so that you have three columns.

In the first column, write out the above competences as a list, include the areas from the RCA project, see Table 5.1 and Table 5.2.

In the second column you can audit your own knowledge and skills against the statements. For example, you could put a tick against the statement if your knowledge matches it, 1 if you have a little knowledge which needs brushing up, 2 if you have some knowledge but need to develop it, and 3 if you have no knowledge at all.

In the third column you can plan how you will develop the areas where you have identified further knowledge is needed.

Doing the above task will help you to feel confident about what you already know, and will help you to see where you need to develop your subject knowledge. Depending on your background you might need to develop your design skills, making skills, theoretical knowledge of fibres and fabrics or industrial practices.

Table 5.1 Aspects of textiles technology

CREATIVE	CONSTRUCTION
Creative exploration and experimentation, personal expression Generating own designs and patterns, Modelling Applying understanding of materials	Understanding physical properties and characteristics of materials (science) Origins of fibres, fibre combinations
Making one-off, art form, new product design	How fabrics are made – weaving, knitting, bonding
Colouring and enhancing techniques, Decoration	Choosing materials to match function, fabric tests
Pushing materials to the limits	Choosing and using sewing machine and equipment
Inspiration from other times and cultures	Pattern designing and using basic construction techniques – joining, reinforcing, finishing, investigating existing products
Emphasis towards creative arts	*Emphasis towards science*
INDUSTRIAL MANUFACTURING	
Understanding industrial processes, designing for manufacture	Modelling and prototyping – model a fabric design, bank of stored designs, pattern lays, colour combinations
Simplifying processes, components, optimum use of materials (nesting), repeatable designs, scaling up for different sizes	Texture mapping of a person/product
Production planning – choosing the best processes and methods to construct the product, the best layout for equipment, materials and people, the best ways to control the quality of the products made (process operation charts) Quality assurance techniques, Costing Health and safety CAD/CAM – using computers to visualise a design, make accurate drawing and models, manufacturing equipment easily, repeat processes accurately and easily	Production line simulation, cell production, team working Testing – technical specifications, for materials, scientific fabric testing (wear; selecting materials according to their working characteristics, combinations of materials for rucksack), prototypes, control manufacturability and maintenance, consumer testing Implications for consumer – safety hazards, environment

Source: Adapted from RCA Schools Technology Project, 1998, p. 99

Table 5.2 Minimum competences for textiles technology

DESIGNING AND MAKING

1.1 Use flat pattern and standard modelling techniques, including drafting, scale blocks, grading, fitting and adapting.
1.2 Understand how models and patterns are drafted in industry (including use of CAD/CAM).
1.3 Construct toiles.
1.4 Show in-depth use of ICT for exploring shape, pattern and colourways.
1.5 Use an in-depth range of cutting tools where appropriate, e.g. knives and rotary cutters.
1.6 Show awareness of industrial processes for mass production cutting.
1.7 Use an in-depth range of techniques for permanent joining.
1.8 Use a range of temporary joining techniques, e.g. tacking and basting.
1.9 Show understanding of industrial processes, e.g. overlocking, flat felling.
1.10 Use shaping techniques (wasting, fabrication and manipulation) to create more complex structures.
1.11 Show understanding of complex shaping processes, e.g. fully fashioning.
1.12 Make a great range of edge finishes, e.g. fully fashioning.
1.13 Apply a large range of fastenings.
1.14 Show understanding of industrial production processes, e.g. quality control and assurance, costing, couture/custom made, batch and mass production.

COMMUNICATION SKILLS

2.1 Use fashion illustration techniques and technical fashion drawing conventions.
2.2 Use a broad range of pattern-marking conventions, e.g. numbered balance marks, placement markings.
2.3 Produce pattern layout for different fabric widths.

PRODUCTS AND APPLICATIONS

3.1 Show a broad and deep understanding of how textiles are used, including examples of industry and advanced technology and make use of this in their designing.

TECHNOLOGICAL CONCEPTS

4.1 *Materials and components*
4.1.1 Show a greater understanding of industrial production of fibres, yarns, fabrics.
4.1.2 Show insight into technological advances, e.g. performance, fabrics, new fibres.
4.1.3 Show in-depth understanding of exploiting properties to create desired effects.
[4.2. is not applicable to textiles.]
4.3 *Energy*
4.3.1 Use fabrics as insulation in products.
4.4 *Structures*
4.4.1 Create complex, appropriately reinforced 3D structures.
4.4.2 Show in-depth understanding of creating fabrics, e.g. use of knitting machine.

4.4.3 Show awareness of industrial testing processes, industry standards and tolerances.
4.4.4 Use complex reinforcing techniques.

INFORMATION AND COMMUNICATION TECHNOLOGY RELATED SKILLS

5.1 Show understanding of industrial uses of information technology in producing textiles products.
5.2 Show understanding of industrial uses of information and communication technology in producing fibres, yarns and fabrics.
5.3 Use computerised knitting and plotting to make products

Source: Design and Technology Association, 1995b, pp. 29–31

Whichever it is you can now plan your own development. Designing and making skills can be acquired through practice – a good way would be to work through school-based projects, designing and making items that pupils will be making. Theoretical knowledge can be acquired through reading textbooks and discussion with colleagues. Companies often produce promotional or educational material which can be helpful, as can reading trade or professional journals. Industrial experience can be obtained through a work placement; talk to your mentor, or whoever is responsible for staff development, about the possibility of arranging this. If it is not possible, then contact local companies yourself and try to arrange a visit, otherwise promotional and educational videos can be helpful.

DESIGNING AND MAKING

As in other areas of design and technology, you will probably be teaching 'design and make' activities, along with focused practical tasks. In focused tasks pupils develop knowledge and skills in specific things, for example a type of seam or a particular method of embellishing fabric. In design and make activities they apply what they know and have learnt to design and make products to meet a specified need.

Designing

The stages involved in designing may seem obvious to you but to the pupil they need presenting, with care and detail, step by step. Although it would be a rare occasion for these stages simply to follow on from one another, whether in industry or making a 'one-off', pupils need to be able to identify each of the processes involved. Taking the activities involved in the design process one at a time, you can see how well they suit textiles.

Identifying the need for design

The need for design is constant, whether in fashion and accessories, interior design or industrial textiles. The fashion industry is huge and *haute couture* designers can command vast sums. Chain stores often adapt many of these designs at more realistic prices for the mass market, as do paper pattern companies. Interior design has also become big business in the last few years, and recent television programmes have fuelled the imagination. Industrial textiles range from bandages to engineering cables, road surfaces and bullet-proof clothing for the services.

Researching

Pupils need to be encouraged to look for wide and varied information which will help them to generate design ideas. This can be two-fold: (a) asking for the public's opinion and (b) finding sources for design. Public opinion could be sought on colour, shape, texture, design. Sources are endless, nature is an obvious first port of call, but the final idea could equally well emanate from a bit of old carpet, a household brick or a tyre tread.

Analysing research information and selecting the most useful

Pupils will quite happily use every scrap of research and you will need to steer them towards using only that which is relevant.

Producing a brief

It is a brave teacher who will give pupils *carte blanche* to write their own brief. In reality, giving them a limited choice of briefs, or even no choice at all, is more manageable in terms of resources and outcomes. For younger pupils you may even write briefs to fit the various elements of the syllabus that you need to address.

Applying theoretical knowledge to the problem

This can be approached in two ways. One way is to teach the required techniques as focused tasks, then write a brief which requires pupils to use them. For example, you could teach methods of decorating fabric with paint or embroidery and then ask pupils to use this technique to decorate an item they make. Another way is to present the brief and demonstrate the techniques as the need arises, for example using a particular seam or putting in a zip. Some documentation, such as making sure the pupils have notes or sketches of these processes in their work books or folders, should be expected to consolidate learning and to provide a ready reference for the future.

Writing a design specification

This can be a difficult task. Perhaps the most understandable approach is to explain to the pupils that it refers to 'a list of features that you want your product to have'. A brainstorming session can help, but you still need to point out that not all features will be required by everyone and that each pupil's specification will be particular to their item.

Generating ideas

This is limited only by the pupils' imagination, but some find it difficult and you may need to guide or prompt them. Using background music can help to provide a creative environment, but you may need to check school or departmental policy on this, and be sensitive to the needs of others if you work in open-plan areas. Revisiting design sources, using fabric and colour swatches, even those little paint charts, may provide inspiration towards combining interesting shapes and textures. Provide as many visual aids as you can to stimulate pupils; these could be posters, pictures or actual products. Using a figure template for fashion designing can save hours of frustration for the pupils. Chapter 7, on the use of ICT, may also give you some ideas for helping pupils to be creative.

Taking account of constraints, materials and equipment

Possibly the two most common constraints are those of time and money; there is just not enough of either. The provision of materials and equipment is constrained by the department budget, but you also need to consider the ability of the pupil to handle difficult fabrics or a piece of machinery efficiently, especially when it is used infrequently.

Selecting and evaluating the best ideas

Much of this happens cerebrally and pupils will probably need prompting by you to record their selection process on paper. Encourage them to think about the reasons for their choices – not just because they like it, ask *why* they like it; encourage them to think about colour, shape, size, overall aesthetic appeal and suitability for its purpose.

Modelling and testing

This includes thinking about the suitability of fabric, colour fastness of paint, anthropomorphic fit or proportion, and can be undertaken at any suitable stage. Encourage pupils to try as many tests as possible in the available time. Results could be presented in a chart, giving pupils an opportunity to use ICT skills, and using the simple headings of 'good points–bad points' for their evaluation.

Product specification, and possibly a working diagram

The difference between a design specification and product specification lies in the detail required. A design specification is likely to be more open, as this will help in the generation of ideas. The product specification should be more detailed as it will say precisely what colours the product will be, its actual dimensions, the actual components to be used, the manufacturing processes.

Task 5.2 Writing a design task

Think of a class that you know, or teach, who have worked through a design and make activity. Think about how the pupils went about the design work.

If you were to teach this activity, think about how you would structure and present the design activities to try and improve pupils' learning and their outcomes.

- Was there evidence that they worked through these processes?
- Were any of the processes omitted?
- Why was this?
- Did the pupils find any of the processes difficult?
- What guidance were they given?
- In what way did their design work impact on their making?

Making

There is a more clearly defined flow to the production of an item than to the designing of it. In a design and make activity pupils should be taught to:

- plan an order of work for the making process
- select appropriate tools and equipment
- decide on the most suitable processes to use
- produce a quality item with a good finish.

There are also other elements which will appear continually, such as:

- amending plans at any point of the making stage
- evaluating the product, for improvement and fitness for purpose
- safe working practices.

Selecting suitable practical work can be challenging. At the back of your mind is the need to choose an inexpensive topic. With the ever-rising cost of fabrics, you may feel forced into making small items and it is tempting always to use calico as it is cheap, will shrink only the first time it is washed or made wet, and it accepts dye well. However, you do a disservice to the pupils if you do not vary the materials they handle and become familiar with. Other fabrics you might try include:

- a cotton/polyester mix, lightweight or a heavier weight, e.g. sheeting
- cotton sateen or even curtain lining
- cotton or nylon twill for less experienced pupils
- fabrics which slip or fray more, such as polyester, for more able pupils.

Choosing a suitable fabric is part of any textiles activity and the teaching of the properties and uses of various fibres (which will help pupils choose a suitable fabric) could be taught in isolation. Pupils enjoy experimental work, in particular identifying an anonymous fibre which they can disassemble, burn or look at under the microscope.

Perhaps paramount to all this must be to ensure the pupils become fully conversant with the equipment, in particular the sewing machine. Frustration abounds when faults cannot be diagnosed or quite simply the pupil has forgotten how to wind a bobbin, and in an effort to get on, winds it by hand – badly!

You might also include a short unit of work, for younger pupils, on the importance of using the right tool for the job. Few pupils will have had the luxury of time spent:

- handling different types of scissors; knowing how to cut out fabric, with long strokes, using shears or larger bladed scissors; using smaller scissors to snip ends of cotton, cut round bends or more intricate shapes (e.g. cutting out a printed design to appliqué on to another piece of fabric); using a stitch unpicker
- becoming familiar with the variety of sewing, knitting and crotchet needles (few can thread a needle with a small eye, such as that of a sharp, so using the larger-eyed crewel/embroidery needle is preferable, say a size 7); understanding why tapestry needles have blunt points; understanding that as a basic rule the size of needle and thread used are roughly in proportion to the weight of the fabric being used
- using thread made of the same fibre as the fabric
- having the opportunity to try more than one type of iron.

Task 5.3 Writing a unit of work

Devise a short unit of work which could be called 'the sewing machine test', with the intention of providing familiarity with the machines in your school. Ideally this unit will be one of the first the pupils experience in the school. Think about how it would be structured and presented to the pupils.

If this unit of work already exists in your school, how could you adapt it to introduce pupils to other pieces of equipment?

INDUSTRIAL PRACTICES

Most of the text books written to comply with the latest textiles technology syllabuses have good sections concerning manufacturing and its component parts. It is worth reading a variety of these (detailed in the Further Reading and reference section at the end of this chapter), to gain the broader picture and an understanding of terms such as systems and control, risk assessment, health and safety, quality assurance and quality control, and the difference between them, and product and design specification.

Task 5.4 Arranging an industrial visit

If there is a textile manufacturer in your area, contact them and ask if you can visit. Ask if you can take pictures of the manufacturing processes; you can then use these to make a display for your room.

If you cannot arrange a visit, borrow any manufacturing videos you can find to help develop your knowledge. These may be in the school, may be borrowed from your local education authority, may be borrowed or bought commercially, or obtained from manufacturers themselves.

If you live in an area with few textiles factories and find it impossible to arrange a visit for your pupils, showing videos provides a really worthwhile alternative. Videos allow pupils to rewind and look again at a process, looking for detail that they may have forgotten or missed the first time. In any case, some factories are short of space and would find it hard to provide a safe visit for more than a few pupils at a time.

Ideally, industrial practices should be introduced to younger pupils, if time permits, as this will give them a greater understanding when they revisit them as part of an examination course. Schools in a manufacturing neighbourhood are at an advantage here and several have managed to set up industrial partnerships to mutual advantage. These enable pupils to:

- present work to real clients
- work with real designers
- use industrial processes
- use the right terminology
- use CAD/CAM.

There is more information about the benefits of industrial partnerships in Chapter 12.

If factory visits or industrial links are not an available option, then consider how you can write a stimulating and realistic unit of work that will allow pupils to experience industrial practices. Start by choosing a small item with few pattern pieces, which can show creativity, such as:

- a set of mug mats (filled with spices?) which allows for printed decoration
- a holder for a small pack of tissues, lined, with a ribbon trim
- an item of jewellery
- Christmas tree decorations
- a tie or bow tie
- small cushions.

Then try to ensure that:

- pupils organise their own team, or cell, working in groups of three or four, and allocate jobs within the team, including a member with responsibility for quality control
- there is a production flow-chart, drawn up by the pupils – to include systems and control. A risk assessment is essential, it covers health and safety (see Chapter 6 for details) and can be done on a spreadsheet, using ICT skills
- you insist on a list of the materials and equipment required being presented to you, to show organisation. You may be required to shop for these, or provide them from the resources cupboard, so advance notice will be needed
- there is a breakdown of costs
- you set a realistic, but brief, time-frame, say three hours' planning and the same for making, to further simulate speed in the industry.

Textiles is fortunate to have, in the form of computerised sewing machines, an affordable example of CAD/CAM which is fun to use and produces good results. Used in conjunction with a scanner, every pupil has the opportunity to experience simulated industrial practice first-hand. Using a digital camera and printing pictures immediately is a wonderful way of providing stage by stage evidence of practical progress.

There is an excellent chapter in *Learning Futures* (NATHE, 1998) which outlines the differences and parallels between industry and education.

TEXTILES TECHNOLOGY CURRICULA

Any textiles curriculum should be regularly reviewed to ensure it is up to date, stimulates creativity, is pertinent and motivating. The curriculum will usually include the study of a range of textiles uses – clothing, household, medicine, sport, protection, geo-textiles for roads, building structures, the car industry, horticulture and agriculture and an appreciation of their diversity. It should also provide an enjoyable experience in a positive learning environment, address values and key skills, and make meaningful cross-curricular connections.

The activities that are chosen will need to contain a balance of compliant and resistant materials to be used together, and experiences that will include:

- knowledge of the origins of fibres and fabrics
- the wide variety of uses for textiles including fashion, household goods and industrial usage
- development of practical skills
- understanding how textiles can be constructed into products
- a knowledge of manufacturing
- encouraging a broad use of ICT and CAD/CAM
- evaluating products and processes.

To ensure that you cover all the required elements when planning a scheme of work from any national curriculum guidelines or syllabus it is a good idea to:

- draw out a time-line showing the length of the course
- use a photocopy of the syllabus to make a cut-and-paste chart to show that you have covered all the syllabus
- find out if there are gaps – perhaps you write another unit of work to cover them specifically, or they could be integrated into other units
- examine past projects and assess their continuing suitability and decide whether newer ideas will work better – always be adaptable
- assess what resources you have or can afford to buy for any new units being developed.

Task 5.5 Reviewing the curriculum

Obtain a copy of the national curriculum or curriculum guidelines which your school follows and look at what you will be required to teach.

Consider how you could sequence this into a meaningful series of units of work. Show the sequence of work you have devised to your mentor and ask her/him to comment on it.

EXAMINATION SYLLABUSES

The syllabuses available for textiles all have subject content which is common, although there are some variations. There is a good range of examination courses to choose from and the department usually has autonomy for its decision.

Task 5.6 Reviewing examination syllabuses

Obtain a copy of the examination syllabus which the pupils follow and read through it to see what you already know and what you need to research and develop.

Repeat Task 5.1, to audit your knowledge, and draw up an action plan to identify areas where you need to develop your knowledge or skills.

The opportunity to study textiles post-16 will be either as an AS/A level or in a vocational course. In England, Wales and Northern Ireland new AS/A level courses start in September 2000, with the first new AS examinations in 2001 and the first new A levels in 2002. Textiles will be available as a focus area within the Design and

Technology: Product Design course, and is intended to provide a logical progression from design and technology examinations at 16. Pupils will study in detail (in addition, of course, to designing and making):

- the classification and properties of fibres and fabrics
- industrial and commercial practices
- quality issues
- health and safety
- historical and social influences on design and production
- consumer issues.

All the new AS/A level courses should also provide opportunities for pupils to develop the key skills of:

- communication
- application of number
- information technology
- working with others
- improving their own learning
- problem-solving.

Design and technology courses are required to ensure that they teach and assess the key skill of communication, so the teaching methods used will need to take account of this requirement.

Task 5.7 Auditing your knowledge and skills against post-16 requirements

Obtain a copy of a syllabus for the AS/A level course in Design and Technology: Product Design, or whatever is appropriate for where you are. If your school does not teach post-16 courses, then you will need to contact the examination board and request a copy of the syllabus.

Carry out an audit of your knowledge and skills, following the procedure described in Task 5.1. You should use the syllabus as your guide and look at both the core content and the focus area of textiles.

There is a natural place for textiles within vocational courses dealing with manufacturing. The textiles industry is very much a major part of manufacturing and if industrial links can be forged, many worthwhile units can be addressed through the medium of textiles.

If you are asked to deliver units of work in a vocational course, it is likely that you will be working with a team of teachers who together would cover the whole course.

CROSS-CURRICULAR LINKS

Pupils sometimes need to be reminded of their prior knowledge of other school subjects during a textiles technology lesson and encouraged to use it to their advantage. Examples of where cross-curricular links can be made are as follows:

- A basic mathematical understanding is essential when drafting patterns, estimating fabric requirements and costing products.
- Scientific experiment principles can be employed to test fibres for their physical properties and understand care requirements for clothing.
- Writing flow-charts, descriptions, explanations and evaluations call on traditional English language skills.

Any training time which you can set aside to foster good working relationships with other departments or faculties in school is seldom wasted.

SUMMARY

Having a thorough knowledge and understanding of your chosen specialism is vital to give you the confidence as a student or newly qualified teacher to perform well in the classroom.

There is something enjoyable about planning a unit of work which neatly covers all the elements of the teaching programme you intended, and that you are happy with. Much has been written about the need to be comfortable with what you teach and this will most often follow on from being familiar with the subject matter and affords you a degree of relaxation in the classroom. You can therefore spend the time during the lesson on, say, trouble-shooting a problem with a sewing machine or doing a short demonstration to a small group of pupils.

Textiles technology may be your specialist area but it is recommended that you also read the subject knowledge chapters on the other areas as these contain other ideas for ways of auditing and updating subject knowledge which you can adapt for your own use. Reading these other chapters will also give you an overview of the whole subject of design and technology.

Belonging to a professional organisation also gives you the opportunity constantly to update your knowledge through reading excellent articles in journals written by other teachers, many of whom are still practising. These articles are written with the sole intention of informing and educating us still further and making life easier!

FURTHER READING

Barnett, A. (1997) *Examining Textiles Technology*, Oxford: Heinemann

Bartle, A. and O'Connor, B. (1997) *GCSE Design and Technology – Textiles Technology*, Ormskirk: Causeway Press

Design and Technology Association (1995) *Guidance Materials for Design & Technology Key Stage 3*, Wellesbourne: DATA

McArthur, A., Etchells, C. and Shepard, T. (1997) *Design and Make It! – Textiles Technology*, Cheltenham: Stanley Thornes

Nuffield Foundation (1996) *The Nuffield Design and Technology Project – Textiles*, Harlow: Longman

Video resources

Designing & Manufacturing Clothing
Fashioning a New Future
Both available from: Boulter-Hawker Films Ltd, Hadleigh, Ipswich, Suffolk, IP7 5BG

Head to Toe
From: CAPITB Trust, 30 Richardshaw Lane, Pudsey, Leeds, LS28 6BN

6 Health and safety in design and technology

Gwyneth Owen-Jackson

INTRODUCTION

In design and technology, health and safety is a vital issue; you are often involved in practical work with pupils using sharp or electrical equipment and in rooms where there are materials, tools, equipment and chemicals, all of which could be a potential hazard.

This chapter covers the health and safety of pupils in your classroom and your legal responsibilities as a teacher. In England and Wales the class teacher has statutory duties under the Health and Safety at Work Act (1974), the Children Act (1989) and the School Teachers' Pay and Conditions Document 1991. It is likely that similar legislation will apply elsewhere. As a student teacher you will not have these statutory duties, these remain with the class teacher, who must be available in the room or nearby.

As a student teacher, however, you will be expected to plan and conduct your lessons with regard to the health and safety of pupils. In England the standards that student teachers have to meet in order to gain qualified teacher status state specifically that you should show that you 'are familiar with subject-specific health and safety requirements . . . and plan lessons to avoid potential hazards' and can 'establish a safe environment' (DfEE, 1998, pp. 10–13). The standards also require a working knowledge and understanding of the legal liabilities and responsibilities relating to a range of Acts, including sections 7 and 8 of the Health and Safety at Work Act, and your common law duty to ensure pupils' health and safety.

Whatever legislation or guidelines apply, you will want to ensure that your lessons run smoothly and that pupils learn. It will, therefore, be important for you to think through any potential hazards in lessons that you plan, in order to minimise the risks.

This chapter covers the legal requirements, risk analysis and management, and suggests ways in which design and technology can be taught safely.

OBJECTIVES

After reading this chapter you should be:

- familiar with general health and safety legislation relevant to design and technology workrooms
- familiar with subject-specific legislation affecting each area
- able to carry out a risk assessment of your planned lessons.

LEGAL REQUIREMENTS

The following information applies within England and Wales. Outside of these areas, similar legislation is likely to be in force, but you will need to check the specific requirements.

The main piece of legislation covering all areas of design and technology teaching is the *Health and Safety at Work Act (1974)*. The main requirements resulting from this Act are for employers to:

- secure the health, safety and welfare of employees
- protect against risks to health and safety
- control the storage and use of dangerous substances
- control the emission of noxious or offensive substances.

This Act confers duties on the employer (in this case, the school or local education authority) to ensure the health and safety of their employees.

Task 6.1 Reading the school health and safety policy

Ask to see the school's written policy statement regarding health and safety and read through this carefully. Note where it relates to you or your teaching.

As an employee you also have duties under this Act. Section 7 requires you to:

- take reasonable care for the health and safety of yourself and others who may be affected by your acts or omissions
- co-operate with the employer, to enable them to comply with the requirements of the Act
- inform the employer of any equipment or procedure which could be a danger to health or safety.

Section 8 states that you must not intentionally or recklessly interfere with, or misuse, anything provided in the interests of health, safety or welfare.

One of the implications of this Act is that if you see a potential hazard in the school you are working in, you should report it to your mentor or the head of department. You may come across defective equipment or spot a hazard in the room layout or working practices. However difficult you may find it, it is important that you report it, as you may be helping to reduce risks and create a safer environment for the pupils.

The Health and Safety at Work Act gave rise to a host of regulations, which set out in some detail the requirements of the law. Again, some of these have a general application across all areas of design and technology and some apply to specific subject areas. One of the main, and more general, sets of regulations is that relating to the *Control of Substances Hazardous to Health*, known generally as the *COSHH regulations*. These apply to all substances that are toxic, corrosive or irritants, and to harmful micro-organisms. Dust, or any other material that could be harmful to health when produced in large amounts, is also covered.

The regulations set out how these substances should be stored and used. They also require that the employer (school) undertake a systematic assessment of the risk to health of the substances used, in order to determine the precautions needed, and should then introduce measures to prevent or control the risk. The employer also has a duty to ensure that these measures are followed and that employees are informed, instructed and trained about the risks and the precautions. There should be a record kept which shows:

- a list of dangerous substances used
- where and how they are used
- who uses them
- the likelihood of danger
- possible harmful effects
- precautions to be taken.

Substances that are hazardous and are to be used should be labelled appropriately, e.g. toxic, corrosive, irritant, harmful. They should be stored in locked cupboards.

The *Provision and Use of Equipment Regulations* place a duty on employers (schools) to make sure that equipment used is safe to use and properly maintained. Information and training should be given to those operating the equipment.

The *Electricity at Work Regulations* refer to electrical equipment, its safe installation, use and maintenance. Guidance is given on the selection, positioning and installation, inspection and maintenance of all types of electrical equipment.

Similarly, the *Gas Safety (Installation and Use) Regulations* cover the installation and maintenance of gas appliances.

There are also regulations that cover the provision, maintenance and use of protective clothing. The *Personal Protective Equipment at Work Regulations* require employers to provide appropriate protective clothing, to maintain, clean and replace it, and ensure that it is properly used.

Other general regulations which apply in design and technology are the *Health and Safety (Display Screen Equipment) Regulations.* These apply to those who work continually with computers and screens, so do not directly affect you or your pupils, who are more likely to be occasional users. However, it is useful to be aware of the guidelines relating to appropriate desk and chair height to give good posture and the need for good vision, good lighting and correct screen position. Other regulations under the Health and Safety at Work Act are referred to later, where they apply to individual subject areas.

Another piece of legislation which has general application to all teachers, and which you should be aware of, is the *Children Act 1989.* This gives teachers a statutory duty to do all that they reasonably can to safeguard or promote the welfare of children in their care. This would require you to assess possible risks and take the necessary steps to prevent, reduce or control these.

There are also sections in the *School Teachers' Pay and Conditions Document* which impose on you statutory duties to 'promote the general progress and well-being of individual pupils, groups or classes assigned to you' and to 'maintain good order and discipline among pupils and safeguard their health and safety' (School Teachers' Pay and Conditions Document, 1991).

In order to make sure that you are safe, both as a student and as a student teacher, in the classroom, it is recommended that you work only with materials and equipment with which you are familiar. If you are required to work with an unfamiliar material or piece of machinery, make sure that you obtain sufficient information or instruction before the lesson, not only in how to use it yourself but also in how to instruct pupils, and what dangers to be aware of. You should also practise using the equipment so that you become familiar with it.

Task 6.2 Reading the statutory documents

Obtain copies of the general legislation and regulations described here (or those that apply where you work). These documents can usually be obtained from a health and safety council, or borrowed from a public library. Usually summary documents have been produced which are simpler and highlight the main points. Read through these documents or summaries carefully.

SCHOOL AND DEPARTMENT POLICIES

When you first start working in a school, it is a good idea to ask your mentor or the school co-ordinator for a copy of the school policy on health and safety. This will contain information that applies to you as an employee, as well as important information for you in your role as a teacher. There should be sections in the policy dealing with equipment and machinery, first aid, accident reporting and procedures, information and training. There will also be information in the statement, or elsewhere, relating to procedures in the event of fire. It is important that you are familiar with these. If you are not totally sure about them, go back to Task 6.1 and read through the school policy on health and safety.

The department policy statement should incorporate aspects of the whole-school policy and include further points relevant to the subject. Additional points may refer to maintenance and safety checks on equipment and machinery, storage and use of equipment, machinery and hazardous substances, protective clothing, classroom procedures, specific information and training.

Task 6.3 Reading the department health and safety policy

Ask your mentor, or the head of department, for a copy of the health and safety policy statement. Read this thoroughly and familiarise yourself with it, particularly the parts that outline your responsibilities. If there are any parts that you are not sure about, talk them through with your mentor.

CLASSROOM PROCEDURES

There are some general classroom procedures that you should be aware of that will help to minimise the risk of accidents. These may be carried out by you, the head of department or the technician: you should check who has responsibility for each of these procedures. They include the following measures:

- all machinery and equipment to be regularly checked for safety
- the position of machinery and equipment checked so that it is safe in use
- safety-guards and dust extractors fitted and used where necessary
- lighting and ventilation checked to be adequate
- pupils not allowed into the room without adult supervision
- when demonstrating equipment use to pupils, make sure that all can see, and that no one is standing in a dangerous position
- during the demonstration remember to stress the safety points
- pupils only to use machinery and equipment they have been taught to use, and to use it only with supervision
- protective clothing available and used
- safety STOP points clearly labelled
- all machinery and equipment to be switched off at the end of a lesson, and checked
- know where the isolating STOP switch is, so that all machines can be switched off if necessary.

You may not have any control over the arrangement and layout of the room, but if you do it is worth taking time to check that it is safe and convenient. What you *can* control is keeping the room clean and tidy, and making sure there are no obstructions in work areas. These simple measures can considerably reduce the risk of accidents.

It is also a good idea to have plenty of safety notices and posters around the room emphasising safe working practices. Make sure these are referred to and used. Checklists for safe working procedures can be displayed and pupils referred to them. As an introduction to health and safety in the room, younger pupils can be encouraged to produce such posters and displays and, because they have done these themselves, it makes them more meaningful to them. Additional, specific notices should be displayed by dangerous machinery and equipment labelling it as such. Remember to check that all the pupils can see and read the notices, especially those with reading difficulties or English as a second language.

Task 6.4 Drawing up your own classroom procedures

Stand in the room in which you teach when it is empty of pupils. Look slowly around the room and note down where you see potential hazard areas: these may be where workbenches are too close together or where stocks are located. Note down any alterations that you can easily make to the room, such as moving furniture, stocks or pupils' work, which would make it a safer environment to work in.

Now look around again, are there appropriate and relevant safety notices? Note down any improvements that you could make to the displays and notices to make pupils more aware of health and safety issues.

If it is your room that you have been surveying, then you can carry out the alterations. If it is not your room, perhaps you could discuss with the classroom teacher, sensitively, your suggestions.

In addition to these general procedures there are regulations, practices and procedures which apply to the different subject areas. The following points made under subject headings apply *in addition* to the general legislation and procedures described above.

FOOD TECHNOLOGY

The *Food Safety Act 1990* makes it illegal, among other things, to sell food either that does not comply with food safety requirements, or that is not of the nature, substance or quality demanded by purchasers, or which is misleadingly labelled or advertised. This mainly covers businesses which carry out 'commercial operations' in the preparation and selling of food. Food technology rooms in schools, therefore, would not normally be covered. However, it may be deemed to apply if the rooms are used to supply food for fund-raising activities, for school events such as governors' meetings, parents' evenings, school social events, mini-enterprise activities or for selling in the school tuck-shop, and possibly if the school stores and sells food ingredients for pupils to use. Whether or not the Act applies, it outlines good practice and its guidelines should be followed where possible.

In addition, the *Food Hygiene (Amendment) Regulations* stipulate minimum requirements for the storage, handling, preparation and serving of food. In food technology rooms these can be applied through:

- ensuring a place for outside coats and bags, away from the food preparation area
- making sure pupils have clean protective clothing
- providing soap and towels and ensuring that these are used before food is handled
- ensuring work surfaces are cleaned down properly
- providing suitable storage conditions, i.e. sufficient refrigerator space, for school ingredients and ingredients brought in by pupils
- ensuring food preparation equipment is clean
- ensuring that sufficient waste disposal facilities are provided and that they are cleaned frequently.

Many of these points will require you to instil good habits in pupils, and to set a good example yourself, for example by wearing clean protective clothing, not wearing nail polish, removing jewellery and washing hands before handling food.

If you devise a set routine for pupils when they are preparing to work with food, they will learn it quickly and it will become easier for you to enforce it. Begin by encouraging pupils to store necessary ingredients in the refrigerator when they arrive in school. A routine for the start of the lesson may include:

- coats and bags to be put away before entering the room
- long hair tied back (have elastic bands ready), jewellery off, nail polish removed (have remover and cotton wool ready)
- aprons or overalls on
- worktops wiped down, with hot water and a clean cloth
- hands washed.

At the end of the lesson:

- check that equipment is left clean
- check that worktops and sink areas are clean
- dirty cloths and clothing should be put aside for laundering.

Where laundering of dirty cloths and clothing is carried out in the food technology area, it should be done away from the food preparation areas.

Once pupils know what is expected of them, most will conform and the more the expectation is reinforced, the better. This can seem like hard work with a new class, but the initial effort will pay rewards later when only a brief reminder will be needed, or none at all!

Food technology lessons may involve experimental work, testing for nutrients for example, which uses chemicals. These should be carefully stored, away from food stores, and should be used in an area away from food preparation areas. If there are no such areas, try to negotiate with the science department to see if a laboratory is available.

As a food technology specialist it will be useful for you to obtain a Basic Food Hygiene Certificate. This is a simple six-hour course followed by a multiple-choice test. It is run by the Institute for Environmental Health Officers and may be offered through your local authority. Contact your local Environmental Health Office for information.

RESISTANT MATERIALS

The school workshop is a particularly dangerous place for pupils with its machinery, equipment, chemicals and fumes. The dangers in the place where you work will depend to some extent on the size and shape of the room, the position of the equipment and the materials used (wood, metal, plastics). What follows gives general guidance; the safety policy in your school and the head of department will be able to give you more specific information and advice.

It is mainly the general legislation already described which applies in this area, in particular the regulations relating to the *Control of Substances Hazardous to Health, Provision and Use of Equipment* and *Electricity at Work.*

Each material used in this area carries some danger. Dust, from wood or plastics, can be allergenic, carcinogenic or flammable. Make sure that extraction systems are used and that there is adequate ventilation. Make sure, also, that the equipment and work areas are cleaned at the end of each lesson to minimise the build-up of dust. Metal shavings can cause serious injuries and the processes of welding and casting, with heat, can be dangerous. Expanded polystyrene produces dust when filed or sanded and irritant fumes when heated, for example with a hot wire-cutter. Fumes from some adhesives, varnishes and plastics can be toxic, irritant and/or flammable. These hazards are all in addition to those that can arise when pupils are using tools and equipment!

The *Protection of Eyes Regulations* require that suitable eye protectors are supplied to those engaged in specified activities. In school this would mean pupils having access to, *and wearing*, eye protectors when carrying out activities such as chipping or cutting metal, removing paint, scale or rust, using a high-speed saw or abrasion wheel, grinding, using compressed air or working at a furnace.

Regulations which may apply if pupils are asked to design and make toys for children (a popular activity) are the *Toys (Safety) Regulations*. Although these apply to commercially manufactured toys, it is useful for pupils to be aware of them and to apply them where possible. The regulations list many criteria to which toys must conform in order to protect children from injury. In brief outline, these state that the toys must:

- be designed and made to minimise the risk of physical injury
- be inflammable

- not contain harmful substances
- be electrically safe
- be hygienically safe.

Daunting as all this may seem, work usually proceeds safely and there are classroom procedures that you can follow to minimise the dangers to pupils. At the start of a lesson:

- pupils should not enter the workroom without supervision
- coats and bags should be stored away from the work space.

During the lesson:

- protective clothing should be worn
- long hair should be tied back, ties tucked in and hazardous jewellery removed
- pupils should only work on machines they have been taught to use
- only one pupil to work on a machine at a time
- pupils working on machines should ensure that safety goggles are worn
- machines should only be switched on when ready for use, and switched off immediately afterwards
- pupils should know where the emergency STOP button is on machines
- care and attention should be paid to the task when pupils are working with equipment.

When pupils are working on electric saws or drilling machines, make sure they use appropriate holding devices. Off-cuts should be stored in a container by the machine, rather than left lying around and all waste should be disposed of regularly and safely.

At the end of the lesson ensure that:

- all equipment is returned and checked
- all machinery is switched off
- if necessary, that the electricity supply to the machinery is switched off.

Establishing safety routines and safe working practices is time-consuming initially and needs constant reinforcement. However, once pupils are familiar with the routines and practices it becomes easier to enforce them and your initial time and effort is rewarded.

CONTROL AND SYSTEMS

This area is again mainly covered by the general legislation, particularly that relating to the *Provision and Use of Equipment* and *Electricity at Work*. If pneumatic systems are in use in the school, then the *Pressure Systems and Transportable Gas Containers*

Regulations may apply. These require that pressurised equipment be regularly inspected, serviced and maintained by a competent person.

If pupils are required to etch PCBs (printed circuit boards), the chemicals used can be corrosive or irritant and special care should be taken and attention paid to the *COSHH regulations*.

With good classroom management you can reduce the risks to pupils working in this area. Try to ensure that:

- pupils do not enter the room without adult supervision
- coats and bags are stored away from the work area
- pupils use only equipment that they have been taught to use
- equipment is not switched on until it is ready for use, and is switched off immediately afterwards.

TEXTILES TECHNOLOGY

In addition to the general legislation, there are other regulations and British Standards which apply to work with textiles. The *Furniture and Furnishings (Fire) (Safety) Regulations* apply to upholstered furniture for use in private dwellings, including children's furniture and bean bags, nursery furniture containing upholstery, scatter cushions, seat pads and pillows. Many of these are items that could be made by pupils in schools. The regulations state that:

- any filling material must be fire-resistant
- cover fabric must have passed a match-resistant test
- the filling and cover together must have passed a cigarette-resistant test.

In schools, where these tests cannot be safely carried out, it is important to check with the supplier of fabrics that these standards have been met.

Several British Standards also refer to the safe use of fabrics, these are:

BS 5665 – safety of toys
BS 5722 – relates to flammability of fabric used in nightwear
BS 5867 – relates to flammability of fabric used for curtains
BS 5438 – gives methods of test for flammability of fabrics.

Information on all British Standards can be obtained from the British Standards Institution, British Standards House, 389 Chiswick High Road, London, W4 4AL.

Where toys are being made in the textile area, the *Toys (Safety) Regulations*, described in the section on resistant materials, would also apply.

In the textiles workroom the main danger points are the use of sewing machines, irons and scissors. It is important that you instil safe working habits in pupils and that you demonstrate these yourself. These will include:

- pupils not working in the room without adult supervision

- pupils only using machines that they have been taught to use
- only one pupil at a time to use the equipment, no queuing for the iron or ironing board
- sewing machines not to be switched on until ready for use
- care and attention to be paid when using equipment.

If you are carrying out batik work with hot wax, there are additional dangers and you should ensure that:

- the pot is secure in its position
- only one or two pupils work at the pot at any time
- the area around the pot is fireproof
- there is a cold water supply nearby.

Textiles work may also involve testing and experimenting. If this involves the use of chemicals then the *COSHH regulations* will apply. When working with chemicals make sure that you have sufficient light and ventilation and a water supply nearby.

At the end of the lesson, have a simple routine to check that all equipment is switched off and put safely in the correct place.

Task 6.5 Observing health and safety points in lessons

Observe a specialist teacher at work in your school, preferably in a practical lesson. Note the health and safety points dealt with by the teacher in preparation for the lesson, the routines followed by the teacher and the pupils at the start and end of the lesson, and how the teacher ensures that the pupils work safely during the lesson.

From this draw up a list of reminder points for yourself when planning and carrying out lessons.

RISK ASSESSMENT

In order to minimise, as much as is practically possible, the dangers in any design and technology workroom, you should carry out a risk assessment as part of your lesson planning. Questions to ask yourself as part of the risk assessment include:

- What are the possible points of danger within this lesson plan?
- What are the possible causes?
- What is the likelihood of the danger occurring?

- How can I reduce the risk:
  — Change the machinery, equipment or resource?
  — Change the teaching strategy?
  — Supervise pupils closely?

An example of a risk assessment form that you could draw up is shown in Figure 6.1.

Figure 6.1 An example of a risk assessment form

RISK ASSESSMENT NOTES

Lesson topic: Date:
Year group:
No. in class:
Room no.:

Check each of the following:

workspace clear —
floor not slippy —
lighting suitable —
ventilation/dust extraction adequate —
storage of tools/materials safe —
protective clothing available —
first-aid facilities available —
fire extinguishers available —
water supply available —

Possible points of danger	Risk
Consider here the materials, equipment, machinery and processes that pupils will use, teacher activities and pupil activities	very low – low – average – high – very high

Amendments to reduce the identified risks:

Lesson notes:

Lessons that involve any of the following are likely to carry risks:

- high-risk foods such as meat
- micro-organisms
- chemicals
- very hot items or equipment
- very sharp items or equipment
- high-pressure equipment
- abrasive items or equipment
- heavy objects.

The level of risk inherent in any particular lesson will depend on a number of factors:

- the room you are working in – its size, shape and layout
- the age of the pupils
- the activity being undertaken
  - whether it is for individuals, groups or whole-class work
  - how much teacher input and control there is, compared to pupil free-choice
  - whether it involves the use of machinery, chemicals, heat
- the expertise of the pupils
  - how familiar are they with the room, the material, the tools and equipment?
- the expertise of the teacher
  - as for the pupils, plus how much do you know about the materials, tools and equipment and how aware are you of the potential causes of danger?

If the risk cannot be minimised to an acceptable level, you have to consider the likelihood of it occurring. If the risk remains high, then you should seek advice about alternative ways of achieving the learning outcome.

Notes relating to health and safety issues should always be highlighted in your lesson plans and on pupil worksheets.

Task 6.6 Risk assessment when lesson planning

Look at one of your lesson plans, preferably for a practical lesson. Undertake a risk assessment of the planned lesson, considering potential hazards, action to be taken to reduce risk to an acceptable level, amendments to your lesson plan and instructions for pupils.

Note any changes you need to make and note on the lesson plan any health and safety points for yourself or the pupils.

Discuss this plan with your mentor to make sure that you have covered all the relevant points.

ACCIDENT REPORTING

It is possible that, despite your risk assessment and safe classroom procedures, an accident may occur whilst you are teaching. What you should do if this happens will be written in the school and department policies, so it is important that you familiarise yourself with these. It is usual practice that all accidents are reported and it is likely that you will need to complete a form with details of the event. It is important that you do this as soon as possible in case there are unforeseen consequences. An example of an accident report form is shown in Figure 6.2.

FIRST AID

The *Health and Safety (First Aid) Regulations 1981* require employers to provide adequate and appropriate first-aid facilities, including first-aid trained personnel. Most schools have a school nurse or central first-aid area – check that you know whom to call on, where they are and what the procedure is for calling them. If a pupil is sent to see the school nurse, it is best that she or he is accompanied by another, reliable, pupil.

The department policy statement should also include the names of trained first-aiders whom you can call on if needed. Again, check that you know who these people are and where to find them. It should also state the location of first-aid boxes in the teaching areas. Every design and technology room should contain a first-aid box, fully equipped and regularly checked, which is in a prominent position. Check that you know where it is in the rooms you will be working in, that it is accessible and suitably stocked.

It is strongly advised that, as a design and technology teacher, you learn to administer basic first aid. This will include dealing with cuts and abrasions, eye injuries, electric shocks, burns or chemical splashes. The school or local authority may offer training, and basic courses are run by the Red Cross and St John's Ambulance (contact local offices for details).

The Design and Technology Association (DATA) have produced standards for health and safety training which exemplify the knowledge and skills required by those teaching design and technology. This lists core standards for all design and technology teachers followed by subject-specific ones. The core standards cover:

- risk assessment
- the workshop classroom environment
- teaching strategies
- equipment, tools and machinery use
- awareness of legislation.

Most aspects are covered in this book and may also form part of your training, but the paper contains a full checklist which you may find useful. Details of the paper are given in the Further Reading section at the end of this chapter.

Figure 6.2 Example of an accident report form

ACCIDENT REPORT FORM

Details of accident:
Date: Time:
Location:
Nature of accident:

Witnesses:

Details of injured person:
Full name: Age:
Address: Gender:

Details of injury:
Nature of injury:
Part of body affected:

Treatment given:	no treatment required	first aid
	sent to nurse	sent to hospital
	sent home	parent/guardian collected

Outcome:	no time off school	absent for less than 3 days
	absent for more than 3 days	temporary disability
	permanent disability, partial	permanent disability, total

Description of events leading up to the accident/incident:

Description of immediate actions:

Description of possible causes:

Recommendation of action needed to prevent re-occurrence:

Signed Date:
Name

SUMMARY

Health and safety is of major concern in design and technology. It means not only knowing the legislation and regulations but also having classroom routines and procedures that encourage safe working practices. These should be constantly instilled, encouraged and reinforced in pupils.

As a teacher, you should exemplify good practice with your behaviour and work and you should be aware at all times of what is happening in the room when the pupils are working. You can do this through *looking* – let your eyes constantly scan the room and move around to watch pupils work – and by *listening* to the sound of machinery and equipment in use. Any unusual or unfamiliar sounds should be investigated as they may be an indication of a potential hazard.

Although this chapter may have caused you to wonder why ever you are entering such a dangerous profession, it is really not so bad. Put together like this, the potential for harm seems enormous, but each lesson will not carry this full range of risks. However, knowing the potential causes of any danger should help to make you more aware in the classroom. With full knowledge of the dangers, how to minimise them and how to deal with any problems, you can go on to create a safe environment for the pupils to work in, teach them safe working practices, and enjoy the subject.

FURTHER READING

British Standards Institution (1984) *BS4163 British Standard Code of Practice for Health and Safety in Workshops in Schools and Similar Establishments*, Milton Keynes: BSI

Consortium of Local Education Authorities for the Provision of Science Services (CLEAPSS) (1990) *Risk Assessments for Technology in Secondary Schools*, Uxbridge: CLEAPSS

Design and Technology Association (1998) *Exemplification of Standards for Health and Safety Training in Design and Technology*, Wellesbourne: DATA/TTA

Health and Safety Executive (1994) *Essentials of Health and Safety at Work*, London: HSE

National Association of Advisors and Inspectors in Design and Technology (1992) *Managing Health and Safety in School Workshops*, Eastleigh: NAAIDT

National Association of Advisors and Inspectors in Design and Technology (1994) *Managing Health and Safety in Food and Textiles in Schools*, Eastleigh: NAAIDT

National Association of Teachers of Home Economics (1993) *Safety in Technology – Food and Textiles*, London: NATHE

Note

Information on legislation and regulations can be obtained from the Health and Safety Executive, Health and Safety Commission, Broad Lane, Sheffield, S3 7HQ (tel. 0114 289 2345)

7 ICT in design and technology

Gwyneth Owen-Jackson and Louise Davies

INTRODUCTION

The use of information and communications technology (ICT) is growing rapidly, and in the world of industry and manufacturing it is transforming the way that products are designed and made. If design and technology is to remain relevant and contemporary, then it is important that pupils are taught how ICT has transformed industry, and how they can make use of it when designing and making in the classroom. Many of the pupils that you teach will be familiar with computers and their many uses, and you will be expected to integrate ICT into your lessons to enhance pupil learning. Information technology is not a separate branch of design and technology, it is a tool which everyone can use to make learning more effective.

As a teacher you may use ICT to do research for lessons, to plan lessons, produce resources and keep records. However, this chapter is concerned with how you can use ICT in your teaching of design and technology in order to aid pupil learning. The different uses for ICT within design and technology will be considered, along with issues for classroom management. It is important to remember, though, that you will have to make decisions about when it is appropriate to use ICT and when it is not. There may be times when ICT facilities and resources are available and you decide not to use them. This is as important as using them appropriately, as you have to decide which resources will best help the pupils to achieve the learning objectives that you have set.

It is assumed in this chapter that you have some basic knowledge and understanding of computer use, that you can switch on and load a machine, use a mouse, run a program, save work to hard and floppy disc, word-process and, print out work. If you are unsure about any of these then talk to your mentor, or the ICT technician, and ask to be shown. It also assumes that you have a basic working knowledge of databases, spreadsheets and word-processing. If you do not, there are several basic level books available to guide you: some are given in the Further Reading section at the end of this chapter. You might also find it useful to read a companion book in this series, *Learning to Teach Using ICT in the Secondary School* (Leask and Pachler, 1999).

OBJECTIVES

By the end of this chapter you should know:

- the departmental policy on using ICT
- ICT provision within your department
- how ICT can be incorporated into the various aspects of the processes of designing and making
- how the assessment of pupils' work is affected when ICT is used
- how you can use ICT in your teaching to improve pupil learning.

SCHOOL AND DEPARTMENTAL POLICIES

There is likely to be a school and departmental policy in place which will outline ICT which the design and technology department is responsible for teaching or using, and how this will be taught.

Task 7.1 Reading the school and department ICT policies

Obtain copies of the ICT policy for the school and for the department. Read through these to find out what ICT the design and technology department is responsible for. This might refer to generic terms, such as design packages, or it may be more specific and name programs that will be used or specific activities that will be undertaken.

Information and communications technology which may be used in design and technology includes:

- design software, 2D and 3D
- drawing and art packages
- graphics software

- CAD/CAM software
- databases
- spreadsheets
- word processors
- desk-top publishing
- systems and control software.

By using a variety of programs and applications, ICT can help improve teaching and learning by:

- aiding creativity in designing
- giving access to more information for research
- speeding up aspects of the making process
- improving the quality of work
- helping pupils to understand its business and industrial uses.

PLANNING TO USE ICT

Before you can begin to plan in detail when and how you will incorporate ICT into your teaching, you should find out where it fits into existing schemes of work and what facilities are available. Your ground research should include:

- how many computers there are in the department, or available for use elsewhere in the school
- where computers, or other ICT resources, are located
- whether computers are linked to other design and technology equipment, such as plotters, lathes, milling machines, sewing machines
- whether the computers are networked, or if they all operate independently
- whether any computers are linked to the internet; if so where are they and what are the procedures governing their use.

You will also need to find out what the pupils already know and can do using ICT. It is likely that you will have to take account of different levels of skills and abilities, but you should try to plan so that each pupil is able to make progress, both in their learning of design and technology and their use of ICT. It will be useful for you to look at any governing guidelines (for example in England and Wales there are national curriculum programmes of study for ICT), as these will help you to judge what is an appropriate level of expectation.

The following sections consider the various aspects of design and technology and how ICT could be incorporated to aid pupils' learning.

Task 7.2 Finding out about ICT resources

Find out what resources are available in the department, or elsewhere for you to use. You can do this by talking to your mentor, the head of department, an interested colleague, the head of ICT or the ICT technician. You should ask the following questions:

- What computers, or other resources, are available and how many?
- What capacity are the computers, i.e. what memory size do they have (some graphics and art packages require a lot of memory)?
- Where are they located?
- When can you use them?
- Who is responsible for maintenance and upkeep?
- What are the virus protection procedures?

Make sure you note down all that you find out.

ICT AND RESEARCH

When pupils have been set a design brief, or have identified a problem or an opportunity for themselves, very often we then ask them to find out more about that particular situation. This can be done through research in textbooks and journals, surveys and practical investigations. It can also be enhanced through the use of ICT, for example searching for information on CD-ROMs or the internet. The internet, and email, can also be used for pupils to communicate with others; these may be other schools, companies or practitioners, who may be anywhere in the world. This direct contact would allow them to ask for information or advice, or allow them to enter into discussion with others which will let them find out more about other contexts, other possible solutions, other values.

Databases can be used to search for information, and can be used by pupils to store their own information. CD-ROMs, which are examples of large databases, are available from commercial organisations. These may be general reference ones or encyclopedias, such as those produced by Dorling Kindersley, or they may be specific to areas of design and technology, such as those produced by the Technology Enhancement Project (TEP). It is also worth remembering to look at CD-ROMs produced for other curricular areas, such as science, art or personal and social education, as these may have sections that are relevant to design and technology. Commercially produced databases contain vast amounts of information, but these will have been structured in a particular way and you will need to become familiar with each one to discover the best way to access the information – for example, the particular words used in a search: does 'wholewheat' produce the same results as 'wholemeal'? Examples of using databases in design and technology include researching information on designers, or the properties of materials, finding information about manufactured foods, investigating the components available to use in a printed circuit board.

Task 7.3 Using a database

Select a topic that you will be teaching and use a database to find information about it. If there are no databases in the department where you work, try asking in the school library. Commercial CD-ROMs are often available to borrow from public libraries.

Think about how you could effectively introduce the use of the database into your lessons with pupils.

You may create a database yourself, for example of materials held in stock by the school. This could contain information about cost, uses and suggested alternatives and pupils could use it when selecting materials for their own work. A database could be compiled which contains diagrams of components, for example in electronics. Pupils could then look through the database for information about the components, their size, shape, uses and properties, before deciding which to incorporate into an electronic circuit being designed for a particular purpose.

Pupils can also construct their own databases to hold information which they have collected through surveys, questionnaires or practical investigations. This could then be used to help them produce graphs and charts, compare information and make decisions about their designs. Information from databases, their own or others, can be used by pupils to justify their decisions in planning and making, when evaluating and when writing reports.

When compiling your own database, or asking pupils to construct one, you need to take time to plan the work carefully. Guidance on compiling a database can be found in the DATA booklet suggested as Further Reading.

A word of caution here about allowing pupils to use the internet, or databases, to gather information. Searching these resources for information is a skilled activity; pupils will need to know how to conduct a search, what questions to ask and how to ask them. They will need to be taught how to discriminate in the information that they find. Allowing pupils free access to these search facilities may lead to hours of 'surfing the net' without producing any worthwhile results, so as a teacher you need to guide them. Table 7.1 shows a number of ways in which you can do this, ranging from very structured guidance to more open access.

If the school has the facility to connect to the internet, then it will also be possible for you to communicate electronically. This will allow the pupils to communicate with other pupils, either in the same country or anywhere in the world. This facility can be useful when they are researching: for example, finding different bread recipes from different parts of the country or the world; finding out what kind of seating is used in different places; or discovering what kinds of fabrics clothes are made from. At the design stage, pupils can send their design ideas to other pupils from different cultures for them to comment on. Pupils can develop not only their design and technology knowledge and skills through this sort of activity, but also their interpersonal skills and their awareness of other cultures and values.

Task 7.4 Searching the internet

If you have not already done so, carry out a search on the internet for websites that are relevant to a topic you will be teaching. If you do not know how to do this, ask for help from your mentor or the ICT technician in the school.

Plan one lesson which incorporates pupils searching for information on a topic; this may include many sources or you may wish to restrict this one lesson to the use of the internet.

Include in your planning how you would provide structured guidance to pupils on how they might perform this activity well. You can use the information in Table 7.1 to help you with this.

Table 7.1 Using the internet in your teaching, from tight control to open use

Method	*Advantage*	*Disadvantage*
You find the information, print it off and copy it, hand it out.	You decide what the pupils see, there is no waiting at the computer and little cost.	The material is not designed for individual pupils. Pupils do not develop information-handling skills. It is less exciting for pupils.
You find the information and download it to your computer, edit it and hand it out.	The information can be matched to the needs of groups of pupils. You can create up-to-date teaching materials.	As above.
You download a website onto your computer system and give pupils access to it.	Pupils begin to learn how to access information for themselves. There are no on-line costs.	Pupils have limited access to the site and will not be able to make links to any other sites shown.
You create a limited list of websites and ensure that pupils only access these.	Pupils can begin to learn how to search available information. The sites are real.	Pupils' work is limited by the the sites you select. There will be costs for on-line use of the internet.
You create a bigger list and allow pupils to choose which they access.	Pupils have greater freedom to conduct a search and have to make decisions.	As above.
Pupils are taught how to use a search engine and how to get the information they want.	Pupils can access a huge amount of information, can develop information-handling skills and have to make decisions.	You may need to 'police' some of their searching, to keep them on task and away from unsuitable sites. There will be costs for on-line internet use.

Source: Adapted from Davies, 1999

ICT AND DESIGNING

Designs can be produced by pupils using computer-aided design (CAD), drawing, art or paint packages. The benefit of pupils using these are that their designs can easily be modified without endless redrawing or redrafting, and they can explore using different shapes, scales, proportions, colours and typefaces. Also, designs can often be more accurate and drawn to scale more easily, and they can be used to produce templates for the making process. These benefits encourage pupils to experiment more with their design ideas, and are especially helpful for pupils with poor drawing skills.

Some pupils, though, will find it just as difficult to sit in front of a blank screen and produce design ideas as they would to sit in front of a blank piece of paper. For these pupils, there are programs, called clip-art files, which contain designs and drawings which they can bring on to their computer screen to provide a starting point for their own design work.

Other ways of starting pupils off would be to give them an image on screen as a first step. This can be done through 'scanning' an image, a picture or photograph. This is similar to taking a photocopy but it is transferred straight on to the computer screen. Digital cameras can be used to take photographs which can then be transferred straight to the computer screen; video-clips can be digitised in the same way. All of these methods would produce an image on screen which pupils could then manipulate and modify to create their own designs. If you are not sure how to use these methods, the school ICT technician should be able to advise you.

Computer-aided designing offers pupils the opportunity not only to create an image, but also to develop a deeper understanding of the product and how it might be manufactured (Davies, 1999).

Task 7.5 Using ICT in design work

Find out which computer program is used in your department for designing. If this type of program is not used, try asking in the art department.

Spend some time working through this program, find out what it will do, and consider the skills and techniques that it covers, and how important these are to your teaching. Does it cover them well or are there other methods that you could use more effectively?

Think about whether your teaching of 'designing' would change if you used this program rather than pencil and paper. If you think it would change, in what way would it be different? Discuss your thoughts on this with your mentor, and try to decide which methods would be most appropriate in which situations.

ICT AND MODELLING

'Modelling is a creative process at the heart of designing and making' (Davies, 1999). It enables pupils to:

- try out their ideas to see if they will work
- think about ways in which their ideas can be improved
- visualise their ideas
- develop their ideas before making final decisions.

Modelling using ICT also offers pupils opportunities to analyse materials, procedures, structures and processes in order to gain a better conceptual understanding of what is happening.

Modelling is often taken to mean producing a three-dimensional 'mock-up' of the intended product. This still has its place in design and technology, but it can be expensive in terms of time and resources, and should only be used when appropriate. Other forms of modelling, using ICT, include producing 3D models on screen, producing simulations on screen and producing information which can be manipulated, for example in a spreadsheet. This could be part of the designing, researching or making process.

When designing, modelling could be done through producing a 3D diagram on the computer, to allow the pupil to 'see' their proposed solution. The model could then be modified, for example in scale, for the pupils to discover what would happen if they made different decisions about size, shape, structure, material. This type of modelling allows sophisticated 'what if . . .' questions to be asked and answered, and can help pupils to develop high levels of analysis and understanding.

One particular type of program, a parametric design tool (PDT) can be used to analyse components and structures in space. This allows for the component parts of a design to be created on the computer screen and moved around to check that they will fit together when the product is made. Modelling in this way saves pupils' time and school resources.

Modelling can also refer to the use of art or paint packages which allow pupils to look at their designs with different colourways, different lettering, different patterns. This modelling can contribute to the design decisions to be made, to the evaluation process and to the making process.

A spreadsheet is also a good modelling tool which allows pupils to see 'cause and effect'. For example, amendments can be made to ingredients in a food product and the effect on its nutritional value can be seen; or the material used for a product can be changed and the effect on its weight or cost can be seen. A spreadsheet could be used to design a manufacturing process, allowing pupils to manipulate it to find out how decisions about changes to the process, or changing the number of products made, would affect the time or cost of manufacture. This would give them an insight into industrial production processes.

With some software it is possible to link a spreadsheet to a drawing, or computer-aided design, and by animating the drawing, a chart or spreadsheet can be produced which models the way in which the design will work (Davies, 1999).

Task 7.6 Using ICT to model

Look at a sequence of lessons that you teach and consider where it would be appropriate to revise it to include some computer-based modelling work.

Re-write an outline of the lessons and discuss them with your mentor.

If possible, carry out the lessons and evaluate them, particularly the learning that took place.

ICT AND MAKING

Traditionally, design and technology has involved pupils in making hand-made, one-off products, or small quantity batch-production. Where large-scale manufacturing is mentioned, the one-off product is referred to as a prototype, but pupils do not really get the opportunity to consider how the prototype would work in scaled-up production runs. With the introduction of ICT in the making process, pupils can be involved in producing products in larger quantities.

Computer-aided manufacturing (CAM) is often linked to CAD work. In the making process, computerised milling machines can be used to shape wood, metal or plastic, and they can be programmed to make products that pupils would be unlikely to be able to make by hand. Computers can aid in the engraving or etching of a printed circuit board. Computerised sewing machines can produce complex pieces of embroidery, direct from the computer design. These machines are reducing in price and more schools are finding that they are affordable and worth buying.

One of the advantages of using CAM is that it allows pupils to make a number of products to a more consistent quality than would be possible through the traditional hand-crafted methods of making. It helps them to understand commercial manufacturing processes and everyday products. It is not always necessary to have this equipment yourself. If the school has appropriate industrial links, it is possible to set up a situation where the pupils create a design on CAD/CAM software in the school, which is emailed to a linked manufacturing company who load it on to their CNC (computer numerically controlled) machine, manufacture the product and return it to the school.

If you have limited access to specialist equipment it is still possible to produce good work with a computer and printer. Some printers or printer drivers allow images to be 'tiled'. This means that several sheets of A4 can be fixed together to produce large posters or patterns for making. Patterns produced on the computer can be printed out, laminated and stuck on to products to give a finish (Davies, 1999).

Graphics and desk-top publishing programs can help pupils to produce packaging and promotional materials for products they have made. Desk-top publishing and word-processing programs can be used to produce instructional leaflets to accompany products.

There is a website which allows pupils to practise computer-aided designing, this is at <*http://www.dtonline.org*> Here they can use design tools and software to produce electronic circuits, nets for boxes and design work for use in textiles projects (Davies, 1999).

ICT AND EVALUATION AND PRESENTATION

Evaluation work can take place at any point in a pupil's designing and making activities. It can involve testing materials, collecting results from user trials, making modifications to their designs, plans or products. Information and communication technology can be a useful aid to many of these processes, for example: conducting tests on the computer which would not be possible in real-time; recording results from tests and trials and analysing and manipulating them; using a spreadsheet to model changes to their ideas.

Pupils are often asked to produce reports describing the context of their work, outlining the work that they have done and evaluating it. Word processors can be used here to help pupils draft work and to edit it until they are satisfied. They can produce the report alongside the work and save it on the computer each week until their work is finished. Desk-top publishing packages and some word-processing programs would allow them to incorporate diagrams, tables and pictures into their report.

Presentations are one area that pupils often find difficult. Frequently they write what they are going to say on a piece of paper and hold it in front of themselves whilst reading it to the class. The use of ICT, from simple overhead projector transparencies to sophisticated multi-media presentation tools such as Powerpoint or Persuasion, would allow them to produce a presentation with tables, diagrams, models and pictures to support their text. Remember, though, that pretty presentation should not be taken as evidence of understanding or good quality work. Evaluation and presentation work should be read for content and for evidence that pupils' knowledge and understanding have progressed.

CLASSROOM MANAGEMENT ISSUES

The management of ICT can often be very different to the management of a design and technology practical work area, yet in some ways they are very similar. Before working with ICT, as with other equipment, you should make sure that you know how the machines work and be able to use them proficiently. With ICT this means knowing where sockets and leads are, checking the software you intend to use, checking on any passwords that might be needed (if pupils have their own password, find out what to do if they have forgotten it), check any peripherals such as printers (which computer it is connected to; who supplies the paper), floppy disks (who keeps them – you or the pupils; where do you get new ones?). It is important to make sure that you know, and follow, any virus protection procedures that the school may have in place. Make sure that you know how to save pupils' work: is this to the hard disc, or will you need floppy disks? This is all preparation which will help you to feel more at ease with the teaching.

You also need to make sure that you are familiar with any health and safety regulations, and that you carry out a risk assessment, for example if the ICT equipment is located near dusty areas or water, as then you will need to take special precautions. All the equipment used will mean a variety of leads, plugs and wires; you need to make sure that these are not trailing or a danger to the pupils and that they are in good condition. Pupils should be able to work comfortably at the machine, so you should check desk and chair heights and that the lighting levels are sufficient. Before working with ICT, check the school and department policy on its safe use.

During the lesson you will need to consider where pupils are seated, which pupils are using ICT resources and which pupils are just watching, and how pupils are interacting. As with any other design and technology work, you have to try to manage each pupil's experience and activities and allow them to work to a level that meets their needs and from which they can make progress. This may mean planning differentiated activities, just as you would for any lesson. You may have basic tasks which you expect all pupils to complete, others which you expect most pupils to complete, and yet others which you know only the more able pupils will be able to do. However, it may be that when it comes to computer use the 'more able' pupils are not those you would normally expect and you should be prepared to respond to individual pupils. It is more difficult to do this with ICT as you cannot always 'see' what pupils are doing. You may have to listen to conversations, or ask questions, to check progress and understanding.

Task 7.7 Providing differentiation in ICT activities

Select one lesson that you teach, or have observed, that includes the use of ICT. Plan how you could provide different activities within that one lesson for a variety of pupil abilities.

There may be occasions when you use whole-class teaching, for example to demonstrate a new piece of software to all pupils. You can do this either by using an ICT suite if the school has one, so that all computer screens can show what you are doing, or by connecting one computer to a large screen so that all pupils can see it. If you use this technique you will need to check that pupils have understood, by asking them questions or, better still, get them to use the software for a specific purpose.

Pupils should be encouraged to 'plan' what they are going to do on the computer: for example, if carrying out a search they should think through what key words might form their search; if they are designing, they should consider basic shapes and sizes, possibly even measurements; if writing up work, they should have notes from which to work. This planning and preparation on their part saves wasted time and helps them to realise that the computer is there to aid their learning and thinking, not to take it over!

If resources are insufficient for the whole class to work with ICT, you may need to plan activities that do not require its use but are an important and integrated part of the work. This may be done through rotating pupils through a number of activities, or by the pupils working in groups with each group undertaking a different activity. If this happens there should be sufficient suitable workspace for the variety of activities being undertaken. Also, remember to check that different pupils have access to ICT in different projects, and that it is not the same ones each time who use the equipment, as these are the ones who are most likely to be proficient already in its use.

Another way of making the management of resources easier is by putting limits on the design work that pupils do, for example you may limit the size of their designs, or the number of colours or shapes that they can use. By doing this you can save time and storage space without any loss of effective teaching.

ICT AND PUPILS' LEARNING

The use of ICT should have an impact on pupils' learning. It is your job as a teacher, though, to assess what learning has taken place. This may mean that you need to reconsider the way in which you teach when using ICT. For example, when pupils are working at a computer screen you need to be able to see what work they are doing in order to be able to judge the progress they are making. When pupils are working in groups or pairs at the computer, which is a common occurrence, you need to be able to judge how much each pupil is contributing and how they are interacting. If pupils are encouraged to save their work as it progresses, you will be able to see how pupils have arrived at their outcome, rather than just the outcome itself. This can be done even more easily if you ask pupils to print out their work as it progresses and annotate it to show their thinking. This will help you to judge if the pupil has understood the underlying principles and concepts involved in the process they have been through. It will be helpful if you have learning objectives and criteria relating to the design and technology work, and which are made clear to the pupils, to guide you in your assessment of their work.

Pupils themselves should be encouraged to evaluate the effectiveness of using ICT in their work. In your teaching encourage them to think about whether using the ICT resources made their work quicker, easier, more creative or of a better quality. Ask if it helped them to understand the knowledge, skills or processes involved in the work.

Using ICT can help you differentiate the work for pupils, for example high-ability pupils may be moved more quickly through a program and be given more demanding tasks to do, whilst others may review sections of their work on several occasions.

Computers and other resources can help many pupils to take part in design and technology activities, where previously they would not have been able to owing physical or educational difficulties. For example, visually impaired pupils can use a computer program to produce designs in enlarged sizes. Pupils with poor manipulative skills can draw and design with more accuracy. Pupils with physical disabilities can use computers to help with designing and drawing; they can use computer-controlled machinery to help in the making of products, and their work need not suffer in quality.

Most, though not all, pupils are motivated to learn when using ICT as learning can be made more interesting and more fun. You should always ask yourself, though, what is the purpose of this lesson, what are the pupils learning, and is using ICT the best way of bringing this about? Don't be afraid if the answer is no – ICT is a wonderful tool, but it cannot teach everything and sometimes other ways will promote your learning objectives more effectively.

The assessment of pupils' work, when they have used ICT, can be difficult. It is inappropriate to assess only the finished work as pupils may have made many changes along the way, all of which could be part of the learning process. Some points to consider are:

- listening to pupils while they are designing and making
- observing and responding to pupils while they are designing and making
- reflecting with pupils on the products during all stages of the designing and making
- involving pupils in the assessment and encouraging them to generate evidence which shows what they can do (Davies, 1999).

Recording these types of assessments can be difficult. You may find it helpful to keep notes of questions or comments, or to annotate pupils' work as a reminder.

Assessing what pupils have achieved will mean being clear in your own mind about what you expect from the lesson, and what part ICT will play in this. You should be clear about particular outcomes that individual pupils may achieve. The following points may help you to think about these:

- How will access to ICT resources affect what you expect the pupils to produce? For example:
  — Do you expect them to produce more?
  — Do you expect them to work more quickly?
  — Do you expect them to produce work of a better quality, and what will that mean?
  — Do you expect them to show more understanding, make more decisions?
- How will you determine the achievement of individual pupils when they are working together? This may be done through observation, questioning, setting individual tasks, homework tasks, pupils keeping a log of their own work.
- What criteria will you use when assessing achievement? (For example, are these related to aspects of design and technology or are they related to ICT?)
- How will you ensure that you assess learning in design and technology rather than the availability and knowledge of ICT? (For example it is relatively easy for a computer-literate pupil to produce a well-finished piece of work, word-processed and with graphics, but you will still need to assess it for content, understanding and suitability. Remember that some pupils will have access to high-quality computers and software and may be extremely computer-literate, but this should not overshadow the content of their work and the understanding and learning which it demonstrates [Davies, 1999]).

Task 7.8 Assessing pupils' work when ICT is used

Look at a project taught in the department that includes ICT in the teaching and learning activities, perhaps one that you will be involved in teaching. Write out what is assessed during the project and/or at the end.

Now look at what is assessed and decide which of the assessments rely on ICT and which relate to design and technology. What evidence will there be for the pupils' learning?

There are some things that you can do that will help to make assessment easier. The following offers some guidelines:

- Encourage pupils to save their work frequently so that they can explain its development more clearly.
- Talk to pupils about their work and listen to their views and opinions; this will help you in making judgments.
- Encourage pupils to review their own work so that they can justify decisions made and actions taken.
- Ask pupils to build up a portfolio of their work which will help you to follow the process and help them to evaluate their work.
- Annotate pupils' work to remind you of activities, comments or achievements that are not written down but which indicate progress or learning (Davies, 1999).

As with all teaching, after teaching a lesson using ICT it will be useful for you to reflect on it and evaluate its effectiveness. Consider whether or not ICT was appropriate: Did it help in the achievement of the learning objectives? Did pupils understand some aspect of designing and making in a better way through using ICT? Was ICT work well integrated with other work? Be honest in your evaluation and consider whether the learning could have been improved through other methods, other software, other tasks. Improvement is always possible, and as ICT continues to develop it will be important to keep on reviewing your use of it, to keep up to date with software and equipment, in order to continue to provide good learning experiences for the pupils.

ICT IN YOUR TEACHING

Although this chapter is not about your use of ICT, it may have encouraged you to explore how you can use it to inform your lesson planning and presentation. Ways in which you might consider incorporating it include using:

- the internet to search for information relevant to lessons
- the internet to communicate with colleagues, experts, companies or other schools to get ideas for projects or resources
- word-processing, desk-top publishing and graphics software to produce resources such as worksheets and displays
- digitised photographs to introduce a project or encourage design ideas.

Once ICT becomes an integrated part of your work it can provide great enrichment and surprises.

SUMMARY

This chapter has suggested various ways in which ICT can be incorporated into the teaching of design and technology and some of the benefits which may result. We hope, however, that it is merely a starting point for you and that you will go on to explore for yourself the many other ways in which it can, and is, being used. Remember, though, that you are a teacher of design and technology and that whenever you plan to use ICT it should result in some learning outcome which enhances pupils' learning or understanding of design and technology. It is as important for you to know when *not* to use ICT as it is to know when it is appropriate.

As with all areas of design and technology, ICT will continue to develop and change and it will be important for you to keep up to date with the equipment and resources available. You will be able to do this through contact with your professional organisation, through reading relevant journals, through becoming familiar with new software packages as they are produced and through practice, practice, practice.

FURTHER READING

Bates, R. (1997) *Special Educational Needs: a Practical Guide to IT and Special Educational Needs*, Oxford: RM

Davies, L. (1999) 'ICT in the teaching of design and technology' in The Open University/Research Machines (1999) *Learning Schools Programme*, Buckingham: Open University Press

Design and Technology Association (1998). Publications include: *Using Databases in Design and Technology, Using Drawing Packages in Design and Technology, Using DTP in Design and Technology, Using Spreadsheets in Design and Technology,* Wellesbourne: DATA

Leask, M. and Pachler, N. (1999) *Learning to Teach Using ICT in the Secondary School*, London: Routledge

NCET (1994) *The DITT Pack*, Coventry: NCET

NCET (1996) *D&T: the Modelling Pack*, Coventry: NCET

Qualifications and Curriculum Authority (1998) *Information Technology – a Scheme of Work for Key Stages 1 and 2*, London: QCA

WEBSITES

www.standards.dfee.gov.uk Information on the curriculum in England and Wales.
www.nine.org.uk The Northern Ireland Network for Education.
www.netschools.org Provides links to websites for all secondary subjects.
www.data.org.uk The professional organisation for design and technology teachers (DATA). Provides information and links to other websites.
www.design-council.org.uk Information about design issues.
www.howstuffworks.com A fascinating site which covers a whole variety of products.
www.tep.org.uk Information from the Technology Enhancement Project.
www.easynet.co.uk/ifst Information from the Institute of Food Science and Technology.
www.iee.org.uk Information from the Institute of Electrical Engineers.
www.technology.org.uk New at the time of printing, no details available.

8 Pupil learning

Jim Newcomb

INTRODUCTION

As you read in the first chapter, there have been several rationales put forward for the inclusion of design and technology in the curriculum. Some focused on economic concerns, some on the development of technological awareness, while others have supported the inherent value of offering pupils opportunities to create and solve problems. The value of 'learning by doing' has also been recognised, as has the significance of the 'concrete language' of design and technology and its relationship to the notion of 'capability' (Kimbell *et al.*, 1996). In view of all these different understandings, the following may help to set the scene for the discussion that follows:

> Learning design and technology helps to prepare young people for living and working in a technological world. It does this by teaching the technical understanding, design methods and making skills needed to produce practical solutions to real problems. It stimulates both intellectual and creative abilities and develops the personal qualities needed to complete a design project from initial to finished product.
>
> (DfE, 1996)

> Notions such as practical learning, learning through doing, and a reaction against didactic pedagogies are implicit in 'practical' subjects. A style and pedagogy of emancipation and liberation from rigidly controlled learning is also implied within such domains: here education is seen to empower the child, and to confer dignity upon the adult by accepting the dignity of the child. Here children can learn to explore, expand and express. Liberation comes through the process of learning to make decisions by making them, learning to cope by coping and learning to co-operate by co-operating.
>
> (DES, 1985)

From these statements it is possible to detect three important and interrelated strands of pupil learning in this curriculum area:

1 *how* pupils learn design and technology, that is the development of what might be called the directly associated knowledge, understanding and skills
2 *what* pupils learn through designing and making, that is their ability to apply a developing range of knowledge, understanding and skills (what they know and can do), including elements drawn from other curriculum areas, in order to resolve practical problems
3 the part that design and technology plays in the development of *key skills* – literacy, numeracy, communication, problem solving, teamwork – and a wide range of attitudes and attributes.

OBJECTIVES

By the end of this chapter you should:

- be aware of what constitutes quality learning in design and technology
- recognise the importance of progression in pupils' learning
- understand the concept of capability, and its importance in relation to effective teaching and learning
- recognise how the role of the teacher will influence effective design and technology activity
- be aware of how learning through design and technology can help to enhance key skills and other attributes and attitudes
- be aware of the means by which individual needs might be supported in the context of design and technology activities.

HOW PUPILS LEARN DESIGN AND TECHNOLOGY

There is a critical relationship between teaching and learning, but how do you know what is effective or quality learning? A consideration of the criteria set out in the *Framework for the Inspection of Schools* provides some indication:

> Good learning in design and technology means that pupils continuously apply and extend their knowledge, understanding and skills when designing and making good quality products. They investigate the capabilities of different materials, use an increasing range of techniques, processes and resources confidently and show creativity in designing products to meet particular needs. Pupils persevere in the organising, planning, making and completion of their products, evaluating them at

> each stage and testing them against identified criteria. They work successfully, both individually and as part of a team.
>
> (OHMCI, 1996)

How then might this be brought about in practice? How can a school department, the individual members of its design and technology team and you as a teacher seek to secure quality learning?

Task 8.1 Reviewing learning outcomes

Have a look at a scheme of work that you will be teaching. In reading through it, can you see what learning is intended to result? How is this information given?

Discuss with your mentor, or the head of department, what she or he regards as quality learning and how it is brought about in the department.

In considering the ways in which pupils can learn the directly associated knowledge, understanding and skills, it is helpful to think about activities which help to develop them. The national curriculum in England and Wales uses the terms 'product analysis', 'focused practical tasks' and 'design and make activities' to describe such activities and these can be a useful way to think about how work is presented to pupils to develop different kinds of learning.

Product analysis

This strand of design and technological activity can be seen to be closely allied to the notion of technological awareness. It reflects the importance given to developing pupils' recognition that design and technological activity is inextricably linked to understanding products and the processes which made them, and that value judgements, the need to make choices, are an essential part of design and technology.

From their very earliest days children are naturally inquisitive and interact with the material world that surrounds them. However, this predisposition to find out more about things and how they work is not sufficient on its own. It needs to be developed over time in order that they can learn the more refined skills of investigation, research and evaluation in order, eventually, to be able to make informed decisions and draw considered views about design and technological development. It is important, therefore, that pupils' analytical skills – their ability to observe, explore, appreciate, empathise – should be given opportunities for expression and enhancement. This can be done by providing them with activities which help them learn:

- how to look more critically at the made world in which they operate
- how to analyse products for fitness for purpose and quality

- that value judgements underpin design and technological development
- how to consider both the benefits and costs associated with design and technological development
- the importance of reflective practice as an aid to their own designing and making.

Product analysis activities could include:

- looking at one product made from a variety of materials, e.g. tables, which can be plastic, wood or metal, and investigating the differences between them
- investigating the range of compact disc holders available and analysing their qualities
- investigating a food product, e.g. muesli, to analyse its constituent parts
- taking apart a garment, or packaging from products, to see how it is constructed
- evaluating any number of products for their 'fitness for purpose', quality, ergonomics, aesthetics, usefulness.

Product analysis could take place at a number of points in your teaching. You might use it as an introductory activity, asking pupils to analyse existing products before going on to design and make their own. It could be a final activity, in which they analyse products and compare them with their own, or they could analyse their own products. It might also be a focused practical task, in which you want pupils to develop particular knowledge or skills (see below for details of focused practical tasks).

These activities will help pupils to develop skills of enquiry, and to understand that in addition to looking at actual products, they can draw upon reference material in books, CD-ROMs or the internet. In order to demonstrate their analytical abilities they should be encouraged to identify, and make purposeful use of, relevant research. This may require a lot of support and intervention from you initially, but you should encourage them to become progressively more independent.

One way of securing an appropriate level of independence would be to develop a 'question bank', as a means of focusing their research work. Initially you may suggest some important aspects for attention, but beyond this pupils could be expected to begin to pose questions of their own choosing. In this way they learn how to:

- organise and carry out research
- set their own criteria for the analysis
- be selective in how they research
- use information effectively.

In short, they learn to think for themselves. Progression here may be achieved through:

- the increasing range and complexity of materials considered
- the ability to identify a greater range of relevant aspects to explore, including the needs of the user

- development from descriptive to more analytical accounts
- the extent to which research findings are purposefully incorporated into their own designing and making.

Task 8.2 Developing pupils' learning through product analysis

Take a scheme of work that you will be teaching and consider where in the scheme you could purposefully introduce an activity on product analysis.

Write the lesson plan for this activity, planning your lesson objectives, learning outcomes, pupil activities and resources.

If possible, carry out this lesson and evaluate how successful it was.

Focused practical tasks

Focused practical tasks help pupils to learn specific pieces of knowledge, understanding and skills. However, you need to think about how you will structure the work to ensure that progressive learning experiences lead to:

- a deepening of knowledge
- greater proficiency in the use of a widening range of materials, tools and techniques
- a growing ability to utilise such knowledge, skills and informed judgements effectively and efficiently to resolve practical problems.

Pupils' learning of specific design and technology knowledge, understanding and skills is usually the result of teacher-guided activities. What specific knowledge, understanding and skills, then, are pupils required to develop through focused practical tasks, and how might these be progressively developed? The knowledge, understanding and skills may be dictated to some extent by national curriculum or guidelines, the examination course that your pupils are following, or the resources that you have available in school. But within these constraints you may have some freedom to decide on the materials you want them to work with, the tools and equipment that you want them to use, and the processes that you want them to learn. You are also likely to want them to develop an understanding of how and why products are made, and the value judgements involved.

Progression in knowledge and skill can be supported in a number of ways, including:

- hands-on experimentation, supported by judicious prompting and questioning from you
- hands-on activity to reinforce, practise and clarify new knowledge or skill
- encouraging pupils to leave their 'comfort zone' of established knowledge and skills to tackle challenges that force them into new areas
- moving from simple, structured tasks to more complex, open-ended ones.

Of course, pupils do not come to school as 'empty vessels'. Rather, they will arrive with a plethora of conceptions and misconceptions that you will need to take into account when planning for and delivering learning experiences.

As a starting point, any national curriculum or guidelines for design and technology will need to be interpreted by teachers and transformed into a set of meaningful and successive learning experiences. As a means of exploring the possibilities here it will be useful to make a distinction, albeit at times somewhat artificial, between aspects of knowledge and understanding and skills.

Knowledge and understanding

Consider, for example, the programmes of study contained within the new national curriculum for design and technology in England. In the section relating to knowledge of systems and control, for pupils aged 11–14 years, is a statement which includes the phrase that pupils should be taught about 'the interconnection of mechanical systems to achieve different kinds of movement' (QCA, 1999, p. 127). How is this to be translated into an appropriate set of activities that will provide progression in the pupils' learning and a suitable foundation for later work? In this case it would be necessary for pupils, for example, to:

- learn about a range of relatively simple mechanisms, such as gears, cams, pulleys
- learn about how they might be linked to produce different kinds of movement, such as linear, reciprocating
- develop associated conceptual knowledge and technical vocabulary, such as force, speed, gear ratio.

Their learning experiences might include:

- teacher exposition or demonstration
- teacher-led whole-class discussion
- paired or group discussion – pupil directed
- experimentation with appropriate resource materials
- completion of a worksheet
- a practical activity.

Task 8.3 Identifying and analysing focused practical tasks

Read through a scheme of work that you will be teaching and try to identify in it the focused practical tasks. Look for key areas of knowledge or skills that are to be covered, how these relate to the overall scheme and how the learning will be assessed.

Skills

It will also be necessary for pupils to develop a wide range of skills in order that they may select and employ them appropriately when designing, planning and making. Some pupils will find these skills easy to learn as they may be predisposed or have a natural aptitude for them. Others will find them more difficult and so it might be helpful for you to reflect upon how you can help pupils learn to plan and make.

Planning, in the sense of organising how to go about an activity, may be a feature of pupils' work at any time during a design and make activity. Here, however, planning for making is the focus and pupils may plan for making by:

- discussing their intentions for the use of materials, tools, techniques and time with their peers or with you
- annotating their design sketches to indicate intentions for materials and techniques to be used
- completing a simple list of materials, tools and techniques
- producing a working drawing with a parts list
- generating a flow-chart to show stages of work in chronological order
- maintaining a log of activities which prompts forward planning.

The learning outcomes resulting from this work might include a recognition of the importance of constraints, the development of technical vocabulary, and a willingness to set and work to deadlines.

Task 8.4 Developing pupils' skills

Consider just one of the areas noted in the discussion of skills and think about how, with one particular group that you teach, you could develop the pupils' skills over time through a series of focused practical tasks.

Discussing your ideas with your mentor to evaluate how manageable they would be.

WHAT PUPILS LEARN THROUGH DESIGNING AND MAKING

Design and make activities

Design and make activities allow pupils to demonstrate their ability to apply what they know and can do, in order to resolve a practical problem. When undertaking a design and make activity, pupils will be engaged in aspects of investigating, generating ideas, planning, making and evaluating. In doing this they will be learning through their engagement in these individual activities and also about the often complex way in which they may be interrelated. In addition they should work in a context where the purposeful use of what they know and can do, in order to solve a practical problem, is paramount. Let's now look at what is involved in developing pupils' holistic capability.

Capability

Education for capability, in the broadest sense, has long been championed and continues to be recognised as providing a valuable contribution to pupils' personal development. Those who have written about this (see Further Reading) suggest, though with differing emphases, that design and technological 'capability' is concerned with the active, purposeful application of knowledge and skills, the movement of thought into action, and the simultaneous use of both thought and action. Furthermore they indicate that it is action-based, relying on 'knowing how' as well as 'knowing that'. Capability is also 'holistic' rather than 'atomistic': it requires pupils to demonstrate not that they can investigate, research, design, plan, make as individual activities but that they can bring these together appropriately and purposefully.

For pupils to learn to be capable, the design and make tasks must provide both the time and space for them to think and do for themselves, and situations where current and developing knowledge and skills can be seen and used by pupils. Such activities should also promote appropriate levels of autonomy in order that pupils learn to feel increasingly confident to take on a task independently from you and a willingness to reflect on, or evaluate, their work as it develops. Pupils can demonstrate, at any stage of their design and technological development, evidence of their capability through their ability to:

- use developing knowledge and skills in a creative and purposeful way
- take responsibility for the form and direction of their work
- make informed judgements
- handle uncertainty
- modify their work in the light of personal reflection.

Task 8.5 Looking for progression in schemes of work

Look at a scheme of work designed for pupils in their first year in the school, then at one covering a similar area for pupils in their third year in the school. Consider how these schemes differ, how the activities differ and how they allow pupils to demonstrate their capability. How is capability in the first year of school different from capability in the third year?

Pupils should also be given opportunities to learn to be selective in their use of resources for action. Here the focus is on the development of their procedural knowledge, for example, pupils may learn a range of ways in which to communicate ideas (see below). As these methods are 'banked' and developed over time, pupils should be encouraged to make use of what they consider to be the most appropriate means to express their thoughts. This may be by talking through the problem, sketching, direct manipulation of materials or use of a CAD package. The important point here is that they learn to optimise their use of knowledge, understanding and skills in the context of a particular problem and set of circumstances.

To summarise, what pupils learn through design and make activities includes:

- to be capable, to apply what they know and can do in order to resolve practical problems
- to optimise their use of knowledge, understanding and skills
- to be increasingly independent and self-critical thinkers and doers.

DIFFERENTIATION

In planning and teaching any project you will need to respect the fact that pupils will be at different stages of development and so will progress and achieve at different levels.

Task 8.6 Pupils with special needs

Talk to your mentor about:

- the department policy on working with pupils with special needs
- the ways in which teachers in the department find out about pupils with special needs
- how you can support pupils with special needs in your classes
- what you can do if you have concerns about a pupil you teach.

Some pupils' special needs will have led to them being given an Individual Education Programme or Plan (IEP). These are given to each teacher of the pupil and they describe the nature of the pupil's needs and what can be done in your lesson to provide support. An example of an IEP is shown in Figure 8.1.

The Curriculum Council for Wales (1993), in their document *One in Five*, provides many suggestions for ways that differentiation can be achieved. Whilst dealing specifically with support for pupils with special educational needs, it offers practical suggestions to aid both planning and classroom practice in general.

Other pupils will have different special needs: they will learn and understand more quickly, they will show insight, be able to make connections and be able to transfer their learning to new situations. These able pupils will also need guidance from you if they are to be challenged and motivated by the work.

Figure 8.1 Example of an Individual Education Programme or Plan (IEP)

INDIVIDUAL EDUCATION PROGRAMME
for
Pupil Name/Form

Date Stage Teacher

This pupil is included on the special needs register for the reasons marked below:

learning	behaviour	emotional	language	dyslexia	medical
visual	hearing	speech	physical		

I have used appropriate, simplified worksheets __
I have used shared reading strategies __
I have used recommended strategies for spelling __
I have given __ keywords to be learnt for
pronunciation __
meanings __
spelling __

I have given simplified homework tasks __
I have carried out advised behaviour management strategies __
I have revisited work to reinforce concepts and learning __
I have found opportunities to celebrate and reinforce success __
I have set small, attainable targets __

Subject goal:

Goal achieved __
Goal partly achieved __
Goal not achieved __

Comment/evidence

Subject goal:

Goal achieved __
Goal partly achieved __
Goal not achieved __

Comment/evidence

Please return this form to **Learning Support** by the following **Review Date**:

Task 8.7 Able pupils

Talk to your mentor about how able pupils can be recognised and supported in design and technology.

Think of the classes you teach and consider whether any pupils display any of the signs.

For one lesson that you teach, plan extension work that would interest and challenge an able pupil and take their learning forward.

Different pupils will also have differing preferred learning styles, for example a predisposition for working independently rather than as part of a team, one-to-one dialogue rather than participation in whole-class discussion, or communicating ideas three-dimensionally rather than through sketching or writing.

Realistically, in the context of large classes and busy environments it will prove very difficult to manage a completely individualised curriculum. Nevertheless, it is possible to support such an ideal through focusing attention on a number of key issues:

- adopting a wide range of teaching and learning strategies
- using appropriate language and presentation techniques
- regularly monitoring pupil progress and providing positive and constructive feedback
- a willingness to support differentiation in a variety of ways.

Differentiation can be achieved by way of task, resource, support and response, for example:

- *By task* The emphasis here is on the degree of openness within a task. The suggestion is that 'in many instances there is scope or flexibility for the teacher to structure different layers within an activity and to guide particular pupils to an appropriate, achievable yet challenging task' (CCW, 1993, p. 7). An example of this in shown in Figure 8.2. Alternatively, you may present pupils with different tasks; a way of planning this is shown in Figure 8.3.
- *By resource* Some children may need the additional use of:
  - — templates and / or cutting jigs
  - — measuring and marking out guides
  - — pictorial labelling and / or large text aid access to materials, tools and technical vocabulary
  - — modified tools and equipment to support those with particular motor skills difficulties.
- *By support* Here you need to consider carefully the extent to which individual pupils are monitored and supported in their progress. What is the level and type of intervention required? Some pupils will deal with high

levels of uncertainty better than others and may be able to make effective progress with little or no intervention. Others may simply need additional guideposts, questions from you such as: Have you considered this? What happens if . . . ? Can you describe the problem you are facing? Your questioning skills become paramount here.

- *By response* Here differentiation is related to outcome, when a class of pupils is working on the same project, each pupil's work will still be different from the others. For teachers, it is important to reflect on the extent of learning that has taken place. This should also reflect the extent to which pupils have met agreed targets, and this is made easier by you making these targets explicit to pupils at the start of the work.

Figure 8.2 Structuring an activity to be more open or focused
Source: Curriculum Council for Wales, 1993, p. 7

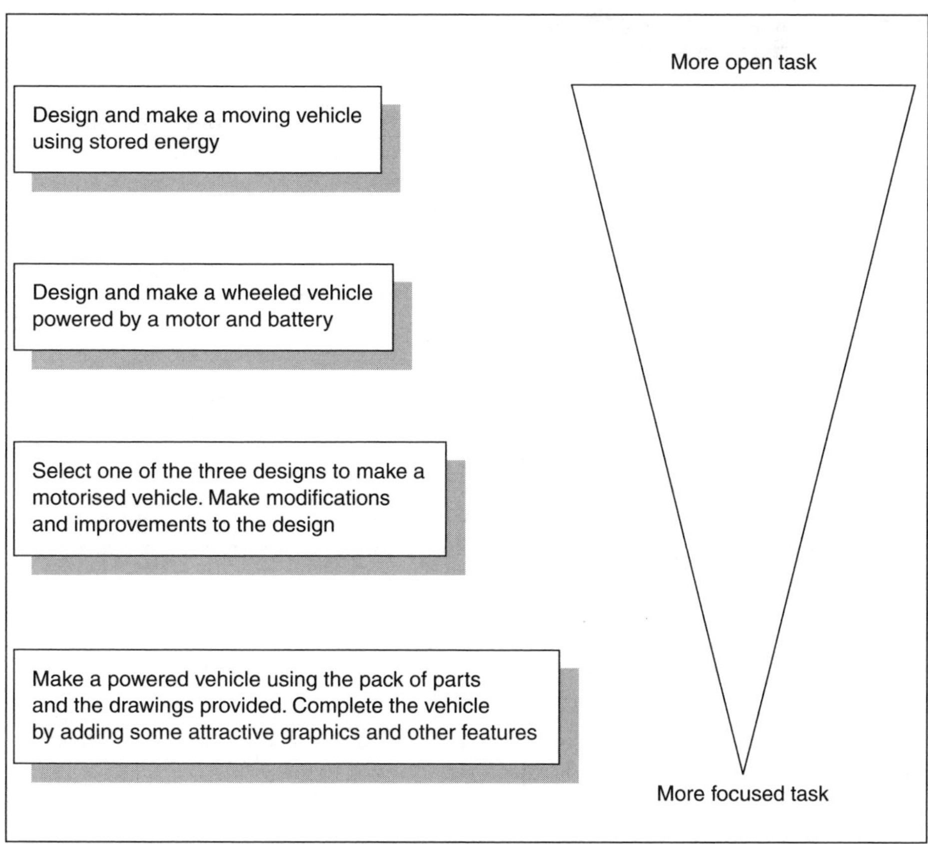
More open task
Design and make a moving vehicle using stored energy
Design and make a wheeled vehicle powered by a motor and battery
Select one of the three designs to make a motorised vehicle. Make modifications and improvements to the design
Make a powered vehicle using the pack of parts and the drawings provided. Complete the vehicle by adding some attractive graphics and other features
More focused task

Figure 8.3 Differentiated learning routes
Source: With kind permission of Stephen Griffiths, Open University PGCE student

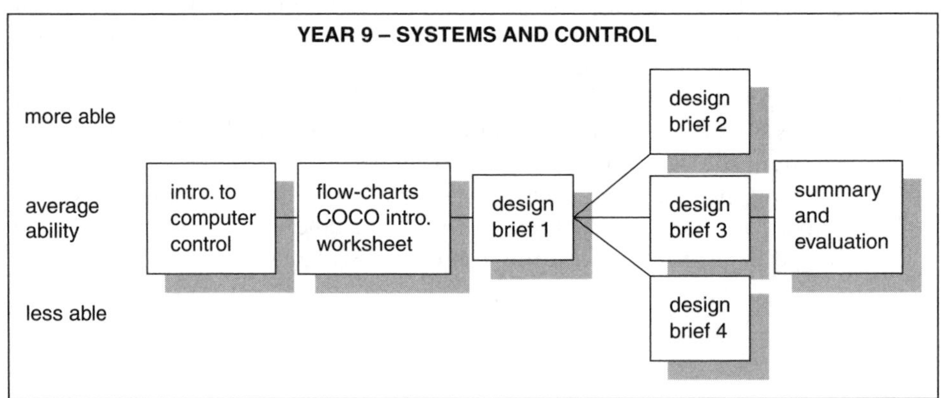

Task 8.8 Planning for differentiation in your teaching

Consider a group of pupils that you teach. Think about each pupil in the group and how he or she may have particular needs which you could support in one of the above ways.

Make a note of your thoughts and ideas.

In your next few lessons with this class try to incorporate some of the above strategies and evaluate their effect on the pupils' learning.

Consider, then, how you might broaden this to work that you do with other groups.

The challenge for differentiation is to retain a balance between respecting the individual differences of pupils and holding a clear view about the essential qualities that they need to develop for technological capability.

All of the aspects considered in the last section suggest that the role of the teacher is paramount, in terms of structuring problem-solving activities at an appropriate level of challenge.

THE ROLE OF THE TEACHER

It is the responsibility of the teacher to create activities that provide suitable levels of challenge yet allow pupils to work through a series of manageable tasks. These points are extended by Ritchie (1996), who emphasises the need for teachers to vary the level and nature of their classroom interventions according to the phase of the problem currently being encountered by their pupils. He sees the teacher's role as involving, at different times, the giving of instructions, demonstrating, facilitating debate, eliciting ideas, advising, encouraging, focusing, clarifying, extending pupils' line of thought, and challenging existing ideas. This means that at times you will be closely involved with the pupils' work and at other times your role will be minimal, in order for them to 'get on'.

Task 8.9 Observing teacher intervention

Observe an experienced teacher working with a class on a design and make activity.

Note how the teacher interacts with different pupils. Consider the type of intervention the teacher conducts; try to think why it was done in that way and how it helped the pupil's learning.

Discuss your observations and notes with the teacher after the lesson and compare your thoughts with the teacher's actual intentions and the outcomes.

You need to strike a careful balance between teacher-led activities and those that promote greater levels of pupil independence. The teacher also has a role to play in terms of motivating pupils as a means of encouraging learning. Pupils who are motivated generally learn more, learn better and are easier for you, the teacher, to deal with. So where does motivation come from and what can you do to encourage it in the pupils you teach?

Motivation can be intrinsic, something inside the pupils which drives them, such as being successful at something which gives a good feeling, or finding the work interesting, exciting or fun, or wanting to do well for you. Extrinsic motivation on the other hand comes from some outside reward, such as wanting to pass the examination or wanting to get a particular job. In preparing your lessons, and in carrying out your role as a teacher, consideration of how to motivate the pupils will require you to think about:

- the suitability of the task: is it pitched to provide appropriate challenge?
- its relevance to the pupils: is it set in a meaningful context?
- its enthusiastic delivery
- the sharing and clarification of objectives
- the early identification of agreed criteria for success – remember to have high expectations
- the organisation of any problem into manageable sub-tasks
- the efficient monitoring of progress and effective feedback, with suggestions for how they might move forward
- the appropriate use of rewards and praise
- the appropriate valuing and stimulating display of pupils' work in order to help establish a classroom ethos in which pupils feel secure about contributing.

These issues are developed further in Chapter 8, in the discussion on planning lessons. There is more general information on learning theories in the core text in this series (Capel *et al.*, 1997).

THE DEVELOPMENT OF KEY SKILLS

Key skills include:

- communication (see below)
- application of number. This arises naturally in much design and technology work when pupils are measuring, weighing out, costing. It occurs in other ways when pupils are researching statistical or numerical data or compiling numerical data from their own research, or when they are recording numerical test results
- information technology (this is dealt with in Chapter 7)
- working with others (see below)
- improving their own learning – this should develop as pupils' capability in design and technology develops and they take more responsibility for their own work
- problem-solving (see below).

Communication

The language of technology is indisputably a concrete one of images, symbols and models. This means that it is important to think about the significance of developing pupils' ability to communicate through media other than the written word, and how this contributes to their general cognitive development.

Task 8.10 Developing pupils' communication skills

Think about a scheme of work that you have taught. It is likely that there was some form of communication skills used in the lessons, but consider whether it was all reliant on written work or whether there was discussion, graphical work or presentation work. Why were the particular communication skills used, and in what way did they contribute to pupils' learning?

Think about whether you could amend the scheme of work to develop pupils' communication skills in a more planned and purposeful way.

Pupils need to develop not only the particular skills associated with communicating, within the context of design-based activities, but also an appropriate awareness of when and how to employ the wide range of strategies available to them. This requires a willingness on your part to transfer responsibility for selecting and using such strategies to the pupil, and to be less prescriptive in your approach to the way in which pupils develop their design proposals. This can only be done, however, when the pupils have acquired the relevant knowledge and skills and when you consider they are ready for this development in their learning.

What, then, are the communication skills that children need to learn, and or that can be enhanced through design and technological activity?

- *verbally:* brainstorming, explaining decisions, discussing ideas, critically evaluating the work of others
- *in writing:* research findings, annotation of sketches, lists of resources, written evaluations
- *drawing:* simple sketches, formalised drawing, presentational work, CAD
- *3D models:* paper and card mock-ups, appearance models
- *ICT:* the use of appropriate word-processing, DTP, CAD, CD-ROM packages and the internet.

Working with others

Pupils usually work on individual projects in design and technology but there will be times when you ask them to work in groups on a joint project. This is particularly important when teaching about industrial practices. In what way will working in groups help to develop pupils' learning?

When working in teams, group discussions can help to promote understanding and pupils learn to develop skills of social interaction. However, the composition of groups, and the degree to which pupils understand and can manage the differing roles that they may have to undertake, will affect significantly the extent to which they benefit. Recent research (Burgess, 1998) noted that group composition has a significant effect on individual performance and that pupils with less confidence and/or skills in design and technology will not necessarily develop them when grouped with more able pupils. Indeed, in terms of kinesthetic learning, through handling and manipulating materials, placing less able pupils with more able or confident ones can be seen to restrict their development. Whilst it is difficult, therefore, to devise any set of definitive rules for group management, the following may be of use:

- ensure that at the outset pupils are fully aware of objectives and criteria for success
- ensure that pupils are fully aware of the roles and responsibilities that they will need to undertake, including valuing co-operation, respecting the views of others, showing a willingness to lead or follow as required
- ensure that pupils are monitored effectively so that that they remain on task, yet maintain as much responsibility for progress as possible
- whilst pupils should be encouraged to take responsibility for deciding how

to proceed with a task, the notion of equal access to and involvement with all elements of the process should remain crucial if breadth and depth of learning are to be achieved by all

- teams of four seem to be ideal, offering good lines of communication
- younger and quieter pupils seem to do better in pairs and the development of co-operative skills may need to be fostered in such settings in the early stages.

Task 8.11 Introducing teamwork

Look at a scheme of work that you currently teach and consider where the introduction of teamwork would enhance pupils' learning. This could range from a simple group discussion to produce an agreed outcome to a full joint project involving planning, designing and making.

If possible, amend the scheme, teach it and evaluate it. If not, then discuss your ideas with your mentor and consider how the planned teamwork would be organised and managed, and what the possible outcomes might be.

Group work is also a good strategy as it provides a reflection of design and technological activity in the workplace. It offers pupils an opportunity to learn about industrial and commercial practice, which increasingly uses team-based methods.

Problem-solving

There is considerable debate over the extent to which it is possible to teach general problem-solving skills (Hennessy and McCormick, 1994). Arguments centre on the extent to which such skills, learnt in specific contexts, are transferable to new situations. Nevertheless, a number of benefits have been suggested to result from pupils engaging in problem-solving activities. Most design and make activities that you set for pupils will involve some form of problem-solving activity. Problem-solving situations may be seen to:

- provide motivation
- be pupil-centred
- require the application of knowledge and skills
- encourage inventiveness
- foster interactive language
- develop social skills
- encourage observational skills
- encourage a multi-disciplinary approach
- help to break down arbitrary curriculum boundaries
- provide concrete experiences

- present concepts in a natural setting
- encourage logical and forward thinking.

THE DEVELOPMENT OF GENERIC SKILLS

In this brief section the focus is on how pupils, through design and technological activities, might develop attitudes and attributes which can be of benefit across the curriculum and beyond. Table 8.1 gives some examples.

Table 8.1 Design and technology activities that develop wider skills

In developing:	*Pupils can learn that:*
Creativity Risk-taking Decision-making	It is possible to move beyond the obvious. In the context of practical problem-solving, there will be solutions which are more or less appropriate. There is merit in taking chances in using trial and error to improve ideas.
Organisational skills	Benefits can be gained from thinking ahead. Being well-organised in terms of time, materials and the sequencing of work will aid successful completion of a project.
Perseverance Industriousness	In order to produce a quality product it will be necessary for them to adopt a diligent approach to their work and to take a pride in the outcomes.
Independence	They can take greater responsibility for their own progress. In so doing, they will develop greater levels of initiative, self-monitoring and control over the direction of their work.

SUMMARY

A central theme running through this chapter has been the need for you to employ a wide range of teaching and learning strategies to help all pupils develop their design and technological capability. Moreover, it has emphasised the need to provide an appropriate relationship between investigative tasks, focused practical tasks and design and make activities. If pupils are to learn effectively in design and technology, they must be offered opportunities to develop relevant knowledge, understanding and skills and be able to apply this in the context of solving meaningful practical problems. Furthermore, there will be a need for them to exhibit informed judgements based upon a growing recognition of the values that underpin design and technological activity at any level.

Such learning is important not only in subject-specific terms but also as a means of encouraging a wide range of attitudes and attributes that will be of value across the curriculum and beyond. Not least of these is the development of key skills such as communicating, problem-solving and collaboration.

In all of this your role as teacher is crucial to achieving a suitable balance between guided activities and those that provide opportunities for pupils to operate at appropriate levels of uncertainty. Aside from the constraints of national curriculum guidelines or examination syllabuses, you should think carefully about what you want the pupils to learn, how you can structure and present this so that all pupils will benefit, and how you will assess what they have learnt. The following chapters will help to guide you through these issues.

FURTHER READING

Assessment of Performance Unit (APU) (1991) *The Final Report of the APU, Assessment of Performance in D&T Project*, London: SEAC

Banks, F. (ed.) (1994) *Teaching Technology*, London: Routledge

Faulkner, D., Littlejohn, K. and Woodhead, M. (1998) *Learning Relationships in the Classroom*, London: Routledge

Kimbell, R., Stables, K. and Green, R. (1996) *Understanding Practice in Design and Technology* Buckingham: Open University Press

McCormick, B., Newey, C. and Sparkes, J. (1993) *Teaching and Learning Technology*, Wokingham: Addison Wesley

Wood, D. (1988) *How Children Think and Learn*, Oxford: Blackwell

9 Planning your teaching

Gwyneth Owen-Jackson

INTRODUCTION

One of the main ways of ensuring that you will feel confident when you go into the classroom is with thorough planning and preparation beforehand. Calderhead, after researching the ways in which teachers planned and prepared lessons, said that 'survival planning' is not to be recommended and that '[e]ntering the classroom with a well-thought-out plan probably provides most teachers with greater confidence and leads to a more relaxed lesson' (Calderhead, 1994, p. 9).

Think of planning and teaching as an iceberg where the tip of the iceberg is what happens in the classroom, one-third of what is seen, but most of the iceberg is made up of planning and preparation, which represents the two-thirds below the surface (see Figure 9.1). Thorough lesson planning and preparation is a major key to good classroom performance.

Most design and technology departments have long-term plans to cover one year or a number of years; medium-term plans to cover a term or a unit of work; and short-term plans to cover individual lessons. The results of planning are usually documents or files, which form the basis of the teaching in the department. These are important documents, since they can be used to provide evidence of what is happening to governing bodies, school leaders, government inspectors and parents. They are also useful for new members of staff joining the department as they give guidance and support, showing what is to be taught. No doubt you were shown the schemes of work which you would be teaching when you started work in the department.

There are, of course, constraints on planning. Departments may have to follow national guidelines, or examination syllabuses for older pupils. Certainly as a student or newly qualified teacher, you will be expected to follow existing departmental guidelines, which can be a source of both comfort and frustration.

Figure 9.1 Planning and teaching are like an iceberg

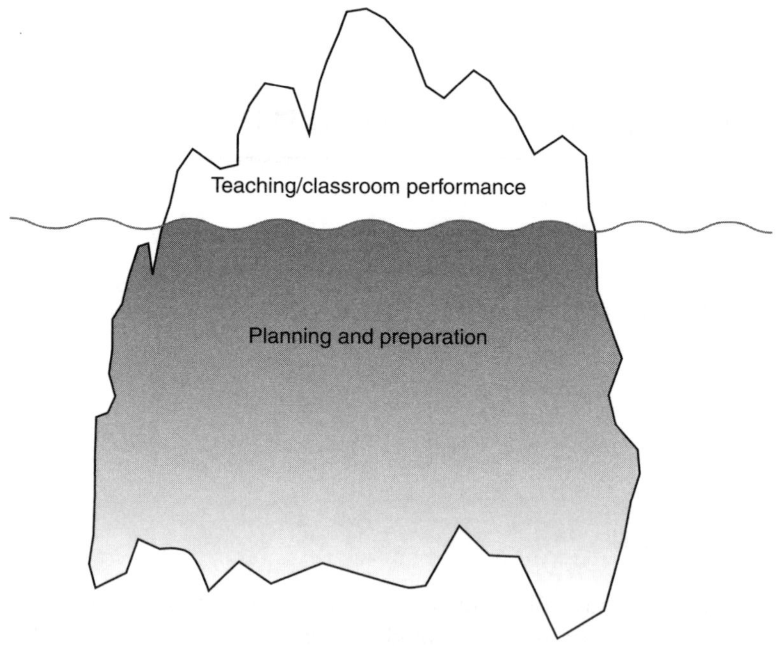

OBJECTIVES

By the end of this chapter you should be able to:

- understand the terms used in lesson planning, such as aims and objectives
- think about the factors involved in planning and preparation
- construct a scheme, or unit, of work
- construct an effective design and technology lesson plan
- link design and technology work to wider issues, such as values and key skills
- evaluate your lessons.

LONG-TERM PLANNING

This refers to plans that cover a whole school year, or several years. In England and Wales, the national curriculum for pupils aged 11–16 is divided into two key stages, KS3 covers 11–14 years and KS4 covers 14–16 years. Schools will often plan work to cover a key stage. Other similar divisions operate in other countries.

In design and technology departments long-term planning is usually a collaborative venture, with specialist teachers from the different areas agreeing the structure and outline content. An example of a plan covering key stage 3 (pupils aged 11–14) is shown in Table 9.1. For older pupils, the plan usually covers the one- or two-year examination period.

Table 9.1 Long-term planning over three years

Year 7	*Food* fruit & veg	*Res. Materials* wall plaque	*Textiles* t-shirt
Year 8	*Systems & Control* signboard	*Textiles* container	*Food* carbohydrates manfacturing
Year 9	*Textiles* charity item	*Food* nutritional analysis	*Res. Materials* chair to scale

Task 9.1 Reviewing the long-term plan

In your school, ask to see the plan for a key stage, year group or examination group. Look at this alongside the relevant curriculum guidelines or syllabus and see if you can match the plan to the requirements.

MEDIUM-TERM PLANNING

This refers to plans that cover a unit of work – this may be a few weeks or a full term. It may also be called a scheme of work. Units of work are usually planned by specialist teachers and cover an area of the syllabus within an agreed time-frame.

When starting to write the scheme of work, it is important that you know where it fits into the long-term plan, and to discover what pupils have learnt previously and what will follow. In design and technology this may be different for different groups of pupils, depending on how their lessons are organised. A scheme of work, though, is designed to achieve continuity and progression in learning, so that skills, knowledge and understanding, and values are all developed in a planned way.

The scheme of work should be cohesive and comprehensive. It should have continuity (or 'flow') and progression. Schools, or departments, usually have an agreed standard format for schemes of work, which may be more or less detailed; one format is shown in Figure 9.2.

Most departments will have schemes of work that are similar in content to the pro-forma in Figure 9.2, if not in layout. Most will include the following elements.

Figure 9.2 Scheme of work for pro-forma

DESIGN AND TECHNOLOGY DEPARTMENT
Scheme of Work

Year group: *Duration*:

Area: Topic:

FT

RM

TT

SC

Aims:

Links to national curriculum/guidelines:

Learning objectives:

Week No.	Lesson content	Resources	Assessment	Homework	Key skills	Differentiation support/ext.

Aims

These refer to what you broadly want the pupils to achieve, describing the purpose of the unit of work and what pupils will have achieved by the end of it. Aims can be described as the destination point of the journey. They are usually written in broad terms, for example, 'pupils will understand how the properties of materials affect their choice and use'.

Objectives

These describe more specifically what you want the pupils to achieve. They will help to define the content and assessment of the unit of work and can be described as the 'map points' showing the route of the journey. They are usually written to say what pupils will know, understand or be able to do as a result of the work, for example:

- 'pupils will be able to define ferrous and non-ferrous metals and name three types of each'
- 'pupils will be able confidently to use a pillar drill'
- 'pupils will be able to choose an appropriate metal for an item of jewellery'.

You should, therefore, when writing the objectives, consider how you will assess whether they have been achieved (this is covered later in this chapter and in Chapter 11).

Links to the syllabus or guidelines being followed

This may or may not be included. it shows you are meeting the requirements of the syllabus or prescribed curriculum.

Time-frame

It is usual to show how many weeks the unit is planned to cover, and/or how many lessons. The length of each lesson may also be given, for example: '12 weeks × 1 lesson/week, 70 minutes'.

Class details

This will show who the unit of work is aimed at, for example: 'Year 9' or 'Class 4'.

Content outline

This may be just a title. Its purpose is to show what material pupils will be working with, or what area of the curriculum they will be covering, for example, 'Food – nutritional needs of different groups' or 'Electronics – printed circuit boards'.

Teaching strategies

This is to show that a variety of strategies are planned for over a period of time. Strategies may include talk, video, written work, research, practical work, investigative work, evaluations.

Assessment

It is a good idea to build assessment times and plans into schemes of work to show that progress is to be monitored. Assessment outcomes should be identified and these may link back to any guidelines or syllabus being followed. For example, the national curriculum in England and Wales gives 'level descriptors' which describe aspects of pupils' work which can be expected at different stages of their development.

The scheme may also show:

- *cross-curricular links*, for example links with science if teaching nutrition or moments; with mathematics if the work involves measuring, costing or surveys; with geography/history/religious studies looking at cultural or historical differences or developments in technologies
- *key skills*, such as literacy or communication if pupils are writing instruction leaflets, or extracting information for research; numeracy skills if they are measuring, calculating or costing; working with others if group work is involved or problem-solving
- *social, moral, spiritual or cultural values*, for example if you are discussing environmental issues, the needs of others or cultural traditions of decoration
- *citizenship issues*, for example if pupils are required to be involved in discussions of issues of general significance; to work with others to meet a challenge; to consider the experience of others, analyse and reflect on significant issues or community events; to collect information from a range of different sources about an issue; or to demonstrate an understanding of the use of statistics.

An example of a completed scheme of work from one school is shown in Table 9.2. This is a short four-week scheme to introduce pupils to the use of the sewing machine.

Task 9.2 Writing a medium-term plan

For your specialist area, select a topic in which you have good subject knowledge and plan out a scheme of work for a class of pupils in their first year in secondary school.

Follow the above guidelines, including in your plan aims and objectives, the time-frame and class details. Outline the content and teaching strategies to be used and how work will be assessed. Indicate any cross-curricular links, key skills or social, moral, spiritual or cultural values that will be covered.

Show your mentor or tutor this scheme of work and ask for comments on how suitable and realistic it is.

Table 9.2 An example of medium-term planning, a scheme of work

YEAR 9 – 1999/2000

Unit: Using the sewing machine – wall hanging, 'the coastline'

Time allocation: 4 double lessons

Aims

1. To develop pupils' design and technology capability through a design and make task
2. To promote co-operative working, and to meet the school aims of developing sensitivity to others and achieving sound personal relationships
3. To make pupils aware of the need to work efficiently and safely
4. To encourage pupils to produce work of high quality
5. To promote equality of opportunity through the presentation of work which allows for, and reflects, individual differences of gender, culture and ability, and allows all pupils to develop their potential

Objectives

1. Pupils should know:
   - how to thread up a sewing machine
   - the variety of stitches available on the sewing machine
   - the technique of appliqué
   - a variety of hand embroidery stitches
   - how to use an eyelet punch
   - the names and uses of common textiles tools and equipment
   - why 'process' is important in practical work.
2. Pupils should be able to:
   - work safely
   - select suitable fabrics for their purpose
   - select and use appropriate equipment
   - use a sewing machine efficiently
   - follow instructions and work through a planned sequence of operations
   - make a product of good quality.

Table 9.2 Continued

Week	*Knowledge and understanding*	*Teaching methods*	*Resources*	*Homework*	*Assessment*	*Differentiation*
1	Room safety and equipment Introduce brief – generate ideas Methods of decoration Threading machines and neatening fabrics	Teacher-led discussion Pupil activity Demonstration	A3 paper Calico and fabrics, threads, exemplars, machines and equipment	Finalise chosen design, and annotate		Individual dem. Teacher intervention
2	Transfer design to fabric	Demonstrations	As week 1	Complete flow-chart	Checking for accuracy	As week 1
3	Use of sewing machine Appliqué and hand embroidery Use of Bonda web Need for flow-chart	Practical activities		Continue practical work		
4	Mitering corners Strengthening top edge for hanging Spacing of and making eyelets	Pupil activity Discussion of evaluation Written work	As week 1 + pre-cut strips of card, eyelet and rope	None	Mark all work for quality Grade pupils for effort	Teacher intervention and quality of outcome

Source: Used by kind permission of Thurston Upper School, Bury St Edmunds, Suffolk

SHORT-TERM PLANNING

This usually refers to individual lesson plans, and is likely to be where you will start with your own lessons. There are many variations on the style and layout of lesson plans; it is best to try different ones from your training institution, other students and teachers before selecting one that suits your purposes. You might also need to discuss with your mentor and tutor what is considered appropriate.

Lesson plans develop from the scheme of work described above, but should be in more detail. As a new, or student, teacher you will be expected to write lesson plans for all your lessons, which your mentor or tutor may ask to look at. What they will be looking for in the plan is evidence that you understand the elements involved in lesson planning, and have taken them into account, that you have good subject knowledge, and that you have thoroughly prepared for the lesson. In order to provide all this evidence your plans must be detailed, and you may supplement them with teacher's notes. As a student teacher you will be required to show your lesson plans to your mentor or head of department before the lesson. Try to agree a regular time when this will take place. The class teacher retains responsibility for the class and needs to be aware of what is being taught. She or he may also be able to give you good advice about the group of pupils, or about the content or activities that you have planned. Be prepared to accept advice and constructive criticism of your planning and try to achieve a balance between working to accepted practice and introducing new ideas. Caution – any advice about safety should always be adhered to (points to consider about health and safety have been covered in Chapter 6).

Task 9.3 Observing what teachers do

Observe carefully an experienced teacher teaching a lesson and make a list of what the teacher does during the lesson. In particular, note what happens before the lesson starts, how it is introduced, what activities the teacher and pupils engage in, how time is used, what resources are used, how assessment takes place and how the lesson ends.

The list that you have from Task 9.3 will give you some idea of the aspects of a lesson that you have to plan and, although it may seem endless, it can be structured into a meaningful experience for both teacher and pupils.

Many of the elements described below are similar to those used in the section on medium-term planning, but with a slightly different perspective and usually with more detail.

Aims

You may or may not have aims for an individual lesson; remember that these are broad statements of what pupils will achieve. You may list aims from the scheme of work which link to the objectives for your lesson.

Objectives

These should always feature in a lesson plan. They are important in describing the *purpose* of the lesson, what you want the pupils to know, understand or be able to do at the end of the lesson. Note that the objectives refer to what you want the pupils to achieve, not what you will do, and they refer to what pupils will achieve or learn, not what they will do. For example, rather than 'pupils will work in groups to write a specification', it is better to say 'pupils will be able to list the factors to be considered when writing a specification'. The first describes what they will do in the lesson, whilst the second is what you want them to learn. Kyriacou says that 'One of the major pitfalls in teaching is to neglect thinking precisely about educational objectives and to see planning as simply organising activities' (Kyriacou, 1993, p. 23). Be wary.

The objectives will be important, too, in helping to determine the content, strategies and assessment you select, as all of these should contribute to the achievement of the learning objectives. It is good practice to share your objectives with the pupils at the start of the lesson, if appropriate, so that they know what to expect and what is expected of them. Don't have too many objectives; depending on the length of the lesson, two or three should be sufficient.

Links to syllabus or curriculum

If your work is governed by the requirement to follow a national curriculum, guidelines or a syllabus, this information will show you are working to the requirements. Don't try to include too much, though – you are likely to cover only one or two aspects in a single lesson. It can also be helpful to use the link as a cross-reference to check back to the original document, to make sure that your lesson does cover what is required.

Class details

It is useful to show the year group for whom the lesson is intended, and details of particular classes, such as how many pupils are in the class. In fact, this might be a major factor in your plan, as the age and number of pupils in your lesson may well determine what strategies you can use, how resources can be used, and what you and the pupils can do. Remember, twenty-six 16 year olds in a one-room workshop can constrain even the most enthusiastic teacher!

It is also useful to have additional information about the class as a reminder, for example the number of girls and boys, the ability level of the class in general, the particular needs of individual pupils, such as those with eyesight, hearing or reading difficulties.

Time frame

There are two aspects to the timing of an individual lesson. It is a good idea to show where this lesson fits into the scheme of work, for example 'lesson 3 of 5' or you could date each lesson plan. You could also put the time of day on the plan, for example, '1.15–2.25p.m.'.

In addition, the content of the lesson should have timings alongside indicating how long you anticipate each part of the lesson lasting. This can be quite difficult initially; it may take you some time to get to know the different classes that you teach, and the different topics, to be able to make an accurate judgement on timings, but it is useful to start with some guide. This may be done in actual times, for example:

1.15	Settle pupils and take register
1.20	Introduce the lesson with a question and answer session on packaging
1.30	Move pupils to watch the video . . .

or you may prefer to use this method:

5 mins	Settle pupils and take register
10 mins	Introduce the lesson with a question and answer session
15 mins	Pupils move to watch video . . .

This shows that you have thought about the pace of the lesson as well as its structure. Sometimes it can be difficult to gauge how long activities will take, and timings may differ with different groups. It is a good idea to have additional work planned, both for use during the lesson and at the end, just in case the pupils work more quickly than you expect. If they take longer, then you can take account of this when planning the following lesson.

Remember to allow sufficient time at the end of the lesson for setting homework, reviewing the lesson and indicating what comes next. Also, in practical lessons, allow time for the clearing away and checking of resources.

Lesson content

There are many factors to be considered here and the plan should be regarded as a summary of what you aim to teach. It should not be a script, nor should it contain all the factual information which you may need. A good way of writing up additional support material for your lesson is through the use of teacher's notes, with more detailed content, to supplement your lesson plan.

The main point to consider is what knowledge or skill will be covered in the lesson. You may be guided in this by the scheme of work operating in the department. You may, however, be asked to produce a scheme of work for a particular year group or topic, in which case go back to the previous section to check what is required and consult with colleagues when drafting the work. It is worth pointing out here that prescribed curricula or syllabuses for design and technology are sometimes written in broad terms which teachers need to interpret. For example, the national curriculum for England includes statements that pupils should be taught to:

- select and use tools, equipment and processes . . . to shape and form materials accurately, and finish them appropriately
- join and combine materials and ready-made components accurately to achieve functional results
- consider the physical and chemical properties of materials . . . and to relate these properties to the ways materials are worked and used.

(Adapted from QCA, 1999, pp. 126–27)

Each of these statements requires the teacher to make decisions about *what* tools, equipment and processes, *what* materials and components, *which* materials and properties to teach about, as there are too many for them all to be covered. It is here that your good subject knowledge will be put into practice, in selecting suitable, relevant and appropriate content for lessons. There are useful commercial resources available which may help you in this, schemes such as the Nuffield Project and the RCA Routes books. One or other of these may be in your school, and it is worth checking to see what texts other members of the department use as reference material.

It may be possible to base your selection of appropriate knowledge or skill on local industry. Check to see if the school has established links with companies in the area and, if so, whether you can make use of them. If not, do you have any contacts or can you make any? In design and technology this can be useful for starting off projects, for speakers, visits to the company or for resources (these ideas are discussed further in Chapter 12).

Important factors to consider when selecting suitable content are the needs, interests and abilities of the pupils. Try to select content that will appeal to both boys and girls or to use examples from their own interests, for example fashionable toys or clothes, packaging of fashionable items. You may also be teaching pupils from different cultural backgrounds, so try to make the work relevant to them, for example discussing traditional fabric decorations or foods. Make sure, as well, that the work is pitched at an appropriate level so that all pupils will achieve something and the more able ones will be challenged (for details on this see Chapter 8).

When you have a general idea of the content to be covered, you then have to decide how to structure it and how to present it to pupils. This is where your own creativity is called for.

Try to plan the lesson so that the content 'unfolds' for the pupils; remember that it needs to be coherent to allow them to construct the concepts appropriately for themselves.

Teacher's notes

These have been referred to several times in the section on lesson content. They can be useful in providing the additional support you may need in the lesson, and will

Task 9.4 Making lessons interesting

Think about your own experience as a pupil. Think of a lesson that you still remember today:

- What was it about that lesson that made it memorable?
- Was it an exciting introduction?
- Was there an outside speaker?
- Did you do an interesting activity?
- Did it relate to things you were interested in?

How can you use this knowledge to help you plan your own lessons?

help your mentor or tutor to see more clearly what you intend to teach. Teacher's notes can contain information such as:

- notes on the knowledge to be covered, e.g. which foods contain vitamin A, the properties of different types of woods, the various ways in which fabric can be finished, the colours and values of resistors
- technical vocabulary that you want to introduce or reinforce
- key words or concepts that you want to introduce or develop
- questions that you will ask at various points in the lesson
- points you will write on the board – this is useful if you are expecting pupils to provide answers, for example in a brainstorm, as you can check your notes to make sure that they cover all the points you want to include
- details of homework to be given, and the date by which it is to be done.

Having prepared these notes, you may find that you do not need to refer to them. Remember to have them by you in the lesson, though, as they are a source of support if you 'dry up' or forget the questions that you were going to ask, and they are a useful checklist to ensure you have covered all the points you wanted to make.

Teaching strategies

Having decided on the content, you then have to decide how the work will be presented. Think about how you can present work to make it interesting for pupils. You have a wide range of strategies to draw on, and will not be too constrained here by prescribed curricula, although departmental schemes of work may have already identified some strategies to be incorporated. The strategies you choose will depend to some extent on your own personality, qualities and skills, as well as on the objectives and content of the lesson. As a student, or new teacher, it is a good idea to try out different strategies to find out what works for you, and what works for the pupils. Remember, too, that pupils will have different preferred learning styles. By providing a range of strategies (over a number of lessons), you will be enabling more pupils access to the work, and the purpose of teaching is for pupils to learn, so if something works for the pupils then it is a good strategy, even if it is difficult or time-consuming for you. Teaching strategies are discussed further in the next chapter.

If you plan to use textbooks or worksheets, video or slides, then remember to check these in advance to ensure that they are appropriate and suitable. Will they cover the content? Are they clear and concise? Will pupils be able to understand them?

You may have planned learning objectives which will affect your decisions about the presentation of the work, for example you may want pupils to consider some of the social or moral values which influence design decisions and so may set up discussion groups in which pupils research and debate the use of hardwoods for toy-making, or the use of additives in food.

You may want to incorporate key skills into the work, so you may ask pupils to produce a piece of work which requires accurate measuring, for example a box with a lid. If you want to develop literacy or communication skills, you may ask them to undertake a piece of research and present their findings.

Classroom management issues

This is often an area of great concern to students and new teachers, but many management issues can be pre-planned. Think back to Task 9.3: which of the activities you observed involved management of the class?

From the moment the bell goes for your lesson, plan how you will manage the group. How, for example, will they enter the classroom – will they line up outside waiting for your instructions or will they wander in individually as they arrive back from the far corners of the school field? You need to check whether there is a school or departmental policy on this, or accepted practice. If there isn't, you can decide what you want them to do, then plan and prepare for this.

Many design and technology lessons take place in workshops or practical rooms and knowing what to do with pupils' coats and bags is an important management and safety issue. Again, check on the practice of other teachers and establish your own guidelines. You may need to include time for this in your time plan.

If you have planned activities for pupils, you need to think about how you will move them around the room: will they work in friendship groups or will you set the groupings? Will they sit where they choose or will you direct them? If you have planned a demonstration or are showing a video, where will the pupils sit or stand? Is there room for all of them and will they be able to see?

In a practical lesson you need to plan how pupils will access and use the materials, tools and equipment. Think about safety issues, pupil movement around the room and where you will need to place yourself. It is easy, sometimes, to get 'trapped' in one place with pupils coming to you continuously for assistance, but it is important that you move around the room and constantly keep checking the room for safety, as well as to ensure that pupils are working.

Think about how you will manage the ending of the lesson: will you give out homework? If so, you need to plan time for this. If resources have been used in the lesson, how will pupils be instructed to clear these away, and who will check this?

Plan how you will dismiss the class – will they all leave at once on the bell or will let each table leave in turn as you have checked their work?

By planning these management issues into your lesson you can feel more secure and confident that you know how the lesson will run, and this will allow you to concentrate more on teaching the lesson for effective learning.

Discipline management

No matter how good a teacher you are, there will always be occasions when you have misbehaviour in your classes. The causes of misbehaviour, and the way it manifests itself, are numerous. Some of the most irritating misbehaviour can be the most trivial, for example the pupil who talks at a low level throughout the lesson. It is possible, though, to plan into your lesson how you will deal with misbehaviour.

Task 9.5 Planning for managing discipline in the classroom

List the types of misbehaviour that might occur in a design and technology lesson. This is list 1.

List the strategies that you have for dealing with misbehaviour. These may be personal ones you have developed yourself or stem from departmental or school policy and procedures. This is list 2.

Go back to list 1 and put the types of misbehaviour into a hierarchical order, from mildest to worst. This is list 3.

Referring now to list 2, match suitable strategies from this list to each type of misbehaviour in list 3.

This will give you an outline for your discipline management plan. Discuss this with your mentor and consider how practical your discipline management plan would be in the classroom.

You need to decide beforehand what behaviour is acceptable and what is not; different teachers may hold different opinions on this. When you have a list of possible misbehaviours you can decide how you will deal with each one, for example if a pupil is talking constantly you may draw up a list of stages for dealing with it, starting with a general warning to the whole class, then a warning to the pupil for all the class to hear, a quiet word in the pupil's ear, taking them outside the classroom and talking to them, keeping them in during a break or lunchtime. You can also make your list hierarchical, as in Task 9.5, so that more trivial misbehaviour does not result in a pupil being marched off to see the school Head!

Remember that praise can also be used in a behaviour management strategy. Praising good behaviour can have a positive 'ripple' effect on others.

Health and safety issues

Although you may be aware of these in your head, your lesson plan, especially for your mentor and tutor, will show that you have thought about these and taken them into account. This is particularly important in practical lessons. Details about health and safety issues are covered in Chapter 6.

Resources

Once you know what you will be teaching and the strategies you will use, you will be able to list the resources that you will need. These may be quite simple, such as a supply of paper and spare pens, or resources which are already in the room, such as tools and equipment. However, it is as well to acknowledge this in your plan.

If you can plan your lessons one week in advance this will give you, and others, time to ensure that the resources you need will be available. This is easily done for the first week, then during each week it is a good idea at the end of each day to plan the lessons for the following week. This is time-consuming, but the rewards are that you are certain of having the resources that you need. Moreover you can remind yourself of the requirements of individual pupils, for example if a pupil was absent you can make a note to make sure they are up to date; if a pupil did not complete a piece of work, you can remind yourself to make sure that they finish it before progressing.

In addition to planning the use of resources, you may need to prepare them or to check them before the lesson. This is covered in the section on lesson preparation.

Assessment

Formative assessment is that which takes place on a continual basis during lessons. Some of it will be informal and unplanned, but it is a good idea to note when you want formally to check pupils' work. You may do this through a question and answer session at the beginning or end of the lesson, or you may go through homework which you have marked, or you may decide to speak to each pupil individually during the course of a practical lesson.

It is also important that you note not only when and how you will assess during a lesson, but also what criteria you will use – for example, will you be checking how much progress pupils have made, or will you be checking what they know? Make sure that the lesson will provide pupils with opportunities to show what they have learnt, and that this will provide evidence suitable for assessment of your planned learning outcomes. More information on assessment issues is covered in Chapter 11.

When you have made your decisions about when, how and what you will assess, it is a good idea to share these with pupils. If pupils know what is expected of them they can often produce better work.

Homework

Note in your lesson plan what homework will be given; this may be included in the scheme of work or it may be dependent on how each lesson progresses. However, *when* you give the homework may vary. It does not always have to be at the end of the lesson – you could start the lesson by giving the homework, as this will put the lesson into context for pupils. If the homework relates to something that will be done during the course of the lesson, it could be given at that point.

The homework should be planned to be relevant to the work that the pupils have done, to extend the classroom work, to apply it or to start a new piece of work. Pupils should also see that homework has value, so remember to collect it in, mark it, return it with feedback and refer to it during lessons. There is more information on homework in the core text in this series (Capel *et al.*, 1997).

The lesson plan in Figure 9.3 is from a student teacher's file. It shows how all the above points have been incorporated into one lesson plan.

Task 9.6 Writing detailed lesson plans

Select one lesson that you may feel unsure about teaching, either because of the subject content, the teaching area or the group of pupils.

Write a lesson plan for that lesson in the amount of detail shown in Figure 9.3. Teach the lesson and evaluate it, particularly in terms of how you performed in the lesson and how well it was managed.

LESSON PREPARATION

Having done all this lesson planning, you are still not ready for the classroom! There are aspects of the lesson plan that require some preparation, mainly to do with resources that you will be using.

Check, first of all, that the resources you need will be available. You may be planning to use textbooks; if the school only has one set, check that these will be available, as other members of the department may have planned to use them. If you will be using worksheets, then give yourself time to prepare these, or make sure that there are sufficient stocks. If you are in a school where photocopying is handed to a reprographics department you may need to hand these in several days in advance.

Some resources, such as the video and television, overhead projector or ICT equipment, may need to be pre-booked with the technician or other member of staff. Remember to allow good time for this, as you will not endear yourself to staff if you ask for equipment which you need 'next lesson'. By giving as much notice as possible you are allowing others to organise themselves.

If you intend pupils to use tools and machinery that are already in the room, check that quantities are sufficient. If not, arrange to borrow from another room, or amend your plan accordingly. Check that the machinery, tools and equipment all work and are safe to use, for example that chisels have been sharpened or that all the ovens work. Check that you know how to use the machines, tools and equipment that pupils will be using. Make sure that you know how to do 'running repairs', for example replacing coping saw blades or sewing machine needles, coping with the oven that won't light or the computer program that won't run. If there is anything that you are not sure about, make time before the lesson to familiarise yourself with it, asking for assistance from other staff if necessary.

Figure 9.3 An example of a lesson plan

SYSTEMS AND CONTROL – MECHANISMS

Class: Year 10 GCSE Date: 5 May 1999
Session: 04

Topic: mechanisms – cams and followers
simple and complex gears

Aims (inc. NCPoS):
NCPoS: 1b, 6a, 6c, 7e (n.b. these are from the 1995 Orders)
Pupils to understand the principles of simple mechanical devices

Objectives:
The pupils should understand:

- types of motion – continue simple/complex gear trains
- the terms 'cams' and 'followers' and be able to describe their use in converting rotary to linear motion and vice versa

Time	*Teacher*	*Pupil activity*	*Resources*
0	Allow pupils into workshop and registration Give back homework	Bags and coats away Take out pens,books, calculator	Register
10	Set objectives for lesson on board – complete work on gears, cams, followers, cranks and slides	Whole-class questions and answer	
	Recap motion and force Types of motion – examples, moments, equilibrium, levers		OHT on moments
	MA, VR, linkages, rotary systems, speed changes, cranks and slider	Whole-class question and answer	OHT on types of motion Crank and slider
15	Set task – simple gear train example, target 5 mins	Individual work	OHT on simple gear train example
20	Debrief example, set task Technical language sheet – target 10 mins		Gear systems worksheet
30	Debrief worksheet		
35	Introduction to cams and followers, cranks and sliders	Whole-class question and answer	OHT cams and followers Visual aid – crank and slider

Figure 9.3 Continued

40	Organise video – cams and followers	Class gather round TV	Video and TV
53	Discuss video	Class discussion	
55	Practical – organise construction kits and workbook – target 20 mins Individual support and monitoring	Practical activity from workbook, activity 5, assignment 7	Mechanisms workbook and kits
75	Introduce changing the profile of the cams, – target 10 mins Framework to be kept for next lesson	Begin designing own CAM profile	Paper and card compasses
85	Discuss assignment 7	Class question and answer	
90	Collect in equipment count back in	Clearing away	
	Set homework	Write into diaries	
	Recap lesson		
100	Dismiss class		

Homework:	Complex gear train example
Assessment:	Q and A sessions Individual pupil disscussions Homework Behaviour record
Differentiation:	Task: focused practical task Support: from teacher and peers Outcome Extension material
Next lesson:	Gears continued + cams and cranks
Cross-curricular links:	Mathematics, English

Source: With kind permission of Stephen Griffiths, Open University PGCE student

If you are using small items of stock, make sure that there are sufficient quantities, or talk to the technician or person responsible for ordering (for example washing-up liquid in the food technology room, LEDs, reels of cotton). Do not assume that everything that you need will always be in stock, make sure you check in advance of the lesson and allow time for ordering if necessary.

You may need to prepare yourself for the lesson content, for example you may need to re-read your own notes, or the school textbook, to refresh or update your knowledge. You may need to familiarise yourself with the textbook to be used, so that you can confidently say to pupils 'if you look at the chart on page 53 . . .'. Note that schools sometimes have different editions of the same textbook, so that what is on page 53 in one edition may be on page 55 in another. This is worth checking because it can cause disruption in the classroom. You may need to watch the video that the pupils will see, so that you know what to point out or what questions to ask.

In the classroom, check that the blackboard or whiteboard is clean and available for your use. Make sure that you have sufficient chalk or board pens, and make sure that the board pens work! Make sure that you have spare books or paper for the pupils, and pens or pencils for those who forget them.

You may need to do other preparation, for example re-arrange the furniture in the room prior to the lesson for group work. You may need to set up a display, or set out resources for pupils. These tasks are important in creating the right physical environment for teaching and learning.

The social environment will also be important, so make sure that you prepare for this. Learn pupils' names quickly, and use them. Plan how you will present yourself in the lesson. Be firm, be fair and be polite. Good social relationships contribute a great deal to good teaching and learning and will help to establish good classroom management.

Task 9.7 Learning pupils' names

One way you can learn pupils' names is to draw a plan of the room(s) where you will be teaching, showing the seating positions. Then write on the plan the name of each pupil in the appropriate place, and refer to the plan if necessary when you are teaching. Your plan will look something like this:

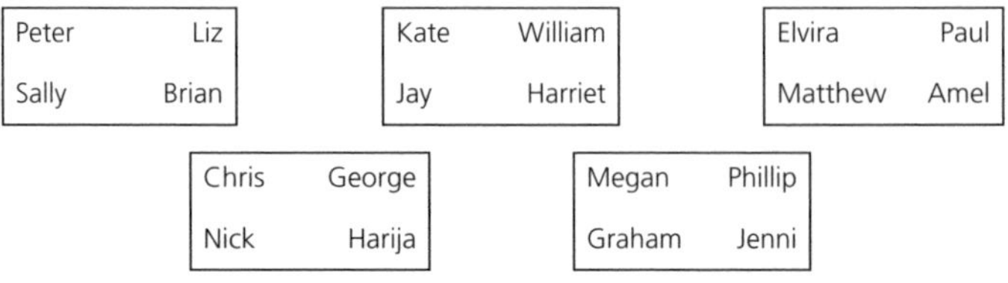

Talk to other staff in the school and ask them what methods they use for learning pupils' names.

Make an effort to learn the names of the pupils you teach. If one method doesn't work for you, try another until you find one that works and that you feel comfortable with.

All this work in advance, although time-consuming, will help your lesson to run more smoothly. This will help you to feel more secure and confident and will show the pupils that you are organised and know what you are doing. This will, in turn, help to produce better classroom performance and more effective learning.

PLANNING PROJECT WORK

Project work has the potential to motivate pupils and integrate learning in a holistic context. It is also the most difficult form of teaching and learning to manage, rather like a plate juggler trying to keep twenty five plates spinning on the ends of long canes! The reasons for this difficulty are:

- the complexity of individual pupils' designs vary, even when they are all working to the same design brief
- the variation in pupils' abilities can be considerable
- rates of progress for individual pupils will vary
- absences, even of one week, can make a considerable impact.

This will tax the most efficient and professional teacher in terms of monitoring individuals' progress and supporting and extending each pupil appropriately.

The individual nature of the work, however, is also its strength. When pupils are working on their own project, it can often generate commitment and excitement for the work. As the work is so varied, you have the opportunity to help pupils share what they are learning so that they all gain from each other's work.

When planning project work there are a number of factors that you need to consider; these are shown in Figure 9.4.

Projects can be tightly or loosely structured: which you choose will depend on the purposes of the project. A tightly structured project will have specific requirements or constraints, for example pupils could be asked to design and make a photograph frame from acrylic materials, to take a 10cm × 12cm photograph and to be free-standing. This will allow for the use of particular materials, tools or techniques whilst allowing some freedom in aspects of design. As a teacher you will have a greater degree of control over a tightly structured project as the materials, tools and techniques can be predicted and planned for. An example of a more open project could be asking pupils to design and make a toy for a child, which has some educational benefit. This will require the pupils to carry out research, design an appropriate toy, select appropriate materials, tools and techniques and plan their work carefully. Here your role is much more difficult to predict and you will need to keep good records to monitor individual pupils' needs, progress and achievements. It might also be

Figure 9.4 Aspects of planning project work

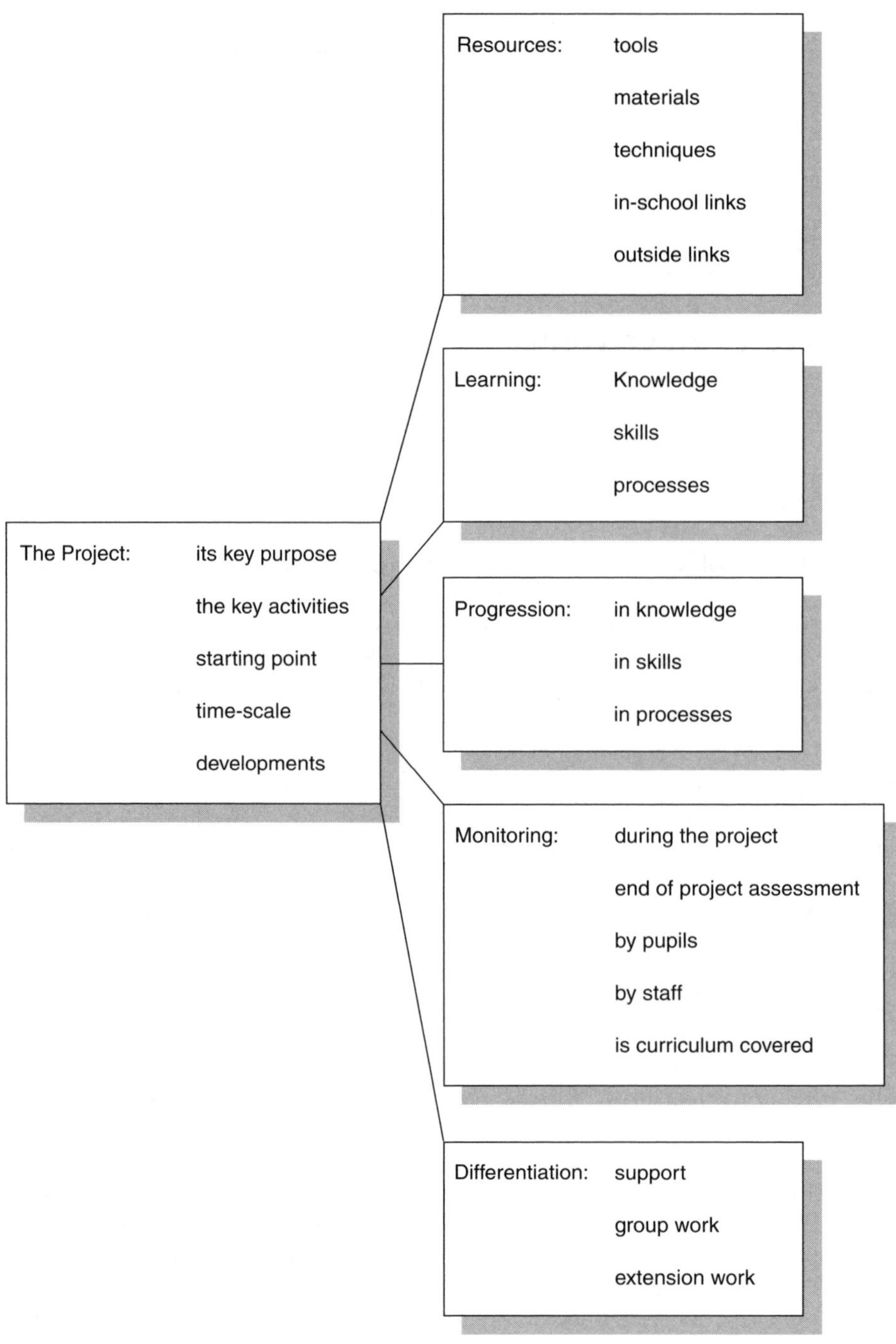

Source: With kind permission of Stephen Griffiths, Open University PGCE student

useful to keep a record of your own comments and observations, for example that 'Megan learnt how to use the lathe this week, following a demonstration' or 'Peter asked about finishes for his game and is researching suitable varnishes'.

Learning can take place during project work in a variety of ways. You might find that a number of pupils are experiencing the same problems or difficulties, so you could stop the whole class and give an explanation or demonstration. You could build relevant learning into the project, for example a topic on adhesives followed by a test. You could ask pupils to give short talks about their work, focusing particularly on what they have learnt.

Don't think that once a project is underway that pupils can just be left to get on with it. They will still need guidance from you and it is useful to start each lesson with a summary of what has been done, what needs to be done, what stage they should be at and what you expect to be done during the lesson. You may have individual objectives for pupils, and you can remind them of these each lesson. If there is time, you can recap at the end of the lesson as well.

Project work can still incorporate homework, and this should be linked to relevant processes. In the early stages focused research could be carried out, information sheets could be given out for reading, and time could be spent practising specific sketching techniques or advancing design work.

Projects can be interesting and motivating; they should also enable pupils to learn a different range of skills from those they learn in focused lessons. However, you do need to plan and prepare thoroughly for project work to be completed successfully and on time.

TEACHING THE LESSON

This is discussed fully in the next chapter, but it is worth noting that, although you have planned this lesson and will use your plan as the basis of your lesson, you do need to be flexible. Perhaps you had planned group discussion work, but find that the group is too noisy to settle down to serious discussion, so you need to think of another way of presenting the work that will achieve the same, or similar, outcomes. Alternatively, you may find that you have set pupils work to do which they are finding too difficult; in this case you may need to stop them and go back over certain aspects of the work in order for them to be able to proceed. Equally, you may find that they complete work more quickly than you anticipated and you need to extend them in some way. So, although you have planned your lesson, be prepared to respond to the pupils in the classroom. Calderhead refers to the lesson plan as a map 'keeping teachers informed of the route but always leaving the option of occasional and necessary detours open' (1994, p. 11).

EVALUATING YOUR LESSONS

This is an important part of the planning process. Before you can plan the next lesson for the group of pupils you should ask yourself the following:

- Was the timing accurate; was the lesson well-paced?
- Was the content pitched at an appropriate level?
- Were the teaching strategies suitable?
- Were pupil activities appropriate?
- Were resources well used?
- Was the issue of health and safety adequately addressed?
- Were the lesson objectives achieved?
- What learning took place and how do I know?

From the answers you can decide what pupils have achieved and what they need to do next in order to progress in their work. You may need to make notes on individual pupils – for example, those who were absent; those who did not complete the work; those who showed some lack of understanding – and you can build into your next lesson plan how you will address these individual needs.

You may find that you are delivering the same lesson to different classes. In this case evaluation is also important, as it is unlikely that you will deliver the same lesson in the same way and have the same responses and outcomes. It is likely that you will need to make adjustments to the lesson, for example adjust the timing, increase or decrease the amount of work to be covered, or use a different strategy. Your evaluations will, over time, help you to know what works and what doesn't and help you to build up a bank of knowledge and skills which you will be able to draw upon in the classroom whenever necessary.

SUMMARY

This chapter has covered a lot of ground. However, if good, thorough planning is the key to good classroom performance, as I believe it is, then it is worth spending time on getting it right. As a student, and in the early stages of your career, you will probably find that you spend huge amounts of time in lesson preparation, but this will diminish as your bank of plans builds up.

Writing lesson plans requires skill and practice and, again, as you become more experienced and more familiar with departmental resources, you will find that you can write your lesson plans more quickly.

I am cautious about comparing teaching to genius, but think that what Edison said about genius can also be applied to writing lesson plans and teaching, that it is '1 per cent inspiration and 99 per cent perspiration'.

FURTHER READING

Kyriacou, C. (1993) *Essential Teaching Skills*, Hemel Hempstead: Simon & Schuster

Kimbell, R., Stables, K. and Green, R. (1996) *Understanding Practice in Design and Technology*, Buckingham: Open University Press

10 Teaching design and technology

Frank Banks

INTRODUCTION

What teaching strategies are appropriate for design and technology? How can you help pupils gain capability in design and technology? What is the best way to use the support that a technician can offer? What can you do to encourage interest and enthusiasm and ensure good behaviour? This chapter will tackle these questions and offer some advice. The core text in this series also gives detailed generic advice on teaching methods and styles (Capel *et al.*, 1997).

As you read in Chapter 1, before the mid-1970s manual subjects were largely restricted to the development of excellence in practical skills. These outcomes were achieved by adopting a pedagogy not so very different to the 'master–apprentice' model of a medieval guild. The pupil would be given a job – perhaps to produce a pipe-rack (now occasionally seen as a CD rack!), coat-hook, pin-cushion or sponge cake – and shown all the skills and techniques necessary to produce a (more or less) satisfactory outcome. The safe manufacture of such quality products is still important but it is only one, restricted, aspect of technological capability.

It is clear that a traditional 'show and copy' apprentice model of teaching is now inadequate as it teaches making skills without any underlying understanding or development of other skills. Today we need teaching methods which match the broader aims that the subject has developed and which will lead to the wider view of design and technology capability. The teaching methods used must be wide enough to embrace attitudes, skills and knowledge for life, and specific enough to meet any curriculum or guidelines which you are required to cover. Remember, though, that the methods you employ will not be fixed and unchanging. Throughout your career your teaching methods will need to be constantly reviewed, and the match between your teaching strategy and learning aims considered.

OBJECTIVES

By the end of this chapter you should:

- be aware of different teaching techniques available
- be able to consider the role of focused practical tasks and design and make assignments to structure teaching and learning
- know some classroom management strategies for practical work
- be starting to consider how to collaborate with technicians and other support staff
- be aware of ways to motivate and manage your pupils.

TEACHING TECHNIQUES IN DESIGN AND TECHNOLOGY

Initially, I would like to review a range of teaching strategies and the techniques of how to employ them effectively. I will describe some strategies for teaching

- a whole class
- pupils working in groups
- pupils working individually.

Task 10.1 What happens in design and technology lessons?

In reading about the different teaching techniques described in the text below, consider the following points and make notes to answer the questions:

- What will I, as the teacher, be doing?
- What will the pupils be doing?
- In what ways am I, as a teacher, conveying messages about the nature of design and technology by how I teach it?

Teaching the whole class

Exposition

As soon as you have more than one person to teach, you need to consider the range of aptitudes, different levels of understanding and variations in motivation of different pupils in the class. Exposition – the teacher standing at the front and talking to the whole group – is sometimes denigrated as 'just chalk-and-talk', which does little to address the individual needs of the pupils. It is, however, very effective and efficient in the following circumstances:

- giving a stimulus or setting the context for a topic, for example, this might involve the use of a video, other audio-visual materials or demonstration and class discussion
- demonstrating a technique or process
- using a question-and-answer session to remotivate the groups or to allow groups to inform each other
- setting general goals of what you hope the class will achieve by the end of the session
- stressing points of safety
- preparing for a visit or the reception of a visitor
- rounding off a topic and preparing for the evaluation and display of the work.

When exposition is used, ensure that it is not a lecture: interact with the class by asking questions and encouraging them to give their ideas and opinions. Eye contact is essential to check that all are paying attention and that questions are being posed which challenge but do not baffle the pupils. Exposition is also most used at the beginning and ending of lessons to help establish teacher control of the group. Workrooms in schools are generally very safe environments and it is the duty of all of us to ensure that this is the case. Strategies for managing pupils are discussed later.

Demonstrations

A demonstration need not be a whole-class activity; sometimes it is better to demonstrate a particular technique or process to a small group or an individual who happens to need that skill. However, in balancing broader tasks, to encourage technological capability, and with focused tasks, to give specific knowledge and skills, a whole-class demonstration may be the most straightforward course of action.

The best way to ensure you give a confident and accurate demonstration is to practise the procedure first. It is essential to go through the demonstration in private and ask a colleague to help you get it right, particularly if the technique is new or unfamiliar. Only by rehearsing the demonstration is it possible to ensure that it can be done and that there are no difficulties with the school's tools or equipment, either in supply or in use. It will also give you an idea of how long the demonstration will take.

Before carrying out the demonstration, organise the components and materials in advance. Make sure that the bench or table surface is cleared as other items can obscure pupils' view and are distracting. Place the items you will need close by you and in a logical order.

All demonstrations should be:

- clearly visible to everyone; if it cannot be seen by the whole class split the group into smaller units
- competently performed and clearly explained so that the pupils understand why they are being shown the technique and how to carry it out themselves
- interestingly executed to keep everyone's attention.

When performing the demonstration, keep the pupils involved. Make sure that they are close enough to see what is happening, but are not in a position to interfere with the demonstration's arrangements. Occasionally a pupil will need to be on the teacher's side of the table to see and interpret the demonstration from the same point of view, but this is the exception rather than the rule. Question the pupils about the materials or components and ask them to link the procedure to similar processes they might have seen before. Discuss what is being done and use diagrams, on an overhead projector or board, to help explain any important or intricate points. A good way to keep pupils involved is to ask individuals to help. They can pass items, take readings if appropriate, and repeat certain tasks or techniques which have just been shown. The pupils can also suggest what should be done next and perhaps use a check list to keep track of the sequence.

At the end of a demonstration, summarise the important points and then control the pupils' return to their workplace. It is obviously a good idea for them to use the technique as soon as possible after the demonstration to reinforce what has been shown, so try to leave enough time for this and circulate around the class to help where necessary.

It is important that you encourage pupils to become independent learners and to consider a variety of ways of gaining knowledge and skills, rather than simply looking on you as the fount of all knowledge. It could be argued that technology projects require so wide a range of knowledge and understanding that one teacher could never hope to supply all that is needed. The individual needs of project work may also reduce the appropriateness of whole-class teaching, but when it is used well it can generate enthusiasm, give a topic a sense of direction, and be efficient in both teacher and pupil time. Most importantly, perhaps, whole-class teaching can give a 'group identity' to help pupils feel they belong.

Teaching using group work

Despite the rhetoric, it is not often that you will see group work in design and technology. Design and technology teachers like each pupil to make a product that 'they are proud of and want to take home to show off', yet this laudable aim often results in a teaching style that neglects the wider issues and focuses on the opinions of the individual. It is also in marked contrast to the group nature of technology projects outside the school workshop or classroom.

Group work is valuable in encouraging co-operative work in planning, sharing responsibility and allocating tasks, and in fostering teamwork. Care has to be exercised, if a group activity is to be assessed, in giving credit for different aspects of the project to the appropriate pupils. Group work need not only be for practical tasks, however, and group discussion is a valuable way for pupils to consider a wide range of issues. Whatever the aims for group work a few points need to be kept in mind:

- Consider the composition of the groups carefully.
  — Is friendship grouping the most appropriate?
  — If not, what criteria should be used to form more effective groups?

— Is the grouping a temporary measure or a more permanent arrangement, which needs monitoring?

- Ensure each group has short-term strategies to achieve long-term goals. This is best achieved by visiting each group quickly once they have started, still keeping every group in view; the different groups must know that their progress is being monitored even though the teacher is principally occupied in a different area of the room.
- Make sure all groups are kept busy and on task. If a group appears too rowdy or too many pupils appear to be moving around on short excursions, check that it is to do with the organisation of their task (see Denton, 1994).

Group discussion

When designing, many people find it difficult to think up novel ideas. Discussion techniques can aid creativity by allowing individuals to trigger ideas off each other. Brainstorming is one simple technique, but organising groups for discussion or brainstorming ideas needs particular care. Pupils do not always discuss well without help.

Establish rules for brainstorming:

- every suggestion is written down
- use words already on the sheet to spark off other ideas
- no one's suggestion is discussed [initially]
- no one's suggestion is ignored or 'rubbished'.

(STEP, 1993)

For younger secondary pupils an initial brainstorm of about five minutes is sufficient before the ideas are developed and explored further. Later, as pupils become more experienced, a more flexible approach may be possible. The techniques where students note ideas individually, then share them with a partner, then in a group of four, and finally report to the whole group can work well. However, the agenda for discussion needs to be tight and the time kept short, especially if pupils are not used to this way of working.

Some of the particular benefits that small group discussion can bring are as follows:

- It enables pupils to contribute their own ideas to less threatening scrutiny before exposing them to a wider audience.
- Pooling ideas can help half-formed opinions to develop.
- It helps the values of different experiences and cultural groups to be considered.

Some occasions where discussion might be useful include:

- product evaluation
- problem identification

- ideas generation
- sorting out roles for a batch production simulation
- preparing a presentation for a group evaluation of an outcome
- exploring the values implicit in a technological solution.

The last point deserves elaboration. There is one aspect of technology education, which perhaps is part of evaluation, where discussion work between pupils and between pupil and teacher is especially valuable. That is, in the consideration of the implications of technology on the community, economy and environment. Such discussion is much more than brainstorming ideas, as pupils need to ponder issues beyond the immediate need to develop the product in hand. The necessary quality of such discussion, and its organisation by the pupils themselves, needs to be of a high order if it is to be worthwhile and meaningful. For example, I was talking about an examination entry by a 16 year old pupil with his teacher. The pupil in question had designed and made a 'panic alarm' in case he was attacked late at night. In a technical sense it was very well done with proper consideration of the alarm's weight, power supply, loudness and so on. If anyone had attacked that boy everyone would have heard about it! However, was it the best solution to the problem? By not considering the wider issues, e.g. few late-night buses or limited and poor street lighting, the solution was in some senses restricted. It provided a partial solution to the youth's problem but certainly did not reduce his fear, in some ways the merely technical solution increased it!

Some teachers have found it valuable for pupils to work out their own rules for discussion work. It is clearly important to find out how much group discussion is already used in design and technology, and other curriculum areas, before making a major organisational issue out of what might well be, for the pupils, a routine learning strategy. However, if little discussion work is used, taking it forward within an agreed framework in small steps is very desirable.

The following suggestions for the organisation of discussion work are adapted from the Science and Technology in Society (SATIS) teachers' guide:

- Seating is important. The usual classroom arrangement, with the teacher at the front facing the students, encourages a flow of discussion from teacher to pupils and back again, but discourages communication between pupils. Wherever possible, discussion groups should be arranged so everyone can see everyone else in the group. [In the final reporting-back arrangement, a circle of seats is best, although the conventional workshop or studio may make this difficult.]
- Discussion rarely goes well without an initial stimulus. SATIS units include many discussion questions and stimuli, but there are plenty of other sources such as newspaper cuttings, pictures from magazines, a recent television programme, a provocative statement from the teacher and so on.
- The teacher's role is very important. He or she needs to avoid dominating the discussion, remember that the teacher's views will carry disproportionate weight. Try to give support and encouragement, and to draw out the quieter pupils.

- It is important to get the right atmosphere at the start. The teacher needs to be enthusiastic, lively and well organised.

(Association for Science Education, 1986, pp. 27–29)

Teaching individuals

Although pupils may share ideas, conduct investigations and brainstorm in groups, much of the detailed production of designs and the making of a product is commonly carried out on an individual basis. Teamwork is very important, particularly as it mirrors the way technology operates outside the school, but teachers always recognise the individual personal investment that pupils put into their work. Pupils gain an enormous sense of personal satisfaction when they feel that their project is worthwhile, but they may experience an equal degree of devastation and frustration when things go wrong. The key to success is the correct matching of a pupil to an appropriate task and ensuring that they have the necessary skills and knowledge to carry out what they want to do. It may seem obvious, but a straightforward way to judge whether a particular design is too cautious or too ambitious for an individual is to talk to them about it! With experience, the matching will be more accurate, but even then a new group of pupils should be questioned about their ideas and plans.

The following are useful strategies when working with individuals:

- Visit each pupil while they are producing and evaluating designs to ensure they have thought through the implications of what they wish to do.
- Encourage pupils to be self-reliant and think for themselves. Do not do the work for them. Give them hints and ideas but encourage them to use the planning techniques and design tools, such as image boards, to make their own decisions.
- Do not spend more time with pupils of one gender than the other; such action gives hidden messages of relative importance (see Riggs, 1994). Catton reminds us that we, often unwittingly, have different expectations of boys and girls with respect to the design and make process, and that we should '[praise] girls for good ideas and practical work as well as neat drawing work. Praise boys for neat drawing work as well as good ideas and practical work' (Catton, 1985, p. 21).

Pupils will need individual help with making techniques and suggestions about procedures, especially when things go wrong. The practical advice which turns a disaster into a triumph is particularly welcome, but the need for such interventions can be reduced if attention is given to individuals when they select their intended design. Go through the plan with the pupil, sitting next to them rather than towering above them. Ensure that:

- their working drawing of what they intend to do is understandable by all involved, including the teacher

- the plan is feasible in terms of materials, time and techniques which they possess or are likely to be able to learn in the available time
- it builds on previous work to ensure progress but is not too risky and likely to fail.

In Task 10.1 I suggested that it was important to read about the different teaching techniques with the following points in mind: What will I as the teacher be doing? What will the pupils be doing? In what ways am I, as a teacher, conveying messages about this subject by how I teach it? The first question is important because when planning to use a particular teaching technique, it is necessary to think through the implications of the strategy as well as the details for implementation (see Chapter 9 about the importance of planning). For example, when working with individuals on their designs, details such as the actual questions to ask, the appropriate standard of the working drawing required, and the procedures to implement if anything is unsatisfactory need to be carefully considered. The implications of the chosen strategy also need to be covered, for example, what are the rest of the class doing while you are involved with an individual? Will the work hold their attention for the time needed? Can they help themselves if they get stuck? These details need to be explained to the whole class early in the lesson so that your discussion with an individual is not continually interrupted by simple management queries. In detailed planning both the teacher's work and the pupils' work need to be considered at times throughout the lesson.

The second question is also important. The way a topic is taught can often have value-added spin-offs, and technological capability requires a sophisticated range of teaching and learning strategies. By choosing a range of techniques over the life of a project, you can balance the contributory elements of technological education and teach not only the necessary knowledge and skills for practical outcomes, but also promote consideration of the relevant social, environmental and economic issues and constraints.

TEACHING FOR DESIGN AND TECHNOLOGY CAPABILITY

Now I would like to consider *when* those different teaching techniques are most appropriate. In particular I want to talk about supporting pupils in doing their practical or project work.

The aim of encouraging pupils to become autonomous – able to plan, investigate and research aspects of their own project – has long been part of the rationale for design and technology education. It has been argued that technology project work is able to encourage people to 'create and do' rather than just 'know and understand'. Such capability is important in many aspects of life and particularly, it is argued, in industry and commerce. Central to the teaching of design and technology is the design and make assignment. This is a type of project work where:

- the exact outcome is unpredictable (although the framing of the task reduces the possible number of outcomes and the risk of failure and disappointment)

- the pupil takes responsibility for the conduct of the project as much as possible; it is based upon a need which the pupil can see and identify with, and is a 'real-life' situation.

Task 10.2 Teaching for pupil learning

You will have read about pupils' learning and lesson planning in previous chapters.

Write down what you think pupils learn when doing practical work in design and technology. In what ways does this suggest you should organise your teaching?

How can you solve the following dilemma? Pupils need knowledge and skills for project work in order to design and plan a response, but their decisions may be limited by their knowledge and skills. Moreover, because 'they don't know what they don't know', they don't ask questions about how they might do their work differently. So do you 'front-load' all your teaching of knowledge and skills just in case pupils might need them, or do you teach them as and when pupils require them?

There are some important differences, however, between what is manageable for a teacher with a large class of 12 year olds compared with a small and self-selected group of older pupils. With younger pupils, assignments are usually chosen by the teacher to highlight aspects of the relevant curriculum or guidelines. The direction and outcome are more controlled than in the open-ended major projects typical of many examination schemes, so that skills and knowledge can be introduced progressively. One drawback is that greater control over the content and timing of what is taught reduces the autonomy of the learner, but the resultant controlled development of learning, and successful management of the project development, may be more beneficial. Clearly, it depends on the degree of prescription versus the degree of openness. The prior experience of the pupils, and your learning objectives, will largely dictate your approach.

How are successful projects organised?

Before considering the organisation at a teacher-in-classroom level, the higher level of planning a scheme of work should be thought through by all the teachers involved. If learning in design and technology is to be meaningful, the work done must:

- be differentiated, able to be tackled at a number of levels so that individual pupils understand what is expected of them and the work makes appropriate demands

- build progressively on previous activities – a new project must offer new challenges which, at least at a general level, are supported by previous tasks; pupils should not 'go through the motions' of a design process where they learn few new skills or ideas
- be relevant to pupils: they must see the point of the project, particularly if it is more open-ended and steered by the enthusiasm of the individual.

Considerable overall planning is required to ensure that this happens in practice before the details of classroom planning and organisation can be considered.

There is a 'chicken and egg' problem when teaching technology. Pupils may know what they want to do but not be able to realise their solution because they do not have the required knowledge or skills. More critically, when planning their work, pupils may not consider certain approaches to a problem because they are ignorant of the existence of equipment or a technique which might help them. For these pupils technological problem-solving is doing little more than applying their common sense. So what is the best approach? Should pupils be taught skills in isolation, which might prove useful later but for which they perceive little immediate value? Should pupils be taught skills 'as needed' within projects, when they appreciate the usefulness of what they are learning but without a coherent structure and without realising that there was something new that they should know, to transfer to future work? The best approach is to steer a middle course, a carefully planned selection of shorter projects or 'focused tasks' that emphasise particular skills and techniques, together with longer, more open tasks which allow pupils to develop technological capability by drawing on their accumulated experiences.

In these longer tasks, new skills and knowledge will have to be covered, just as the shorter tasks will need to be meaningful and situated in an appropriate context to make sense. Teaching skills for skills' sake, as sometimes happens when pupils have to move from teacher to teacher in a 'skills circus', can be unsatisfactory as the point of the activity is lost on some.

The problem of balancing focused and more open tasks has been recognised by the Nuffield Design and Technology Project which refers to two sorts of task:

- *resource tasks* – intended to help pupils acquire the knowledge, skills and values necessary for capability. There are many types of resource task but all have a clear teaching intention
- *capability tasks* – further divided into 'identified open tasks', where a pupil engages in a complete project which has been placed in a context created by the teacher, and 'spontaneous open tasks', where the complete task has been identified by the pupil.

The interplay between resource tasks and capability tasks enables design and technology capability to be developed progressively. If you set the context of the open task, the learning intentions remain clear. If pupils choose a project, they may be more motivated to work independently and with interest but they may have insufficient knowledge and skill to complete it successfully. A teacher-decided project may be better suited to build progressively on the pupil's previous work, be more controlled in the materials and equipment needed to resource it, and easier to manage as part of a whole class's work, but pupils may not be so interested in what they have been asked to do. This issue assumes a great importance as pupils progress and are required to engage in more open project work, but the issue is still relevant in earlier stages. The careful introduction of the project is vital and the way in which the pupils can themselves identify a need to investigate and work on is important. Brainstorming work in small groups will help an individual identify a possible line of work, but a teacher's knowledge of a pupil's background and interests certainly smoothes the negotiation of a project, and this is worthwhile from everyone's point of view.

Organising project work in the classroom

I use the word 'classroom' here to denote any space where design and technology education takes place. It has already been suggested that much of the strategic planning of project work should be done at a team level. What is left for you to organise? You will be responsible for the conduct of the project, and the teaching and implementation of what many books refer to as the 'design process'. There are as many different interpretations and critics of this process as there are different definitions of technology! The criticisms centre around the simplistic use of the design process as a linear movement from 'identification of need' to 'ideas' to 'specification' to 'product' to 'evaluation of product'. People do not actually design like that. The design process is not linear but a complex activity where new possible solutions and evaluations of current ideas continually circle back and permeate every part of the activity at every stage. The over-emphasis on particular aspects of the process, perhaps because of a need to give marks, can be unhelpful in the teaching of design and technology and leads to such distortions as pupils inventing 'initial ideas' after their design is finished! While accepting the shortcomings of the descriptors, many design and make projects will contain the following activities:

- researching, finding out information from books, magazines, CD-ROMs, the internet
- investigating, experimenting with materials, processes, etc.
- specifying, stating clearly the criteria that the chosen solution has to meet
- developing ideas that might make a contribution to the chosen solution
- optimising ideas to formulate the details of a chosen solution
- planning the making or manufacture of the chosen solution
- making
- evaluating.

(Barlex, 1987, p. 18)

Your skill will be in integrating these activities within the constraints of the materials and equipment available and the timetable. However, a well-planned scheme of work, a lively introduction, carefully prepared resources for skill enhancement and teacher inputs, and a good balance of activities will still produce disappointing results if there is insufficient attention paid to the allocation of short-term targets within the long task. There should be a clear purpose to each lesson. By helping pupils to know what they need to have accomplished at strategic points throughout the project, they can be guided to a successful outcome. This does not mean that all pupils should do exactly the same thing in a rigid and undifferentiated way, but you should be aware of the way pupils can get side-tracked by a particular facet of the work and lose sight of the whole task. Your role is to help them keep focused and to guide them to a successful outcome.

WORKING WITH SUPPORT STAFF

Workshop and classroom technicians can significantly increase the quality of teaching and learning in design and technology lessons. In England and Wales technical support is still considered something of a luxury, although that is changing as schools increase generally the number of teacher assistants. So what does a school technician do?

Task 10.3 Observing the departmental technician

Arrange to spend a day alongside the departmental technician, starting and finishing when he or she does. Some of the tasks that you might see done are:

- the ordering of equipment or materials
- administrative tasks
- preparation of resources for practical lessons
- cleaning and clearing away of equipment and materials at the end of a lesson
- safety checks and maintenance work being carried out on equipment
- support in lessons being provided.

Talk to the technician about other tasks that are carried out, and how staff in the department can help the technician to do the job efficiently.

Task 10.4 Preparing for teaching

Think of a practical lesson that you have observed or taught, for example, it might be an activity on bending plastics, preparing a printed circuit board, making chicken burgers or using batik to decorate an item.

List all the preparatory activities which you, or the teacher, had to do. How many of them did you need to do to ensure you had 'ownership' of the lesson and which could have been done by the technician?

A technician who is able to take on the routine maintenance of the tools and equipment is able to liberate a teacher from a large number of tasks, but can also be of help to the pupils. I have lost count of the lessons I have seen where pupils use blunt saws and get progressively more desperate in their attempts to make an impression on a small block of fibreboard. A pupil who lacks confidence in their making skills needs well-maintained tools to prevent frustrations being wrongly attributed to their own inadequacy.

A technician can also work on a day-to-day basis in preparing materials and equipment for your lessons. There is usually a system for booking the technician's time, and that implies long-term planning by all staff. If the department has a scheme of work for a project, and the resource tasks needed to support it, the technician can plan ahead and suggest when a project in Year 8 will need equipment which is currently being used by Year 10, for example. That overview across the department is invaluable. But what can you do to help the technician?

Most departments have a booking form which details the day and lesson that you might need particular specialist equipment or materials. You need to ensure that the technician gets that form every week and that you give special notice for any big job. This may seem common sense, but some teachers who use the weekend as the time for their detailed planning often arrive first thing on Monday morning and expect the technician to have been a mind-reader for what is needed in the first lesson.

Technicians are often very skilled and experienced with machines and tools and delight in helping with practical lessons. This is a most valuable resource and it is a wise teacher who makes the most of all teaching opportunities, but remember you are the teacher and you direct the lesson.

Forming appropriate relationships with pupils and colleagues in school is an important personal quality which all teachers need to develop. The quality of the working relationship that you form with the department technician may be the most valuable for your well-being and for the quality of learning of your pupils.

MANAGING PUPILS IN YOUR CLASS

You might be wondering why I have taken so long to get to this most important topic. In surveys of new teachers it is classroom management and discipline that is of principal concern. The question inevitably posed is 'Will I be able to keep control?' My answer is that it is impossible to isolate classroom management from the way in which you teach and from the wider issues, attitudes and values in which you have to operate in school. If you have a different ethos of how pupils and teachers should interact to that prevalent in other areas of the school, then pupils will be unsure how to react in your classes. That is not to say you are wrong, just that it will take longer for the pupils to work out the ground-rules, and indeed they may never do so. As a trivial example, if you think that pupils should call you by your first name, but the rest of the school operates a more formal code, then pupils will be confused, in fact they may mistake such informality with a *laissez-faire* attitude to discipline. It is a mistake to try to work in isolation from the school support structures that surround you and against the norms and routines of the school and department.

Norms and routines can work at a number of different levels. For example, for safety considerations, it is often the expectation that pupils will line up outside the door and wait for the teacher to signal entry to the lesson. Here it would be unwise for you to change this. As a student teacher, it is important for you to follow the practice of the class you teach and to ensure that you are consistent in the way you sustain the code of practice.

Task 10.5 Classroom routines

From your observations of colleagues' lessons, note down what happens during the 'routine' parts of the lessons:

- Do pupils line up outside the teaching room? Where are bags and coats left?
- How is the taking of the register organised?
- How are resources distributed and collected in?
- How are lessons ended and pupils dismissed?

Make sure that you follow the standard codes of practice for these routine procedures in the lessons that you plan.

Difficult times for a teacher in managing pupils are the beginning and end of lessons and transitions between activities during the lesson. I look at each of these now.

Beginnings

To help reduce the number of opportunities for misbehaviour, remember to:

- arrive before the class – be in the room waiting for them
- always make sure that the class is quiet, with bags put away and coats off before you begin
- scan the whole class regularly (see what I said about whole-class teaching and demonstrations above)
- make eye contact with as many individuals as possible
- keep the lesson introduction short
- make the first pupil activities clear and straightforward
- be clear about the sequence of activities, 'what happens next'
- tell latecomers to sit down, don't let them interrupt your flow, but find out later why they were late.

Endings

Again you will be wise to draw on the usual school routines here, but it is essential in design and technology lessons that you leave enough time to collect in resources and clear up. It is still a source of amazement to me how different the time for this is between pupils who are 11 years old and those just a couple of years older! Some points:

- Think how some of the 'ending tasks' can begin well in advance of the end of the class; perhaps you collect up some of the tools yourself, or perhaps someone who has finished early can helps others.
- Don't try to do too much yourself at the end.
- If something took longer than you expected, don't try to rush to do everything you have planned.
- Get everyone quiet at the end before they go to summarise the lesson and give a word of encouragement and praise.
- Control the exit – this may be more important with a lively and large group of 12 year olds, but even with older pupils make sure you are the one to dismiss the group.

Transitions within lessons

Moving pupils from one activity to another or from one place to another, for example to watch a video or demonstration, can give an opportunity for misbehaviour, so you will need to consider how to carry this out. Some general points:

- Make sure you are ready and have everything to hand before you stop the class.
- Warn everyone that they only have a few minutes to finish what they are doing, and plan what you are going to say to those who have not finished.
- It is easier to 'come round the front' or 'get into discussion groups' if this is an established routine.

Many teachers spend a considerable time at the start of the academic year establishing the classroom routines and procedures. This takes time initially, but saves so much time later. As a new or student teacher you may not have set this up but you can draw on existing classroom norms to help you. It soon becomes second nature, but at the beginning everything has to be thought through and planned explicitly.

Dealing with classroom management problems

The vast majority of schools are well organised and disciplined. Design and technology appeals to most pupils, particularly to those who have found the practical and realistic nature of the work a welcome change from the tasks set elsewhere in school. However, you will inevitably meet some pupils whose behaviour is unacceptable.

Kyriacou (1991, p. 82) suggests that teachers most commonly have to deal with seven types of pupil misbehaviour:

- excessive talk or talking out of turn
- being noisy
- not paying attention to the teacher
- not getting on with the work required
- being out of their seat without good cause
- hindering other pupils
- arriving late for lessons.

It is sometimes a combination of these factors that creates a general feeling of unease and discontent on the part of both the class and the teacher. This raises the stress level and leads you to forget where you are in your lesson plan, or that piece of advice you read about what to do with difficult pupils!

Unfortunately, there is no 'golden rule' for establishing and maintaining classroom discipline. However, most teachers would give the following basic advice, which is far more sensible than the weary time-worn shibboleths such as 'don't smile till Christmas':

- Find out the school and department procedures for handling disruptive pupils.
- Decide what you are going to accept as your basic standards of behaviour and politeness.
- *Insist* on those standards.
- Avoid confrontation.
- Have a behaviour management plan prepared (see Chapter 9) so that you know how you are going to deal with any misbehaviour that you may come across.

Strategies that may help you maintain good discipline include using your voice, making good use of non-verbal communication, and positioning yourself in the classroom.

Using your voice

Regard your voice as a teaching tool; it can be very effective. The pitch of your voice can express a range of emotions: calmness, urgency, enthusiasm, displeasure. Try to vary it when talking to pupils as this will help to maintain their interest. The speed of your voice is also important; when explaining, demonstrating or questioning, you may need to speak more slowly. When encouraging a pupil to work more quickly or to clear away at the end of the lesson, talking more quickly will express a sense of urgency. The projection of your voice is obviously important and again you should try to vary it. There may be times when you choose to speak quietly, for example to quieten pupils or when talking to an individual. At other times a loud voice may be required, for example to give instructions when pupils are engaged on practical work, or to call for attention. Try not to strain your voice when projecting it and try not to raise the pitch when you raise the volume or you will find yourself shrieking. It takes practice, but it is possible to talk more loudly but keep the pitch low.

Task 10.6 Using your voice

Record yourself reading a text or speaking in your usual voice. If you have not heard yourself before then you may be surprised by what you hear, you will sound quite different from what you expect. This is because you are hearing your voice coming back to you rather than going out, as you normally do.

Now record yourself whilst practising with the pitch, speed and projection of your voice. Try to make your voice sound interesting, calm, urgent, in command. Are you achieving the sounds that you want? Continue practising until you feel that you can 'use' your voice.

Non-verbal communication

As well as your voice, you will communicate with the pupils in other ways, for example your facial expressions and your posture. Be aware of these and try to make them match your verbal communication, for example don't smile whilst you are reprimanding a pupil, as this will give confusing messages. Make eye contact with pupils when you are talking to them and try to 'scan' the room constantly, and let pupils see you doing this so that they know that *you* know what is going on! Sometimes letting a pupil know that you are watching closely will forestall any thoughts of misbehaviour. In your posture, try to show that you are open and approachable by keeping your arms by your sides or behind you, not defensively crossed in front of you.

Task 10.7 Your non-verbal communication

Ask your mentor to observe you teaching a lesson and to focus on your non-verbal communication.

Discuss with your mentor the notes he or she has taken and use them to improve your classroom management through your non-verbal communication.

Positioning yourself in the classroom

Where you stand in the classroom can be an aid to your classroom management. In design and technology, especially with practical work, it is easy to move around rather than be confined to your desk or the board. Try not to get 'hemmed in' to one place, with pupils continuously coming to you so that you cannot move – tell pupils that you will come to them. Try to move purposefully around the room. Watch the pupils to see if you need to be nearby to support a pupil; listen to the class and move to where you think pupils might be getting too noisy or are becoming distracted, your presence will quieten them or return them to their task. Always try to position yourself so that you do not have your back to any pupils, so that you can see, and be seen and heard by, all the class.

It is most important, though, to exercise common sense. Teaching is a 'people profession', and using common sense in dealing with people is what remains when all the do's and don'ts of advice have been long forgotten.

SUMMARY

The main message from this chapter is that classroom teaching methods and classroom management are closely intertwined. If you teach in an interesting way, catering for the aptitudes and motivation of your pupils, you will have a relaxed classroom atmosphere which enables you to handle people and equipment effectively. Good classroom teaching and good classroom management go hand in hand. The best advice to people concerned about how to discipline pupils is to 'make your lessons interesting and well organised'. Relationships between you and the pupils are also important, and you will need to work at these: you will need to understand each pupil and what works best with them. Pupils work well for teachers they like – unfortunately there is no magic formula for how to be liked, but you could try being firm, fair and friendly.

The following summary may be used as a checklist for organising lessons in design and technology. For every lesson, ensure that you have:

- prepared and checked all the resources you need, including useful stimulus material
- worked out the routines of bringing the class into the room and settling them to work
- thought about the start of the lesson and how you will quickly get the class engaged and working
- shown clearly in your plan what you and the pupils are doing for each activity and the time you estimate each activity will take
- considered how you will change from one activity to another
- allowed for the differing needs of the different pupils in the group
- tried out any demonstration and any practical techniques you expect the pupils to perform
- worked out what you will say when giving instructions
- decided how you will distribute and collect resources
- planned the ending of the lesson, allowing time for the clear-up routine
- worked out an assessment routine to look systematically at the progress of some of the pupils in the lesson
- considered what the homework will be, either for the class as a whole or for individuals, as appropriate.

As you become familiar with the checklist you will need to refer to it less. However, you should continue to do the checking as it will help you to be well organised, and so more confident in your teaching.

FURTHER READING

Banks, F. (ed.) (1994) *Teaching Technology*, London: Routledge

Bryson, J. (1998) *Effective Classroom Management*, London: Hodder & Stoughton

Kyriacou, C. (1991) *Essential Teaching Skills*, Oxford: Blackwell

Petty, G. (1998) *Teaching Today*, Cheltenham: Stanley Thornes

11 Assessment

Chris Hopkins

INTRODUCTION

Design and technology teachers are very aware of the key role of analysis and evaluation in the design process. Pupils of the subject are constantly reminded of how the development of artifacts relies on good critical examination, to highlight the positives and remove the weaknesses. This examination is carried out by the designer but also relies heavily upon testing and the views and opinions of others. It is only by taking into account possible alternatives and improvements suggested, arising from this process, that products develop. For designers to continue with the development of a product, constructive criticism is essential. Assessment in design and technology provides the analysis and evaluation upon which the designer relies.

This idea, that in the design process to get a quality product we need constantly to assess, can easily be transferred to the teaching and learning process. The role of assessment within design and technology is key to the successful teaching, learning and development of the subject. Whatever form the assessment might take, it can be used in a constructive fashion to guide the future direction of the pupil and the teaching of the subject.

The range of methods available for assessment, their application and uses, need to be understood so that the teacher can use them to their best advantage. Assessment methods poorly used can be destructive and central to the failure of pupils and courses. Analysing the reasons why teachers assess, and how it applies to design and technology, will provide guidance to the correct use and outcome.

You are also referred to the core text in this series (Capel *et al.*, 1997), which has a comprehensive section on assessment, looking at broader issues as well as the practical ones.

OBJECTIVES

By the end of this chapter you should be able to:

- understand the reasons for assessment
- understand the importance of assessment to the learning process
- be aware of the methods of assessment used in design and technology.

THE RATIONALE OF ASSESSMENT – WHY ASSESS?

Teachers assess so that they can:

- record the progress and achievements of individual pupils
- analyse strengths and weaknesses of individual pupils
- give pupils the opportunities to review their own progress
- highlight the next steps in the development of each pupil
- highlight the learning objectives, knowledge, skills and attitudes required in a particular course
- analyse strengths and weaknesses in the teaching of the subject
- inform pupils, parents, teachers and other agencies of the progress of each pupil
- assist with guidance for pupils, parents and other authorities on the suitability of future courses.

ASSESSMENT POLICIES IN SCHOOLS

Every school will have documentation that gives guidelines on the methods and process of assessment. The design and technology departmental policy on assessment should be linked to the school policy, although there will be differences to take account of the nature of the subject. For example, in many design and technology departments pupils visit a range of different areas – food technology, textiles technology, resistant materials – and it is important for each area to keep records that are fed into the pupils' formative assessment. Very few other subjects in a school will operate such a system.

It is important that every teacher is familiar with, and uses, each of the following:

- the school and department policies on assessment
- methods of recording and rewarding pupil achievements
- agreed marking or grading schemes

- agreed methods of reporting to pupils, teachers and parents
- any agreed curriculum plan for design and technology and the approved assessment methods and systems.

Requirements of an assessment policy

Assessment should allow for:

- progression within the subject
- monitoring of the development of the pupils' abilities through a carefully planned sequence of experiences
- differentiation between pupils, highlighting different procedures for each pupil
- clear profiling of pupils' strengths and weaknesses, allowing focused development to take place.

Task 11.1 Reviewing the school and departmental assessment policies

Obtain the assessment policies for your school and department and read these carefully. Then answer the following:

- What differences can you identify between each policy?
- Is the assessment procedure clearly identified in the department policy?
- How should you record the progress of each pupil?
- What methods of reporting are used for parents?

METHODS OF ASSESSMENT

There are a number of ways of assessing; they are all inter-linked and rely on each other to be successfully completed.

Formative assessment

This is an ongoing process that helps the teacher to build an overall view of a pupil's ability, to monitor his or her progress, highlighting their strengths and weaknesses and emphasising the next steps to take. It also helps the teacher understand how his/her teaching might be modified to be more effective. It is a method of assessment that is very focused on teaching and learning. The following strategies of formative assessment will help you to build an assessment of each pupil:

- Watch carefully when pupils are working to see how they are applying new knowledge and skills.
- Discuss the progress of work with pupils, using questions to find the level of understanding and how they feel work is progressing.
- Use question-and-answer sessions to examine pupils' understanding.
- Assess homework tasks.
- Mark design work and practical tasks; to be effective this needs to be a process that the pupils are involved with and it can form the basis of discussion between you and the pupil.
- Mark written or practical tests that are focused on a particular area of the course.

The key to the successful use of many of these strategies is the feedback that you give: a mark without a comment can often have a negative effect on a pupil, as can comments that focus on pupils' failings. Emphasising the positive, even though on some occasions it can be difficult to find, can help motivate pupils and move them on several stages. Feedback can be oral or written as notes on the pupils' work. It is equally important that pupils' progress is recorded and rewarded, showing them that their achievements have been recognised and have value.

Good formative assessment is linked directly to diagnostic assessment, which focuses more on the reasons why pupils might not be achieving. If formative assessment identifies a possible weakness, then you need to find the cause – this could range from a simple misunderstanding of instructions through to language or specific learning difficulties. Although learning difficulties might have been highlighted in other curriculum areas, design and technology brings many new learning methods and styles that are specific to the subject and difficulties in these might not have been previously identified. By working with the special educational needs co-ordinator (SENCO) it might be possible for support to be provided to help the pupil overcome difficulties.

Task 11.2 Observing formative assessment

Observe a design and technology lesson in your specialist area, taught by an experienced teacher.

How many opportunities for formative assessment did you observe throughout the lesson? What methods of formative assessment were used? How many of the opportunities required the teacher to record the information?

Summative assessment

This is the assessment method by which most pupils will eventually be judged. It comes in the form of tests set by the teacher at the end of a unit of work, as part of the school examinations at the end of each year or as a final, externally set examination. Summative assessment is often the method of recording overall achievement in a systematic way. It will measure the progress of individual pupils over a period of time, allowing teachers to monitor the progress of particular groups in relation to others and providing the school with information about the overall progress of the subject and monitoring the strengths and weaknesses of individual teachers.

Every pupil will arrive in the design and technology department at the beginning of secondary school with some knowledge and competences that have already been assessed. It is important to take into account previous experiences and knowledge and to make an initial assessment. This assessment can be made from:

- primary school reports
- links with feeder schools
- records of achievement
- results from national tests
- talking to pupils about previous experiences
- asking pupils to demonstrate previously made items
- questionnaire sheets.

This initial assessment is vital to the development of both the pupil and the department. It can indicate appropriate levels of work and give the department the opportunity to plan and set targets for pupil achievement.

Task 11.3 Making the initial assessment of pupils

Try to find out what design and technology work pupils experience in your local primary schools.

What forms of assessment are used for determining pupils' achievement in design and technology when they first start at the secondary school?

Involving pupils in the assessment process

Assessment is one area in the educational process that we all worry about. Examinations cause worry and concern for most pupils, as will the value and quality of a piece of course work. It is therefore important for teachers to inform pupils of the criteria and expectations against which they are being judged.

Pupils can be involved if you:

- provide information sheets outlining the criteria
- provide exemplar material that meets those criteria, showing how the marks were gained

- use time plans that show when assessment will take place
- explain what evidence will count towards assessment
- supply worksheets giving help and direction
- talk to pupils about your perception of their progress
- demonstrate and encourage self-assessment techniques (see below)
- encourage assessment by peer group (see below).

Task 11.4 Involving pupils in assessment

Think about a unit of work that you have taught.

- Did you explain the methods of assessment to be used to the pupils, and the criteria for assessment?
- Did the pupils' work indicate that they had understood what was expected?
- If you were to teach this unit again, how could you improve pupils' work through the assessment process?

Self-assessment

The process of independent learning relies heavily on each pupil's ability to apply self-assessment skills. These skills help the pupils to:

- plan their work
- plan the progress of project work
- be self-motivated
- identify personal strengths and weaknesses.

Owing to the nature of design and technology, and the length and complexity of some examination project work, self-assessment should play a major part in the development of the pupil. The process can be formative, throughout a project, and summative, which often uses a pro-forma requiring the pupil to consider their response to the process of learning. Figure 11.1 shows an example of a pupil self-assessment pro-forma that was used at the end of a project.

The structure of a pro-forma prompts the pupil to think about strengths that they might not immediately identify in their own evaluation of a project, which is often directed at the final product, rather than the learning process that they have gone through.

Self-assessment is a learned procedure and needs to be taught throughout the design and technology course. Pupils will not be able to guide and direct their project work for examinations if they have not had control of aspects of their work in earlier years.

Figure 11.1 Example of a pupil self-assessment pro-forma

SELF-ASSESSMENT SHEET

Name: ______________________________

Subject: Design and technology – electronics   Topic: Theory/revision

Please give a mark out of 5 for how well you think you have progressed over the last few weeks. If you think you have done something really well put 5, if you think you could have done much better put 1, for somewhere in-between put 2, 3 or 4.

How much did you understand about time delays, security systems, etc., *before* you started this topic? ____

How much do you think you understand about time delays, security systems, etc., *now*? ____

How much effort did you put into writing notes in class? ____

How much effort did you put into answering questions in class? ____

Did you ask questions in class if you did not understand something? ____

How hard did you work on the tasks set in the lessons? ____

How hard did you work on the design work in the topic? ____

How hard did you work on homework assignments? ____

What did you find most difficult in the lessons (taking notes, working out maths, design work, IT, soldering, tests, something else)? ____

What did you enjoy most in the lessons (taking notes, working out maths, design work, IT, soldering, tests, something else)? ____

What do you think that you learnt most from these lessons? ____

What could you put more effort into to improve your learning next time? ____

Assessment by peer group

This method of assessment allows for the development of group attitudes, awareness of assessment criteria and the development of values. Often self-assessment will focus the pupils directly to their own work, but they need to moderate their work and assessment by looking at the work of their peers. The process will need to be carefully handled by you. You should guide the type of assessment that will take place, perhaps through a pro-forma that will focus pupils' attention on the work rather than the personalities that created the items. The criteria used may be developed by the group in a discussion about key aspects of the work. The pupils then need to be observed in the evaluation process – working in pairs will often promote good discussion.

The use of displays of pupils' work also promotes peer group assessment and this can have a beneficial effect on the quality of future work.

WHAT IS ASSESSED IN DESIGN AND TECHNOLOGY?

Design and technology requires pupils to develop capability through combining designing and making skills with knowledge and understanding in order to design and make products.

Key areas in designing capability are the ability to:

- identify design needs and opportunities
- use and apply research skills
- generate a range of different solutions to situations
- develop their ideas in relation to the original brief
- produce a clear and reasoned proposal
- evaluate their proposals and the suggestions of others
- analyse and evaluate products that will help with their designing.

Key areas in making are the ability to:

- plan a sequence for production
- select and use appropriate making methods
- use equipment and associated skills, techniques and procedures
- work safely and with an understanding of health and safety procedures
- use quality control and testing procedures
- produce high-quality outcomes.

Assessing skills, knowledge and understanding are interwoven in designing and making and can be assessed by looking at the pupil's ability to:

- apply previously learnt skills of techniques and procedures to new situations
- use learnt information to make decisions and to help in the solving of problems
- use learnt knowledge and understanding in evaluating their work.

The ability to apply experiences and knowledge that have been learnt to new situations is key to the development of the pupil in all aspects of design and technology.

Alongside the development of the design and technology skills outlined, there will be development of other skills that are the basis for much of the work carried out in the area. You will need to focus on assessing these skills, and the progress of individual pupils and groups of pupils. They include:

- *Attitudes to work:*
  — Is the pupil or group focused on the task?
  — Do pupils listen to instructions?
  — Are pupils willing to act on information given?
  — Is the behaviour of pupils appropriate for the activities being undertaken?

— Is homework produced that reflects thought and effort?
— Is the pupil adaptable to new situations?

- *Organisational skills:*
  — Does the pupil arrive with all the correct equipment and materials?
  — Are homework tasks completed regularly?
  — Does the pupil take responsibility for his/her working environment?
  — Does the pupil plan ahead for the preparation of materials?

- *Personal skills:*
  — Does the pupil relate to others in the group?
  — Does the pupil help others?
  — Does the pupil take part and contribute to group discussion?
  — Is the pupil patient?
  — Does the pupil take into account the health and safety of others?

ASSESSMENT EVIDENCE

You can employ a number of different assessment methods to gather information about the progress of your pupils. Choosing the correct methods of assessment is important to give you a complete picture of the pupils and their abilities. Evidence of pupils' abilities can be obtained through:

- *teacher observation and oral evidence:*
  — questioning
  — listening to pupils without prompting
  — observing pupils working
  — observing group activities
  — pupil presentations

- *written and graphical evidence:*
  — tests and examinations
  — design folders
  — homework
  — questionnaires set for the pupils
  — notes made in design folders and link books or diaries
  — use of drawing techniques
  — use of information and communications technology

- *product evidence:*
  — final products
  — models
  — test pieces.

Task 11.5 Evidence indicators

Select a project you will teach this year, that will run over a number of lessons.

Before starting the project, write a list of the types of assessment evidence you will be looking for.

When you have taught the project, consider – did you find all the evidence you required? How did you record the evidence?

PLANNING ASSESSMENT

To obtain the above evidence, it is essential when planning a design and technology course to build in methods of assessment. Every project or experience a pupil undertakes should help to build a profile, and all the teachers who work with that pupil should have a role in building the profile. The work that is planned should:

- be at the correct level
- have an intended, assessable outcome
- fit within the overall programme of study
- be directly linked to any agreed curricula or guidelines
- allow evidence to be produced which will meet the assessment requirements, for example the level descriptors in the national curriculum for England and Wales.

Every teacher needs to be clear about their contribution to constructing the profile of each pupil. Good planning ensures that the same knowledge and skills are not repeatedly taught and reassessed in different areas of design and technology. One education authority in England compiled a *Record of Achievements and Profiling Document* (Hampshire LEA, 1988) and suggested the following list of areas to be considered when planning assessment:

1. What do we want pupils to learn? How can we share learning goals with pupils in language they understand?
2. What activities can we devise which will enable this?
3. What activities can we collect which will tell us what has been learned?
4. What do we do with the evidence?
5. What do we record? We can't record everything!
6. How can we involve the pupil in recording?
7. How can we give space for learning which was not pre-specified to be recorded?
8. How can we help pupils review and clearly understand what has been learned?

9 How can we help pupils set future learning goals?
10 What does profiling tell us about our teaching?

Task 11.6 Planning assessment

Look at a scheme of work that you already teach, or are intending to teach. Go through the document and apply the above questions. Also consider:

- Is it clear what the scheme intends to teach?
- Is it clear how you will assess each part?
- Is the assessment clear to pupils?

ASSESSMENT AS MOTIVATION

If used in a positive framework, assessment can motivate and encourage pupils. To do this it is important to focus on some key issues that will develop the pupils' responses and therefore their understanding. It is essential that pupils' responses are considered and valued. Remember the response given indicates their understanding, which has been developed through your teaching. Ways to encourage pupils to respond include asking questions that enable a variety of responses:

- Tell me about the design you have been working on.
- How will it work?
- Have you had any problems?
- How did you cope with problems?
- What are you going to do next?

This process allows pupils to develop self-assessment as a positive experience, showing that from examining their problems they can find solutions. Here are some ways to help this to happen:

- Allow pupils time to respond to questions, as they need to construct their thoughts about issues.
- Provide feedback to pupils about their successes.
- Discuss with pupils targets, or future areas for focus, and the reasons for making them so.
- Make feedback regular throughout the process, as this will help to guide pupils.
- Reward positive achievement through the use of school systems, such as house points, merit marks and commendations. This method of reward is

often under-used by teachers but it is highly valued by pupils and parents and often provides an excellent indication of achievement.
- Use departmental rewards for achievement. The use of certificates for major achievement is of value in the short term, on the successful completion of projects, but also in the long term for building Records of Achievement.
- Take care with rewards that you do not simply recognise the best example of work – try to recognise the effort and progress made even when it has not produced a successful outcome, since the pupil could have learnt more through trying to overcome problems and struggling with the understanding. The pupil self-assessment pro-forma in Figure 11.1 shows that the effort the pupil made has been recognised and thought has been given to how the pupil might set targets to improve their own learning.

RECORDS AND RECORD-KEEPING

All teachers need to develop record-keeping techniques that:

- are easy to complete
- record all the evidence that will be required for making an assessment of achievement and report writing
- allow for individual reporting of pupils' experiences
- are easily accessible to other teachers.

Records of pupil achievement can be found in a number of different formats. School reports are an important record of a pupil's achievement. The format will usually be devised by the school and, if available, computerised statement banks compiled by each department can focus on key areas for assessment. School reports in design and technology are often a summary of the pupil's year in the various material areas. To be able to produce effective school reports, accessible methods of recording pupils' achievements and progress are needed and this can be achieved through the use of record cards; an example is shown in Figure 11.2.

To be successful record cards should be easy to use, and prompt completion at the end of a unit of work will allow the information to be used by the pupil's next teacher. You will probably be expected to keep a mark book recording lesson attendance and this can also be used to record classwork, homework and other information to provide an accessible record of every lesson, which will help you to complete record cards. An example from a teacher's mark book, shown in Figure 11.3, demonstrates how you might efficiently record all this information.

Pupils need to be encouraged to keep logs, diaries and portfolios to record their progress and development. These provide evidence that will reinforce assessment made by you, or any other teacher. Some departments keep a central file of pupils' work while others rely on pupils being responsible for their own work.

Figure 11.2 Example of a design and technology record card

Source: With kind permission of Rooks Heath High School

DESIGN AND TECHNOLOGY RECORD CARD

Name: ____________________ Form: __________

Project Number	1	2	3	4	5	6	7	8	9
Teacher (initials)									

Year 7	Effort	Behaviour	Attainment	Homework	Test	NC level	Absences
Food tech.							
RM							
Textiles tech.							
Year 8							
S&C							
Food tech.							
RM							
Year 9							
Textiles tech.							
S&C							
Choice:							

A–E: effort, behaviour, attainment, homework test score 1–8 NC level

Examination option: ____________________

Year 10
Year 11

Comments/problems/support

Figure 11.3 Example of a teacher's mark book

Year 9 Group 2 Topic: plastics/photo-frame

Name	2-Mar	5-Mar	9-Mar	12-Mar	16-Mar	19-Mar	23-Mar	26-Mar	30-Mar
Nick Harris	\	\ 2	\ nh	\ 2	\ gw	\	\ 2	\ gw	\ 4
Chris Matthew	\	\ 2	\ 2	\ 2	\	\	\ 2	\	\ 3
Ann McDonald	\	\ 3	\ 3	\ 3	\	\	\ 3	\	\ 4
Damian O'Con	A	\ 3	\ 2	\ 3	\	\	\ 3	A	\ nc
George Rayme	\	\ 2	\ nh	\ 2	\	\	\ 2	\	\ 3
Sevda Ryalls	\	\ 2	\ 2	\ 2	A	\	\ 2	\	\ 2
Lesson	plastics theory + graphic communication	processing plastics	plastic fabrication + dem filling, cutting, abading etc.	design brief + first ideas	orthographic + working drawings	photo frame mini task + dem marking, cut file, abrade, polish	continue mini task + dem building plastics	complete mini task	evaluation of work
Homework	complete class work	research on ideas	complete worksheet	review ideas	complete final design	none	complete worksheet	evaluation notest	none

Note to marking guide:
1 – little or no understanding of point
2 – basic understanding with some misunderstanding
3 – good understanding of most concepts
4 – good understanding and depth of knowledge

nh – no homework
nf – no folder
nc – work not complete
gw – good work in class

Task 11.7 Understanding reporting and recording methods

Read through the school and department policies on record-keeping and report-writing.

Note down when you are required to write reports, and what you are required to report on.

Look at examples of the reports and record cards that you will be using. Consider the different styles of reporting and whether the reports give pupils, parents and other teachers adequate information.

Choose a range of pupils from a class that you teach and write example reports. Do your comments inform pupils, parents and teachers? Have you included targets?

Discuss your reports with your mentor or head of department and ask her/him to comment on them.

EXTERNAL EXAMINATIONS

Assessment of pupils aged 14–16 is directed by the requirements of the examination board that your school has chosen. In England and Wales the examination boards are monitored by the Qualifications Curriculum Authority (QCA); there will be similar regulatory bodies in other areas. The QCA assesses the work of the examination boards and ensures that the performance of boards' syllabuses and methods of assessment are within the regulations. The syllabuses of different examination boards vary in their content and the levels of understanding required in various aspects of the subject. In design and technology they nearly all rely on two forms of assessment, namely a written paper and a course work project. In addition some boards include a specific design and make or investigation task.

The choice of examination board is left to the discretion of individual schools and departments, and the requirements of the boards do differ. The department needs to make their choice carefully, considering the needs of the pupils, resources available, policy of the school and the expectations of the community. The choice of syllabus will directly influence what you teach and, therefore, what you assess.

Getting to know the syllabus you use and the methods of assessment used by the board is essential. The boards will publish a range of support material including:

- exemplar material assessed at various levels
- previous examination papers
- examiners' reports
- moderation meetings (see Consistency of Assessment).

You will need to guide pupils through this assessment process by clarifying the assessment criteria, examining the required level and type of work and pre-assessing pupils' work. Your knowledge of the examination assessment criteria, therefore, can have an important effect on the examination results of your pupils. After a few years in the profession you might consider becoming an examiner for the syllabus that you teach. This is not easy work, and is undertaken in addition to your teaching at a busy time of the year, but it does give you a useful insight into the way that the examination is structured and what the expectations of the board are.

Task 11.8 Understanding examination marking criteria

Collect together the syllabus, exemplar material, examiners' reports and examination papers from the examination board that your school uses.

Read the syllabus content.

Complete an examination paper.

Using the examiners' reports, mark your paper, look carefully at how the marks were awarded and the style of answers required.

General National Vocational Qualifications (GNVQ)

GNVQs have been introduced in the 14–16 curriculum in England and Wales to provide an alternative course for pupils; they also provide alternative methods of assessment. There are three levels of GNVQ: foundation, intermediate and advanced (advanced level is only available to post 16 pupils). There are several GNVQ courses available. Those likely to be found within the design and technology area include: engineering, manufacturing, information technology, construction and the built environment, health and social care, hospitality and catering. Each course requires the pupils to learn and demonstrate, in addition to knowledge and competence in the subject, competence in the key skills of communication, application of number and information technology.

At foundation level the course combines the key skills with three vocational units, and at intermediate level, there are key skills and six vocational units. GNVQs require pupils to provide a range of evidence which shows understanding of the areas covered. There are also short tests taken at the end of each unit.

CONSISTENCY OF ASSESSMENT

Each area in design and technology – food technology, resistant materials, textiles technology and systems and control – will be looking for different applications of the design process and will rely on the skills of the teacher to identify the development of each pupil's ability. Standardising and moderating the work across the different areas helps to gain consistency of assessment. The School Curriculum and Assessment Authority in England and Wales produced a booklet, *Exemplification of standards for Design and Technology KS3: Consistency in Teacher Assessment* (SCAA, 1996), that looked at several projects exemplifying different levels of attainment in different areas. The booklet points out that judgements about the level of each pupil's work rest on professional decisions, taking into account how pupils perform in the various aspects of the subject and balancing weaknesses in one area with strengths in another.

Standardisation and moderation across the department are best achieved through departmental discussion, using examples of the pupils' work as a focus for discussion, to gain agreement on the level of achievement reached. Once the discussion has taken place, it is useful to compile a departmental portfolio, with work from all areas, that exemplifies the standards expected at each level. This portfolio is useful not only to the teachers involved with assessment but also to new members of the department, other teachers in the school and local authority and to parents. It also serves as exemplars to pupils to help their understanding of what constitutes 'achievement'.

Task 11.9 Moderating your assessment

Choose the work of three pupils from one class that you teach. Mark the work, recording your assessment on separate paper.

Ask your mentor or the head of department to assess the work and explain the criteria you were using.

Compare the assessments and use the comparison as a basis for discussion.

SUMMARY

This chapter has looked at the way that assessment is used and how it is closely linked to styles of teaching and methods of learning. Learning how to assess, and remain positive, is an essential ingredient for successful teaching. On many occasions this may prove difficult, but the advantages to the pupil are many.

In the publication *Design and Technology: Characteristics of Good Practice in Secondary Schools* (OFSTED, 1995, p. 53) OFSTED produced a checklist which is a useful tool for examining your own understanding and practice. Questions to ask include:

- Is there an agreed departmental assessment policy?
- Are assessment criteria for each project decided and agreed at the curriculum planning stage by all the staff teaching the same element of the course?
- Are assessment criteria given to the pupils before they start their work? Are they reminded of them as the work proceeds? Is there planned discussion and feedback as they work to help them make good progress towards meeting the criteria?
- When reviewed over the medium term, can assessment criteria be seen to be increasingly demanding in their expectations of the pupils' performance?

- In what ways are formative assessments used to encourage the pupils and help them improve the quality of their work?
- Is there a standardised portfolio of work to help teachers achieve consistency when moderating the pupils' work?
- Does the range of assessment methods used enable teachers to record the many facets of the pupils' progress as they work on designing and making activities?
- Do assessment records give an accurate account of the pupils' work, including examination results, to evaluate the success of teaching and the curriculum?
- Does the assessment system enable teachers to give parents a clear and accurate picture of their child's progress and design and technology capability, with advice about how improvements can be made?

The statutory requirements for assessment may change over time and place, but the reasons for assessing, the methods that you can use and the importance of assessment for improving pupil and teacher performance will remain constant.

FURTHER READING

Design and Make It (1998a) *Key Stage 3 Assessment Resources: Food and Textiles*, London: Hodder & Stoughton

Design and Make It (1998b) *Key Stage 3 Assessment Resources: Product Design*, London: Hodder & Stoughton

Design and Technology Association (1997a) *Assessment Handbook: Promoting Achievement through Assessment*, Wellesbourne: DATA

Design and Technology Association (1997b) *The Design and Technology Secondary Head of Department Handbook*, Wellesbourne: DATA

School Curriculum and Assessment Authority (1996) *Non-Statutory Tests and Tasks for Design and Technology KS3*, London: HMSO

12 Design and technology and the community

John Young

INTRODUCTION

Design and technology is all about 'the real world', so making links with what happens in the community should not be difficult. In Chapter 1 you read about how design and technology has been defined and the rationales that have been given for its inclusion in the curriculum. You may remember that these involved links with the real world, the impact of technology on the development of society, and the need to prepare young people for the technological world.

It is one thing to hold this view, but how can you bring 'the real world' into your teaching? You can tell pupils about your industrial experience; you can tell them about how industry works; you can show them videos of manufacturing. Surely, though, it is better to get them more fully and actively involved. This chapter will consider ways that you can do this, through making links with industry, arranging for visitors to come into the school, and for pupils to visit places out of school. Other external links may be made with community groups, to make design and technology work purposeful, to introduce a consideration of 'values' into their work, and to help them develop the skills and aptitudes, knowledge and understanding they will need for 'citizenship', such as an understanding of the economic system and knowledge of the 'global community' (QCA, 1998, p. 50).

In this chapter I shall refer to links with business and industry, sometimes using one term sometimes the other, but each time referring to the totality of 'business and industry'.

OBJECTIVES

By the end of this chapter you should:

- be able to use a wider range of teaching strategies
- be aware of opportunities to develop business and industry links
- know how to organise and manage visits out of school
- know how to integrate external links into a scheme of work
- know the safety and legal factors to take account of when pupils are out of school.

THE PURPOSES OF EXTERNAL LINKS

Why would you want to involve other people in your teaching? You have the subject knowledge and teaching skills to be able to deliver the curriculum but, as was considered before, design and technology relates to the real world and by involving people from industry in classroom work, you can make it more relevant and purposeful for the pupils. In this way you can increase their motivation and enrich their learning by providing a breadth of up-to-date knowledge and experiences. You can also allow pupils to talk to designers and manufacturers of products, to enable them to see how school work relates to what happens in industry.

When planning a strategy for an industrial link you should consider what benefits there are for the pupils, the industrialist and the teacher. Benefits for the pupils include:

- work experience opportunities
- industrial site visits
- work simulation
- school enterprise links
- using industrial resources
- using an industrialist as a personal advisor
- special events, e.g. courses, competitions, curriculum development projects.

Benefits for the industrialist include:

- developing a favourable local reputation
- helping local recruitment
- the possible development of new skills
- providing the industrial contribution to pupil and teacher activities
- acting as an advisor to pupils
- development of industry-based learning materials.

Benefits for the teacher include:

- attachments to industry
- attending company training courses
- additional resources.

The opportunities offered by industrial links, to all parties, have meant that many schools are involved in them in some form or another. Although many of these activities can be of benefit on their own, they are all much more effective if part of a planned programme of objectives, firmly based in the curriculum. Schools–industry work is about achieving a better understanding of industry among young people, but it is also about enriching the curriculum and making it more relevant to preparation for a rapidly changing world.

Task 12.1 Finding out about local businesses

Find out what local industries there are in your area. Consider which of these may have some relevance to the topics that you will be teaching. What would be the benefits of developing links with these companies?

MAKING THE LINKS

The onus of developing industrial links almost invariably rests with the schools. It is important, therefore, that there are clear objectives and well-marshalled arguments for why the business should get involved. There are equal benefits for business as for education (see the section above), but you do need to spell these out in order to sell your idea to the business people.

Education–industry activities are geared to achieving educational aims that will benefit everyone. While this may be an attractive reason for a large company, it may not be so for the majority of smaller businesses, whose interest it is vital to attract. Many business people get involved with education for personal reasons and individual satisfaction and it may be worth considering this as a benefit. Education's strongest asset is the challenge, stimulation, pleasure and responsibility of working with young people and there are many people in the business world who can be similarly motivated.

Some business people may find excuses for putting off becoming involved with education; the excuses will include:

- fear of schools
- fear of failure
- anti-teacher prejudice
- never did it when they were at school
- can't see what they, or the company, will get out of it

- no time
- focus only on financial results.

These barriers can be overcome with patience, determination and encouragement on your part. One strategy is to ask those already involved to accompany new business people into schools to show them what really happens. This, of course, will take time but the benefits will make it worth your while.

Ways that you might go about forming links include:

- cold-calling local businesses and industries
- contacting organisations who deal with business and industry, for example the Chamber of Commerce
- formal link organisations, such as Education–Business Partnerships.

Task 12.2 Preparing to make links

List the possible external links that you might make; this might mean looking through directories or local business papers.

Find out about any Education–Business Partnerships already operating in your locality or local education authority.

When you have decided which companies might be worth contacting, you should first of all telephone the company to find out the name of the person you need to contact. You could then telephone this person or write a letter explaining, in general terms, the reason for your approach. Make sure that you include the benefits for the company as well as for the school, and make the educational purposes clear. From this initial contact it is important that you then meet the person to discuss the purposes of the link, how it might work, the requirements on the part of the company and the benefits that might accrue. It is important to listen, too, as the company may offer other things that you had not considered, or legitimate reasons as to why your suggestions are not possible.

Organisations such as Education–Business Partnerships may have already done the groundwork for you, by finding out what the company can offer, how much time they are prepared to commit, and then acting as 'broker' when a school needs to make a contact.

ACTIVITIES INVOLVING EXTERNAL LINKS

Worthwhile programmes of study can be based in school or in the industrial workplace. Many design and technology projects for younger pupils are designed to teach particular specialist knowledge or skills, whilst those for older pupils taking examinations tend to be more open and individual. Activities which may be developed to enhance either of these types of projects include:

- *Work experience:* Usually for older pupils, this can give them some understanding of the manufacturing process, how the various sub-sections link together, the importance of costing and quality assurance.
- *Work-shadowing:* Again, usually for older pupils, this can give an insight into the role of one of more individuals within a company, helping them to see how an individual interacts with others and how the various sections of the manufacturing process interlink.
- *Work-based projects:* These can be used to give purpose and meaning to pupils' work and are often linked to work experience. Pupils could be asked to undertake research, complete design work, plan a production process or check on quality control systems. Projects can vary in length and complexity, but usually provide the pupil with a greater understanding of the industrial process.
- *Industry-based work:* Pupils could visit a company for the initial starting point of the project, or at some point within it, for information, but carry out their work in school. This provides the industrial context without the length of time spent in industry.
- *Workplace visits:* These can be used to focus on specific aspects, for example, quality control or batch production, or can give pupils a general overview of the manufacturing process. Pupils could work in groups to visit different parts of the company, or even different companies, and report their findings back to the whole class. Visits are discussed in more detail in the next section.
- *Guest speakers:* Local business people can be invited in to the school to provide the starting point for a project or they could discuss one of any number of issues, for example the role of design, product development, marketing, costing, quality assurance, production methods.

Task 12.3 Integrating external links into a scheme of work

Write out or adapt an existing scheme of work to show how local industry could be integrated into the work. This may include one or more of the above activities, or others.

Show this to your mentor and discuss how realistic and achievable it is, and what educational aims it would fulfil.

VISITS OUT OF SCHOOL

Taking pupils out of school requires a lot of careful and time-consuming preparation and planning. Before embarking on it, therefore, you need to consider its educational value, for example:

- What is the purpose of the trip and how does it fit into the department scheme of work?

- How does the visit contribute to course work or examinations?
- What experiences and opportunities will the visit offer that could not be achieved in the classroom?
- What preparation and follow-up work will need to be done with the pupils?

Having decided that this is the best strategy, you need to liaise with the company and ensure that they, too, are clear about the purposes of the visit and what it is expected to cover. Agree with them, in advance, the programme for the visit, including timings and personnel involved. There are then the practical arrangements to be made. First of all, check the school and department policy to ensure that you follow the correct procedures and inform all the relevant people.

Task 12.4 Reviewing policy documents on out-of-school visits

Obtain a copy of the school and department policy documents on out-of-school visits and read them through carefully. Make a checklist of what you would be required to do if you were to arrange an out-of-school visit.

The procedures contained within the policy are likely to include:

- a letter to be sent to parents informing them of the visit and asking for their written permission for their child to attend; a standard letter is often provided
- permission for you to act on behalf of the parent, if necessary, during the visit, for example if the child should fall ill; this is usually included in the standard letter but do check
- collect any required payments
- arrange transport and insurance
- make sure pupil–teacher ratios are met
- inform school staff if pupils will be missing any lessons
- inform canteen staff if pupils will be away over break or lunch, especially if numbers are substantial.

Attention to health and safety is very important. Local education authorities and schools have a common law duty to look after children in their care. Local education authorities also have a duty under section 3 of the Health and Safety at Work Act 1974 (in England and Wales) not to expose any child to any situation where their health and safety will be at risk. The school or authority must, therefore, take reasonable steps to satisfy themselves that any visit or work placement which is arranged will be safe for the pupil.

Pupils are especially at risk because of their inexperience and immaturity.

Preparation through risk assessment sessions and safety briefings should reinforce pupils' awareness of employers' high expectations of safe working practices and behaviour in the workplace.

Preparation also means preparing the pupils for the visit. They need to be informed of the purpose of the visit. Point out to them what they need to look for; describe any activities they are to undertake; prepare any surveys or questionnaires which are to be used; prepare note-taking forms. Also, advise pupils of the protocol for visits, for example in wearing school uniform if appropriate and in displaying good behaviour. Ensure that pupils know the practical arrangements for the visit, such as meeting places and times.

After the visit, remember to thank the company. If the visit has gone well they are likely to have invested much time and effort into making it work and a letter of thanks will be much appreciated. Pupils will need to be debriefed: they can discuss their findings, perhaps present their work to the class, and discuss the relevance of what they learnt to their design and technology work.

VISITORS TO THE SCHOOL

As with visits out, consider carefully the educational purposes of having a guest speaker, and inform the speaker of these. Agree with your visitor the timing and content of their visit.

Again, pupils will need to be prepared. They, too, need to know the purpose of the visit, what to expect and be prepared with any questions. On the day of the visit, arrange for the speaker to be met; this could be done by you or the pupils, and make sure that the room and any resources are ready. After the event, again write to thank the speaker and debrief the pupils by discussing what they learnt from the speaker and its relevance to their own work.

EXAMPLES OF EXTERNAL LINKS

Food product development

In preparation for their own food product development work, two groups of pupils were taken to a local factory. They looked at the development kitchen and listened to a talk from the employees which covered how they got their ideas for new products, how they tested and trialled them, using ordinary kitchen facilities, and how they scaled up the recipes once a product had been accepted.

The groups then walked around the factory to see how the food products were made, packaged, stored and dispatched. This was extremely useful in showing pupils that the work that they were doing in school mirrored that in industry. They understood the importance of research and how recipes could be adapted, the need for testing and trialling, the importance of the specification and how to scale up recipes.

Back in school, pupils applied what they had seen on the visit to their own project work.

Business display

This project required pupils to design a display for a business to promote the business and the product being manufactured.

Pupils visited a local business to collect information on the products being manufactured and the range of activities taking place. They then worked, over a ten-week period, in groups of five to produce their displays. These showed the name of the company and the products being made and were made to look attractive and promote the business. The manager of the business was invited into the school to see the displays that had been produced and to make his comments on them.

Quality assurance and quality control

A group of pupils aged 14–15 years were taken to a food manufacturing company to look at quality control issues. They were prepared by a lesson on the legal requirements that food producers have to meet and the preparation of observation and note-taking forms.

During the visit they were given a talk about the vital importance of quality control in food products, how staff are trained for this and how it is carried out. Then they were walked around the factory, with points of quality control being pointed out to them, making notes of their observations and any comments.

The value of this visit was in showing pupils that the regulations are important to manufacturers and how the theory they had been learning was applied in practice.

Glider project

This activity involved links with the local air museum, local aero-modelling enthusiasts and parents. A group of pupils took part in a one-day activity constructing and testing a glider. Two teachers worked with each group of twenty four pupils while museum staff, modellers and parents acted as specialists and consultants, available to give advice and guidance to the pupils.

Each group was required, within the day, to design and construct a glider with an approximate wingspan of 1.2m, and a design folio describing how it was made.

Product design

For a group of pupils aged 15–16 years, about to embark on an examination course, a product designer from an electrical manufacturing company was invited in to give a talk about his work. The talk covered how designs are developed, how materials are researched, how production and costing have to be considered, and how the brief and specification are important to the designer. The designer also talked about how his work was presented, from rough sketches in the initial stages to more detailed and accurate graphics later.

This was valuable for pupils to help them understand the importance of some of the aspects of design which they find difficult or boring, such as the research element. It was also helpful for them to see that not all work has to be perfectly presented, that initial sketches can be quite rough and can be annotated to show the thinking behind them.

SUMMARY

At the core of educational–industrial links lies the need for the two different cultures to understand each other. Traditionally separate and wrapped up in themselves, many schools and business organisations have now begun to realise the importance of developing links and encouraging mutual understanding.

When two different cultures meet in order to work together, it is important to recognise each other's differences and try to use them creatively. To attempt to minimise them and brush them aside can lead to superficial camaraderie, but rarely a productive working partnership. A basis for comparison of the two cultures could be consideration of the outputs or products of the school or business, and the elements which drive them.

Business is driven by its 'bottom line', i.e. financial results. Almost all business people will tell you that a positive financial result is essential for survival and that other, longer-term considerations must take second place. Yet business ignores those other considerations, such as education links, staff training, environmental issues and equal opportunities, to the potential long-term detriment of its overall performance. Although longer-term and less easily measured, these other considerations can add to a company's performance. If business people get them wrong, it can cost them dearly.

Similarly, a school is drawn hard by its most obvious performance indicator, examination results. Like some of those in business, some teachers say that everything must be subordinated to this 'bottom line'. Yet any school that ignores other issues, such as communication skills, economic awareness, industrial understanding, health education and a range of other skills and attitudes, works to the detriment of a rounded education for its pupils.

Examination results are, of course, still very important and employers will continue to use them as indicators of performance. However, over the past ten years school–industry work has revealed a growing interest by employers in the other skills that pupils have, such as communication and economic awareness.

This chapter should have encouraged you to explore the possibilities for including links with industry in your teaching. The benefits and rewards it brings, in terms of providing relevance, purpose and motivation, make the effort that is entailed worthwhile. Links with industry also help to keep your own knowledge of materials and manufacturing processes up to date and this can benefit all the pupils you teach.

FURTHER READING

Department for Education and Employment (1995) *Looking at Values through Products and Applications*, London: DfEE

Department for Education and Employment (1996) *Learning to Compete. Education and Training for 14–19 Year Olds*, London: DfEE

USEFUL ADDRESSES

Young Engineers
University of Surrey, Guildford, Surrey, GU2 5XH

TEP
The Engineering Council, Essex House, 12/13 Essex Street, London, WC2R 3EG

The Engineering Council (books and resource packs)
Middlesex University, Teaching Resources, Bramley Road, Oakwood, London, N14 4XS

13 Continuing professional development

Gwyneth Owen-Jackson

INTRODUCTION

On completion of your initial teacher education course you will have been assessed against the competences or standards currently in operation, and so can be confident that you have the ability to be an effective teacher. You will also have ideas on areas where you feel you still need to develop. In England and Wales this will be formally written down in your Career Entry Profile. So, during your first year of teaching (the probationary period in Scotland is two years) you will have guidance on how to continue with your professional development. This chapter will consider what you can do to help yourself in this process, and directs you to resources that will help you.

First, though, consideration is given to how you will obtain your first teaching post. The core text in this series (Capel *et al.*, 1997) covers general information about looking for posts, writing your application and curriculum vitae and attending interviews. In this chapter the discussion is focused on how you can apply this to specific design and technology posts.

OBJECTIVES

By the end of this chapter you should:

- be able to apply confidently for your first post
- know how to prepare for an interview
- be aware of the need to keep your subject knowledge up to date, and have ideas on how to do this
- be aware of the relevant professional organisations and how they can help your development.

OBTAINING YOUR FIRST TEACHING POST

It's never too early to start looking for your first post. You can start looking in January and not be in the classroom until September. The best places to look for possible jobs are *The Times Educational Supplement*, the education supplements of the *Guardian* and *The Independent* and your local press. The school in which you have been working may also have the local education authority *Vacancies Bulletin*, and talking to other teachers and students can alert you to opportunities.

When looking at advertisements, you need to be aware that they may be advertised under the headings of 'design and technology', 'technology' or 'food technology'. Some areas may also continue to advertise for home economics staff. Remember to explore all possibilities when searching.

When looking at a particular advertisement, there are certain pieces of information that you should look for, for example:

- Is the school state maintained, grant maintained, aided or independent?
- Is it a City Technology College (CTC) or does it have Technology status?
- Is it a grammar or comprehensive?
- Is it a mixed or single-sex school?

The answers to these questions may have some bearing on the resources available in design and technology and the ethos and status of the subject within the school.

You might also want to consider the age range of the pupils in the school. Do you want to teach pupils from the age of 11, or would you be happy with a middle school system where they transfer at 12 or 13? Do you want to teach pupils to the age of 16, or would you prefer to teach post-16 as well?

In England and Wales more detailed information about the school and the design and technology department can be obtained through reading the OFSTED report. This is a public document and all reports are now available on the internet. Remember, however, to check the date of the OFSTED inspection as it may have been a number of years since it was produced.

Finally, remember to check if the school is advertising for specific design and technology skills. The advertisement should state that they require a person with skills in resistant materials, electronics, textiles technology or food technology. If no specialism is mentioned, it may be better to telephone the school and ask them if any specific skills are required – you could save yourself some time!

The application form

Once you have found a post that you are interested in and have received the details from the school, it is a good idea to photocopy the application form and complete it in draft, to make sure that you do it correctly and make good use of the space provided. There will usually be a section in the application form which asks you to say something about yourself and your suitability for the post, and this is where you have the opportunity to sell yourself. You can say something here about any previous relevant experience that you may have had, for example in youth work, as a classroom assistant or any relevant industrial experience. This can be particularly important in design and technology with its greater emphasis now on industrial production. You can also refer to the schools in which you have trained, their type and location, the age range that you taught and areas of the curriculum or syllabus that you covered. If you have completed a Career Entry Profile, you can refer to the areas of strength identified by your mentor. If possible, look at the job description, and person specification if there is one, and try to tailor what you write to address these points.

You will be asked to provide the names and addresses of two referees, i.e. people who can comment on your teaching competences and personal qualities. You can use one of your training schools and your training institution, but seek permission from people before putting their names on the form.

You may or may not choose to include a curriculum vitae (c.v.) with your application. If you do, make sure that you have included all relevant information and that it looks professional. Guidance on writing a c.v. is given in the core text (Capel *et al.*, 1997).

Task 13.1 Writing an application

Bellarmine Comprehensive School
Walton, Eastshire

11–18 co-ed comprehensive school 2000 on roll (sixth form 200)

TEACHER OF DESIGN & TECHNOLOGY

Required for September, an enthusiastic and committed teacher to contribute to the development and growth of the D&T department. *Please state your specialism* when applying. The department has excellent facilities and D&T is a popular subject in the school, with high status and good results. In addition to a *full GCSE programme, GNVQ Manufacturing and Health and Social Care* are also offered.

The department takes part in many *national projects and competitions*, with success, and there are *opportunities for further development* here.

Look at the post advertised above and draft a letter of application in response to it. The sections which are italicised are those that you should particularly comment upon, including your experience in those areas. You may wish to include other relevant information such as other experiences, strengths and interests, and you may want to refer to your educational philosophy and aspirations. Remember, though, that the school will be looking for an applicant who best meets their own needs and will fit into the design and technology team.

When you have drafted your letter show it to your mentor and other colleagues. Ask them for comments and try to get as much varied feedback as you can.

When sending off your application, it is good practice to enclose a covering letter with it. If you have not had an opportunity in the application form to write about your strengths and experiences then you can do that in the letter. Alternatively, you may wish to highlight points in the letter, or simply draw attention to the fact that certain details are covered in the application form. The letter of application should interest the school, make them want to read your application and invite you for interview, so say something about what you have to offer the school. Remember also to refer to the job description and person specification when thinking about what the school will be looking for.

Preparing for the interview

If called for interview, try to arrange to visit the school before the formal interview date. This will give you an opportunity to meet some of the staff and pupils, possibly observe a lesson and see how the department functions. This will help you to get a feel for the school and the way that it operates. It may also suggest questions that you may be asked at the interview, or raise questions that you would like to ask, for example to do with technician support, resources, schemes of work or the examination board that is used. If there are any aspects of the teaching with which you are not familiar, take the opportunity to find out about them before attending the interview. You may want to find out whether you would be expected to teach just your specialism, or whether you would be asked to teach in other areas of design and technology. Think about how you would feel about this. During the interview you may be asked to teach a lesson, or part of a lesson. If you have visited beforehand you will have some idea of the resources and space available when planning your lesson.

If you cannot visit the school in advance, ask them to send you a copy of their school prospectus. This will give you some idea of the facilities, the philosophy and policies of the school, as well as information about the subjects taught within design and technology, the structure of the department and the examination success rates.

In preparation for the interview, put together a portfolio of your own work. This will allow the interview panel to see the knowledge and skills that you have, as well as giving you something concrete to talk about. The portfolio could consist of work that you have done at your own level, for example for your degree, as well as work that you have done during your course, for example a selection of lesson plans, worksheets or other resources, visual aids or examples of project work that you have made for teaching aspects of your specialism. If you have further qualifications, for example in ICT or health and safety, include the certificates in your portfolio.

The interview

The interview itself is likely to last for most of the day. When you arrive at the school you will meet other candidates for the post. Most likely you will all be shown around the school together, either by a member of staff or a pupil. There will probably be time for informal conversations with staff, and possibly pupils. If this opportunity arises, use it to find out about the department and the school – you could ask about current projects for example. Depending on the timing of the interviews, you may be given lunch, again as a group and possibly accompanied by school staff. Remember, throughout all this informal time, you are making judgements about the school and they are making judgements about you.

Many schools now are asking candidates to deliver a lesson, or part of a lesson, as part of the interview process. If this is the case, then you will have been given information in advance about the topic, timing and class. If you have not received this information then telephone the school and ask for it when preparing for the interview.

The formal interview panel is likely to consist of, at least, a governor of the school, the Head and the head of department. There may be other staff there, perhaps from the pastoral side of the school. It is difficult to give a definitive list of the sorts of questions that you may be asked at the interview, but the questions are likely to cover the areas set out in Table 13.1.

There may be other questions, specific to the school, for example: how willing you would be to teach in other areas of design and technology; how you would deal with pupils with English as a second language; how you would deal with a highly gifted pupil. You may also be asked about things you have put on your application form, c.v. or letter of application, so be prepared to talk about these. Interviews can be unpredictable and are always stressful, especially the first one. Thorough preparation, reading all the information you have, re-reading your own application and having some answers prepared, will help to reduce your stress levels and encourage you to feel confident and professional. Other ways to help yourself include arriving in plenty of time, dressing so that you feel confident and comfortable and being organised with your portfolio.

When invited into the interview room, wait to be asked to be seated, try to make yourself comfortable and put your portfolio in a convenient position. Try not to fiddle with your clothing or papers, try to sit still and relaxed. The first question you will be asked is likely to be whether or not you are still interested in the post. As each person asks you a question, look at that person and respond to them. Be honest when answering questions, do not be afraid to pause and think about your answer, or to say if you do not understand. It's unlikely that you will be asked a question to which you do not know the answer, but if this does happen then, again, be honest and say that you do not know and that you would have to think about it or find out (I actually did this in an interview once, and was appointed!). If possible, in your answers refer to information about the school, for example, if you know that they run lunch-clubs or after-school clubs, could you contribute to these; if you have seen an interesting display of design and technology work in the department or elsewhere in the school you could refer to it. When you are asked if you have any questions, make these relevant to the school, the department or the post, for example, if it has not been covered you could ask about post-16 work or the range of examinations available for pupils at 16. If you do not have any questions, then you can thank the interviewing panel for being so thorough in the information they have given you that they have covered everything that you wanted to know.

When everyone has been interviewed, you may be asked to wait until a candidate

Table 13.1 Questions you may be asked during a job interview

Issues	*Specific questions*
Subject knowledge	You may be asked direct questions to test your knowledge in your specialist area, for example to describe the process of vacuum-forming, or how you would produce a French seam.
Teaching your subject knowledge	For example, how would you introduce Year 9 pupils to the feedback in control systems, or how would you teach Year 7 pupils about nutritional values?
ICT skills	For example, how would you integrate the teaching of ICT skills into a Year 10 lesson in your specialist area?
Curriculum or syllabus knowledge	You may be asked about particular commercial schemes or examination syllabuses that you have used, or that the school uses, in terms not only of your knowledge of it but also your evaluation of it.
Evaluation of lessons	You may be asked to describe a lesson that you taught that went particularly well, why you think it went well and what contributed to the success.
Safety issues	You should ensure that you have the relevant safety certification and can talk confidently about risk assessment, planning for safety and working safely with pupils using machinery, equipment and materials.
Class management	You may be asked how you would work with a group of pupils all engaged on individual project work, to ensure that each pupil worked to the best of their ability.
Equal opportunities	There may be questions on how you would integrate pupils from different social and cultural backgrounds into your classroom.
Special needs	This is a wide field but, for example, you may be asked how in practical lessons you would support a pupil who was confined to a wheelchair.
Your experience as a form tutor	What do you think you will bring to your role as a form tutor?

has been selected. Whilst this can be a nerve-racking time, at least you do not have to wait for days to know the outcome. If you are successful, the school will then negotiate contract details with you. In making the appointment, the school will be looking for someone who will fit into the existing team and meet certain needs: it may well be that they regard you as an ideal candidate, but that you do not meet their particular requirements at that particular time, so do not feel that you have failed if you are not appointed. If you are not successful, you may be offered, or can ask for, a debriefing session, in which they will say why they did not appoint you. This can be a useful learning experience, and will help you to prepare for your next interview.

YOUR FIRST POST

Before taking up your post, if it is possible for you to visit the school then it is a good idea to do so. These visits will allow you to become familiar with the layout of the school, the location of various places, and help you to find your way around the design and technology department. You can meet members of staff and find out what the routines are. You can begin to become familiar with the schemes of work, textbooks and resources available. When your timetable is available, you can begin to prepare lesson plans and resources for the classes you will be teaching and there are likely to be many questions that you want to ask.

Task 13.2 Preparing for your first post

If you are able to visit the school before starting your first post, in addition to your teaching timetable, find out about and make notes on the following:

- the location of your teaching room, or rooms
- the need for any display materials in your room
- the textbooks used by the school, and where these are stored
- any video resources available, and how these are booked
- what materials, tools and equipment the department has, and where these are
- the procedure for photocopying worksheets
- ICT facilities (see Chapter 7 for the details of what to check)
- the procedure for ordering anything you might need, stationery, materials, etc.
- registration and dismissal procedures.

There will be many more things that will arise as you begin to teach, but these will form the basic knowledge that you will need to perform confidently in the classroom at the start of your first term.

Once you begin teaching in your first full-time post you will be in a probationary period, one year in England and Wales called the induction year, two years in Scotland. If you have a Career Entry Profile, the support you receive from the school will help you to develop in the areas identified in that. Figure 13.1 shows an example of pages from a Career Entry Profile, identifying a student's strengths and areas for development on completion of their course and how these feed into an action plan for their induction period.

If you do not have such a document, then you could negotiate with the school, or identify your own training needs. This will help you, and the school, to select and plan appropriate training sessions for you.

Task 13.3 Planning your professional development

Look at the strengths and areas for development identified in your Career Entry Profile. If you do not have one of these, then write your own list of what you consider to be your main strengths and areas for development.

From these identify two or three targets which you think you could achieve in your first year of teaching, taking account of your own capabilities and time, and the school's resources and facilities. Your targets should focus on specific skills, knowledge or experiences which you wish to acquire or develop.

Discuss these targets with your induction mentor or head of department, how feasible are they and what will you, and the school, need to do to realise them. From this discussion you can agree with the school your action plan.

It may well be that you are not the only new member of staff at the school and there may be an induction programme organised for all new staff, to give information about school policies, procedures and facilities. These are extremely useful sessions, not only for the information they give about the school but also for meeting other colleagues.

You are likely to have a varied timetable, teaching younger pupils and examination classes. You may be asked to teach aspects of design and technology that are outside your specialist area. If this is the case then do not be afraid to ask other members of the department for advice and help; they will probably be flattered to be asked and only too pleased to help. Before teaching the new topic, familiarise yourself with any textbooks that will be used, and any machinery, equipment or materials. If possible, especially if there is a practical element, work your way through the lessons yourself, or try to observe another teacher teaching the same topic.

As well as learning from the department, it may be that you also have something to offer; you may have been appointed because of your particular subject knowledge or skills, your industrial experience or ICT skills. These may 'fill a gap' in the department and they may be looking to you to make a contribution in this area. Some

Figure 13.1 Example of a Career Entry Profile
Source: Teacher Training Agency, 1999

NEWLY QUALIFIED TEACHER'S STRENGTHS AND PRIORITIES FOR FURTHER PROFESSIONAL DEVELOPMENT DURING INDUCTION

Areas of strength in relation to the standards for the award of Qualified Teacher Status

1. Sevda has excellent subject knowledge, her knowledge and understanding of D&T in general is sound and she is always striving to keep abreast of changes
2. Excellent production of a range of learning resources, appropriate to a wide range of different groups in age and ability
3. Very effective ability to cope securely with pupils' questions and misconceptions, she understands and analyses pupil responses and makes her answers constructive
4. Sevda has kept a comprehensive record of pupils' work to inform pupils, parents and colleagues

Areas in which the standards for the award of QTS have been met but where, as a priority, the NQT will benefit from further development during induction

1. More experience in post–16 teaching would help to further develop Sevda's subject knowledge
2. More use of ICT in her teaching would increase the range of strategies she can use
3. Sevda needs to develop a consistent approach to the appropriate use of reward and sanctions
4. Sevda would welcome the opportunity for developing expertise within a pastoral system

TARGETS AND ACTION PLAN FOR THE INDUCTION PERIOD

TARGETS	ACTIONS TO BE TAKEN AND BY WHOM	SUCCESS CRITERIA	RESOURCES	TARGET DATE FOR ACHIEVEMENT	REVIEW DATE
1 To co-teach an AS/A class	Timetable to include 6th form – HoD	Appropriate grades obtained by pupils		July 2001	December 2000 and April 2001
2 ICT to be written into lesson plans	Lesson plans written by Sevda, seen by HoD	Pupils successfully using ICT	ICT resources	April 2001	December 2000
3 Sevda to be form tutor	Form group to be allocated and monitored	All tutor work completed	School hand-book Meeting time with Head of Year	July 2001	December 2000 and April 2001

departments look to new teachers to bring fresh ideas for projects, new ways of teaching projects or new external links, so do not be afraid to make suggestions. Remember, however, to be sensitive and do not openly criticise existing schemes of work, as you need to work as a member of the team and it will be important that you all work together to develop and improve the teaching.

DEVELOPING YOUR SUBJECT KNOWLEDGE

You probably have become aware by now that design and technology does not consist of a static body of knowledge. It is an important part of your role that you keep up to date with developments in your specialist area. As I write, the newspapers are full of stories about genetically modified foods, which a food technology teacher should be informed about in order to be able to discuss the subject with pupils, from a scientific and objective viewpoint. In other areas there are continual developments in materials and processes. There will be information in relevant professional journals, which are discussed later, and in quality newspapers and even television programmes. The local authority where you work may also offer in-service training courses. Ask about information on these from your head of department, as there may be courses that will help you to develop areas of knowledge or skill.

In earlier chapters in this book you will have reviewed your subject knowledge. If you only looked at your specialist area, you could now look at other aspects of the subject and begin to develop your knowledge and skills in other areas. The more you can offer, the more employable you will become.

Whatever your level of knowledge, schools will use different topics to teach the subject content so it's likely that you will need to spend time familiarising yourself with the projects in your new school. For example, processes in textiles technology may be taught through pupils being asked to make a garment, a container of some kind, a decorative item, a gift item or an item for the home. The list is endless, and each project, although requiring the same knowledge and skills, will require you to present it in a different way, and have different resources to support the learning. Prepare for this as much in advance as possible.

RESOURCES

This is a major area in design and technology. Depending on the projects being taught in school you may be looking for examples of pens, hats, children's toys, sandwiches, chair designs, ties, packaging, pizza toppings, kettles, Indian embroidery – again the possibilities are endless. Looking for resources becomes a way of life: you may not need it this year, but it might come in handy for next year's topic. So always be on the lookout for resources, whether you can see any immediate relevance or not.

DEVELOPING YOUR TEACHING

Just as you will want to continue to develop your subject knowledge, so you should look for opportunities to develop your teaching expertise. There is a saying that you can have 'twenty years' teaching experience, or one's year experience twenty times'. As you become more familiar with the school routines, resources, schemes of work and calendar of events, your teaching can be developed in a number of ways. You might look for opportunities to teach in unfamiliar areas, for example in post-16 classes or a vocational course. You might try to make links with other departments, for example science. You might try to work more with pupils with special needs.

With your own classroom performance you could try small-scale research to look more closely at what is happening. It would be helpful if you could identify a colleague who could become a 'critical friend', someone whom you trust and respect. This colleague could observe you teaching, focusing on your area of interest, for example your interactions with girls and boys, your questioning or demonstration techniques. The notes made by your critical friend should highlight strengths and areas for improvement. You could discuss with your colleague ways in which you could improve and try them out in the classroom. There is more information about carrying out small-scale action research in the core text (Capel *et al.*, 1997).

Evaluation of your lessons is a time-consuming task as a student, but it provides invaluable information. If you do not continue with written evaluations it is still worthwhile to reflect on your lessons, thinking seriously and critically about what happened in the classroom, what worked and what didn't, why events occurred as they did and how you could change, develop or improve what happens. It can help to talk through with your mentor, or induction tutor, your reflections. She may be able to guide your thinking or offer suggestions that you had overlooked. Informal talk in the department, for example over coffee or lunch, often involves talking about classroom events or particular pupils, and this might also be a useful forum.

You might also want to spend some time reflecting on wider issues, for example your philosophy about design and technology and how this is represented in your teaching, or the social, moral, ethical and environmental issues which are important to your teaching.

Many schools now operate appraisal systems, which means that your performance will be monitored and discussed on a regular basis. During the appraisal cycle you will be asked to note down your achievements and developments since the last meeting, and your targets for continuing development. Your appraiser will talk to other nominated staff and will then meet with you to discuss all the information. The result of an appraisal is usually agreed targets, with an action plan, and resources allocated, similar to the induction plan for your first year. Appraisal is a useful instrument for helping you to chart your development and to keep you moving forward.

PROFESSIONAL ORGANISATIONS

It is crucial that you are aware of the importance of joining a professional association. As a member of a union, you will have access to insurance cover and professional advice should you need it. This is particularly important in design and technology, where health and safety issues are a vital part of everyday teaching.

There may also be relevant associations for your specialist area, for example there are associations for electrical engineers, mechanical engineers, textile specialists. Being a member of a specialist organisation will give you access to relevant information, new developments and, possibly, resources.

In addition, the professional organisation for teachers of design and technology is the Design and Technology Association (DATA). As a member of DATA you will receive regular journals and newsletters, information about relevant courses, invitations to attend design and technology conferences, and be able to talk to like-minded colleagues.

SELF-MANAGEMENT

Your first year of teaching is likely to be extremely stressful and tiring. It is important, therefore, that you take care of yourself during this year. Simple things like eating properly, taking exercise and getting sufficient sleep will help. Try to be organised and avoid last-minute panics; prepare your lessons and resources in advance; keep up to date with marking work and keeping records. Learn to prioritise your work; obviously being in the classroom when you are teaching is one thing that you cannot change. In the remaining time have three checklists, one for things that you must do *now*, one for things that you must do, and one for things that can wait until you have the time. Make sure that every day you complete the must do *now* list, even if all you do is transfer it to tomorrow's list. At least that way it remains a priority. This is important because you need to meet deadlines and be seen to be doing your job properly. Information provided by you may be needed so that someone else can get on with their job, for example completing a report on a pupil for the special needs co-ordinator or preparing a display for the department to use. Many tasks that you are doing will take longer the first time that you do them, for example, keeping departmental records up to date. Once you become familiar with the systems, the tasks become easier and quicker. It is also a good idea to keep a diary and to write in deadlines, and schedule time before the deadline for completing the task, for example writing the Year 7 reports or preparing for a parents' evening.

Do not be afraid to ask for help or advice if necessary. If you are not sure how to do a task, ask before you attempt it; getting it wrong could waste hours of time. If you are not sure where to find information, ask instead of searching round. If colleagues are doing a task more quickly than you are ask how – is there something you can learn from them?

Make time to relax, either at the end of each day or at least one day over the weekend. You need to have time to recharge your batteries. Working with hundreds of children all day, every day, is a draining experience and, if you want to be able to give something of yourself in the classroom, there has to be something to give. Keep your sense of balance and perspective, keep your sense of humour and keep some sort of social life. If you don't then your teaching will suffer, and so will you.

SUMMARY

Having a commitment to being a good teacher means having a commitment to keeping up with changes, both in the education scene in general and with developments in design and technology. Presumably you became a teacher of design and technology because you have an interest in the subject. It is important therefore that you keep that up and show your interest and enthusiasm in the classroom.

There will come a time when you may want to move on from the classroom, develop your career in the pastoral side of education, or move into management. A successful classroom career will help you to do this, and will provide you with the knowledge and skills for any further study that you wish to undertake.

Design and technology is a demanding subject, but also an innovative and exciting one. I wish you well in your career.

USEFUL ADDRESS

Design and Technology Association (DATA),
16 Wellesbourne House, Walton Road, Wellesbourne, CV35 9JB
tel: 01789 470007, fax: 01789 841955
email: *DATA@data.org.uk*

References

Assessment of Performance Unit (APU) (1991) *The Assessment of Performance in Design and Technology*, London: SEAC

Association for Science Education (1986) *Science and Technology in Society: General Guide for Teachers*, Hatfield: ASE

Barlex, D. (1987) 'Technology project work' in *ET887/897, Units 5–6, Module 4, Teaching and Learning Technology in Schools*, Milton Keynes: Open University Press

Burgess, S. (1998) 'Effects of group composition on individual learning/performance', *The Journal of Design and Technology Education*, vol. 3, no. 3

Calderhead, J. (1994) 'Teachers planning' in The Open University, *Secondary Facsimile 4*, Buckingham: Open University Press

Capel, S., Leask, M. and Turner, T. (1997) *Learning to Teach in the Secondary School*, London: Routledge

Catton, J. (1985) *Ways and Means: the Craft, Design and Technology Education of Girls*, York: Longmans, for SCDC

Curriculum Council for Wales (1993) *Design & Technology. One in Five*, Cardiff: CCW

Davies, L. (1999) 'ICT in the teaching of Design and Technology' in The Open University/ Research Machines, *Learning Schools Programme*, Buckinghan: Open University Press

Denton, H. (1994) 'The role of group/teamwork in design and technology: some possibilities' in Banks, F. (ed.), *Teaching Technology*, London: Routledge

Department for Education/Welsh Office (1992) *Technology for Ages 5–16*, London: Department for Education

Department for Education/Welsh Office (1995) *Design and Technology in the National Curriculum*, London: DfE

Department for Education (DfE) (1996) *Why Design and Technology*? (leaflet), London: DfE

Department for Education and Employment (1998) *Teaching: High Status, High Standards*, London: DfEE

Department for Education and Science (DES) (1985) *Education 8–12 in Combined and Middle Schools*, London: HMSO

Design and Technology Association (DATA) (1995a) *Guidance Material for Design and Technology*, Wellesbourne: DATA

Design and Technology Association (DATA) (1995b) *Minimum Competences for Students to Teach Design and Technology in Secondary Schools*, Wellesbourne: DATA

Dickinson, C. and Wright, J. (1993) *Differentiation: a Practical Handbook of Classroom Strategies*, Coventry: NCET

Hampshire Local Education Authority (1998) *Design and Technology 11–14 Teachers' Guidelines*, Winchester: Hampshire LEA

Harrison, M. (1996) *What Is Design and Technology in the Curriculum?*, Buckingham: Open University Press

Hennessy, S. and McCormick, R. (1994) 'The general problem solving process in technology education: myth or reality?' in Banks, F. (ed) *Teaching Technology*, London: Routledge

Kimbell, R., Stables, K. and Green, R. (1996) *Understanding Practice in Design and Technology*, Buckingham: Open University Press

Kyriacou, C. (1991) *Essential Teaching Skills*, Oxford: Blackwell

Kyriacou, C. (1993) *Essential Teaching Skills*, Hemel Hempstead: Simon & Schuster

Leask, M. and Pachler, N. (1999) *Learning to Teach Using ICT in the Secondary School*, London: Routledge

NATHE (1998) *Learning Futures – Textiles – a Teacher's Guide to Good Practice in Textiles Technology*, London: NATHE

National Curriculum Council (NCC) (1993) *Technology Programmes of Study and Attainment Targets*, York: NCC

OFSTED/DfEE (1995) *Design and Technology: Characteristics of Good Practice in Secondary Schools*, London: HMSO

OHMCI (1996) *Framework for the Inspection of Schools*, Cardiff: OHMCI

Qualifications and Curriculum Authority (QCA) (1998) *Education for Citizenship and the Teaching of Democracy in Schools*, London: QCA

Qualifications and Curriculum Authority (QCA) (1999) *The Review of the National Curriculum in England. The Consultation Materials*, London: QCA

RCA Schools Technology Project (1997) *Control Products*, London: Hodder & Stoughton

RCA Schools Technology Project (1998) *Textiles*, Hong Kong: Hodder & Stoughton

Riggs, A. (1994) 'Gender and technology education', in Banks, F. (ed.), *Teaching Technology*, London: Routledge

Ritchie, R. (1996) *Primary Design and Technology – a Process for Learning*, London: David Fulton Publishers

Sage, J. (1996) 'Developing capability in technology through collaboration with maths and science', *The Journal of Design and Technology Education*, vol. 1, no. 1, Spring

Sage, J. and Thomson, D.S.C. (1996) *Electronic and Control Systems*, Cambridge: Cambridge University Press

School Curriculum and Assessment Authority (SCAA) (1996) *Exemplification of Standards for Design and Technology KS3: Consistency in teacher Assessment*, London: SCAA

School Curriculum and Assessment Authority (SCAA) (1997) *The Contribution of Design and Technology to the Curriculum*, London: SCAA

Scottish CCC (1996) *Education for Teaching Technology Issues and Possible Ways Forward*, Glasgow: Scottish CCC

Somerset County Council (1990) 'Somerset County Council curriculum statement' in Banks, F. (ed.), *Teaching Technology*, London: Routledge

STEP (1993) 'Card 47 – brainstorming' in *Datafile for Key Stage 3*, Cambridge: Cambridge University Press

Teacher Training Agency (1999) *Career Entry Profile Pack*, London: HMSO

Index

Note: main chapter pages are shown in **bold**